PROPERTY OF _____

TITLE _____

COMPANY _____

THE

EXECUTIVE

DESKBOOK

Second Edition

Auren Uris
Research Institute of America

VAN NOSTRAND REINHOLD COMPANY

NEW YORK   CINCINNATI   ATLANTA   DALLAS   SAN FRANCISCO
LONDON   TORONTO   MELBOURNE

HD31
U66
1976

Van Nostrand Reinhold Regional Offices:
New York   Cincinnati   Atlanta   Dallas   San Francisco

Van Nostrand Reinhold Company International Offices:
London   Toronto   Melbourne

Library of Congress Catalog Card Number: 76-4074
ISBN: 0-442-28812-3

Manufactured in the United States of America

Published by Van Nostrand Reinhold Company
450 West 33rd Street, New York, N.Y. 10001

Published simultaneously in Canada by Van Nostrand Reinhold Company, Ltd.

15 14 13 12 11 10 9 8 7 6 5 4 3 2

Library of Congress Cataloging in Publication Data

Uris, Auren.
  The executive deskbook.

  Includes index.
  1. Management.   I.   Title.
HD31.U66   1976   658.4   76-4074
ISBN 0-442-28812-3

PREFACE TO SECOND EDITION

In the six years since *The Executive Deskbook's* appearance, new factors have entered the business scene. A combination of economic sag and inflation has brought enormous stress to corporate life. High levels of unemployment, unprecedented situations ranging from material shortages to skyrocketing costs have created new needs for executive excellence. In this new world, the original design and aims of the *Deskbook* take on increased potency. Today's executive has an even greater need for information, and practical solutions to immediate problems.

Of course, it is the success of the first edition in satisfying executives' information, idea and tool needs that supplies the impetus for this update. The second edition has new material in four areas—meetings, memo-writing, women in management, and fair employment practices. Your access to these can be gained quickly through the table of contents and the newly revised and comprehensive index.

This book is planned as a tool to help executives work their way more effectively through the routines and problems of their day-to-day operations. This enlarged second edition should optimize the process by which you get your own and the world's work done.

Auren Uris

Grand View-on-Hudson, N.Y.

v

PREFACE TO FIRST EDITION

"I wish I knew a better method of handling my paperwork."
"I must learn how to systematize my decision making."
*"I've fired three secretaries in the last month. My fault? I wish I
knew. . . . "*

Executives *need* to know. They must have the best methods, the
latest ideas, the most helpful insights and information available to
handle the problems and obstacles that throttle day-to-day job effectiveness; or, stated more positively, executives must acquire the
know-how to seize the many opportunities that arise daily for improving performance, theirs and their subordinates'. The difficulties
come in all shapes and sizes, and run from frustrating to costly, often
both.

In a world undergoing a technological revolution, many aspects of
management tradition have been destroyed. The foundations of yes-
terday's executive leadership—company loyalty, paternalism, even an
honest concern for the individual employee—have been shattered by
the attitudes, values, and behavior of today's work force. New methods are essential for the executive to perform at the levels expected
today. And executives must have what they need *quickly*. The pressure on the manager today leaves no time for waiting. Accordingly,
The Executive Deskbook has been organized to put at your fingertips
the exact information you are seeking, rapidly, succinctly. You don't
have to wade through a sea of prose to find the solid information
you seek. Brevity, compactness, clarity, make the material easily available. And you get to the subject you want two ways:

- a *complete table of contents,* in exact sequence, as the material
has been organized and developed
- an *exhaustive alphabetical index,* that permits you to zero in on
the subject of interest immediately

To provide in-depth coverage of the broad range of executive concerns, *The Executive Deskbook* is organized in an unusual way. It
does not consist of a series of chapters, but of *four major sections,*
each with a separate and distinct purpose:

Section I Areas of Management Action—The 12 headings represent a practical division of executive activity. And under each of the
12 headings will be found recommendations for dealing with specific
situations: how to take the five basic steps of executive time saving;
how to handle the flood of executive paperwork; how to handle the

uncertainty factor in decision-making; how to plan; the six steps to successful delegation; how to stimulate creativity, and so on.

Section II   Reviews and Appraisals—Every executive, one time or another, asks himself, "How am I doing?" or he wonders how well his staff is performing. This section provides the executive with twenty checklist and self-rating items to help him assess performance and potential. Some of the appraisals yield numerical scores.

Section III   Key Management Concepts—Today's management thinking is based on a number of ideas developed by management experts and behavioral scientists. Every executive, present or future, should have the keystones of contemporary management theory available to him in brief outline. The most important contemporary ideas are described clearly and concisely. This section represents a view of the current state of management for the busy executive.

Section IV   Management Tool Kit—Every professional is a tool user. Just as the doctor has his medical kit, from stethoscope to headlight, so too the executive has available to him a wide assortment of tools to increase his capabilities. A group of tools in the form of charts, check lists, and so on, help the manager solve many of his key problems in communications, planning, and self-scheduling.

Jimmy Walker, colorful mayor of New York in the late 1920s, said during a discussion of pornography, "I never heard of a girl being ruined by a book." Surprisingly, we hear little of executives *saved from ruin* by a book—even though the meat of management wisdom often reaches executives in book form. Books on management not only advance the art, but doubtless have helped in countless crucial professional victories, and will continue to do so.

You may read, browse, through these pages. But this is less a book to read, than an instrument for the myriad challenging situations that confront the working executive. The insights of the behavioral scientists, the experience of hundreds of perceptive executives and management experts have been refined and compressed to give this volume practical, quick-reference, authoritative usefulness. Its ultimate goal is to assist the executive to function at his highest level of capability, thereby enhancing his own fortunes and the vital profession on which the world of business, indeed the world, depends.

Auren Uris

Grand View-on-Hudson, N.Y.
March 1970

ACKNOWLEDGMENTS

Many people helped shape and complete this work. Authorities in the field as well as executive practitioners shared their insights with the author, and their contributions are acknowledged at appropriate points in the text. And my gratitude for assistance in sharpening and refining much of the content of the *Deskbook* is gladly conveyed—

To my friends and colleagues at the Research Institute of America, especially Bill Case, Joe Cowley, Marjorie Noppel, Barbara Whitmore, Mary Jollon and Rayna Logvin.

For assistance in preparing the manuscript, thanks are due Doris Horvath, Marie Stancarone, Jessica Miller, Angela Rapuano, Carol Korula, Beth Harding, Rosalie Miller, and Betty Russo.

To Evelyn Sheehan and Barbara Price, my appreciation for library assistance, the supplying of key references and news materials.

And finally, to my family for the interest, encouragement, and accommodation to the difficult schedules which the production of this book required.

Auren Uris

Grand View-on-Hudson

CONTENTS

THE
EXECUTIVE
DESKBOOK

1

AREAS OF
MANAGEMENT
ACTION

The executive's job can be sliced up in a variety of ways. For example, the field of general management has traditionally been divided into planning, organizing, implementing, and controlling.

For purposes of *The Executive Deskbook*, twelve functional areas have been developed which more clearly relate to the executive activity as the executive practitioner tends to see it in his day-to-day operations. Here are the twelve areas:

Time Saving and Self-Scheduling
Effective Communication
Decision-Making and Problem-Solving
Planning
Delegation and Assignment
Building Group Effectiveness
Leadership and Motivation
Dealing with Problem People
Dealing with Interpersonal Problems
Improving Your Own Effectiveness
Women in Management
Fair Employment Practices

Under each of these parts you will find specific, practical suggestions for handling the most typical and common difficulties. While many of the recommendations are based on the insights of behavioral science, the recommendations themselves are spelled out in clear operational terms.

* * * * *

1. Time-Saving and Self-Scheduling

Most executives would agree to the following propositions:
- There's never enough time.
- Interruptions and other unforeseen developments threaten or destroy executive schedules.

It is precisely because executive time is of such supreme importance—after all, whatever the executive accomplishes, he does *in and with time*—that it deserves your special attention. The catalog of ideas in the pages ahead have worked timesaving and effortsaving wonders —and can work for you. Consider the suggestions on a purely pragmatic basis—if they suit you, they're "good." If not, pass them by. But remember that the successful adaptation and application of just one idea can save hours of precious time—and be worth thousands of dollars to you and to your company.

⊃ FIVE BASIC STEPS OF EXECUTIVE TIME SAVING

   1. Develop an overview of your responsibilities.   Your job requires that you perform a particular set of activities—for example, if you're a line executive, you are responsible for overseeing the output of your department, division, and so on. But also, you must maintain contact with other company departments—Personnel, the treasurer's office, Production Control, and so on—and long range, seek to improve the production capabilities of your unit. As you consider all these obligations, and the activities they suggest, you clarify the picture of your job, see it in helpful perspective, and get a line on your time requirements.

   2. Set priorities—pattern your work schedule according to overall organizational needs.   Obviously, all elements of your job have some importance. But in developing a realistic work schedule, it's essential that either on paper or in your mind you set the various elements in a hierarchy according to importance. By setting priorities:
   a. you know how much relative time to assign to an activity;
   b. you can reschedule; in case an item of higher priority "heats up," an immediate low-priority task can be set aside.

3. Schedule your routines. Most executives follow both a daily and a weekly schedule. Typically, correspondence is handled first thing in the morning, ongoing tasks checked, progress reports read, communications with other executives made for a variety of operating reasons, and so on, through the day. Weekly items, regular weekly conferences, for example, are fitted in on appropriate days, as required. In developing your schedule, observe two points:

a. *Consolidate like tasks.* For example, all correspondence should be done in a single sitting, all phone calls made consecutively, as far as possible.

b. *Allow for the unexpected.* As experienced executives know, their jobs are prone to emergencies, interruptions, even sudden changes in direction. Be prepared to juggle items on your schedule, as necessary.

4. Delegate. Assigning specific tasks for which you are directly responsible is a major factor in executive time saving and job accomplishment. (Because delegation is a crucial factor in executive job performance, you'll find it covered at length, starting on page 59.)

5. Review periodically. Few executive jobs remain the same, year in, year out. That's why, every six or twelve months, it's desirable to assess your job for changes in responsibility and activity. When changes or trends toward change, are spotted, you can make appropriate adjustments in your work schedules.

For those executives who want to really dig into the whole problem of self-scheduling in depth, the item on page 15 offers help in conducting a self-time study.

➲ THE IMPORTANCE OF PACE AS A TIME-SAVER

> *"He's a man on the move."*
> *"He's got a lot of executive drive."*

Labels like these are thought to spot the outstanding executive. Maybe. Maybe not. The inexperienced manager who says with pride, "It's drive, drive all day," may feel he deserves high marks for performance. But the effective manager is one who paces himself: who may be going like a jet for a while, working at a leisurely pace a bit later, and completely relaxing (yes, during working hours) after that.

Athletes understand the need for pacing. The miler doesn't knock himself out of the race by trying to burn up the track the first quarter. Similarly, the real champion has a sense of pace that is partly attuned to the competition, partly to the need for outstanding performance for its own sake.

In your own case—

- Only go all out for the tasks that demand it.
- Take breaks—coffee, a walk down the corridor or another building, a feet-on-the-desk interlude—*before* you reach the exhaustion point.
- Add a relaxation period, when you feel either physical or mental fatigue beginning to appear. *How* and *how much* you relax—ten minutes, two hours,—depends on your preference. The rest may take the form of a prolonged lunch, or conversations with colleagues or on-the-job friends. One executive, enmeshed in a month-long grueling project, found a stimulating movie a perfect workbreak and mind refresher.

The above points tie in to the matter of your daily energy cycle, the next item.

➜ ADUSTING YOUR SCHEDULE TO YOUR PERSONAL DAILY ENERGY CYCLE

Undoubtedly, you've observed it in yourself: your energies have fairly regular peaks and valleys. There are times during the working day that you feel up to anything, at other periods you would just as soon coast along.

The well-known industrial psychologist Norman R.F. Maier studied the working efficiency of a group of executives, and charted his findings, as illustrated below.

Remember that the curve represents the rise and fall in efficiency of the "average." Your own personal energies may closely resemble those charted, or deviate somewhat. In any event, the same factors apply:

Warm-up period. Note the rise from the morning start. Physiologists explain the warm-up on a partially physical basis. Muscles must be limbered; changes in blood pressure and circulation take place.

Fatigue drop. Fatigue is the usual explanation given for the lowering of efficiency in the course of the working period. In some cases, this tends to be cumulative.

End spurt. Although not shown on the chart, there is a tendency for efficiency to increase as the end of the work period is approached. In some cases, a similar increase may occur before breaks in general—lunch periods, completion of a task, and so on.

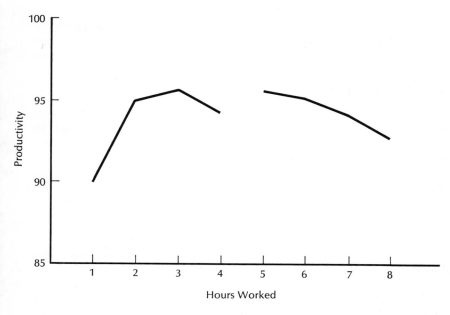

Personal Efficiency Chart.

Your own peaks and valleys. To chart your own ups and downs of daily efficiency, keep a brief record, noting:

- the hours you feel the peppiest
- the times fatigue catches up with you
- the periods you feel most at ease mentally
- the times you find it difficult to work

Tabulate the results over several days to pinpoint your strong and weak periods. Then, the final payoff step:

Tailor your daily working schedule to your personal chart. For instance, save tough, demanding jobs for high-energy periods. Fit routine tasks into low-energy periods. Fill in mental doldrums with the tasks that almost "do themselves." Tackle new projects, or mentally taxing ones, when your energy peaks are highest.

➲ ONE EXECUTIVE'S TIME TEASER

"May sound like kidding yourself," says James R. Kray, president of a Los Angeles department store, "but when I have a rush project for my office staff, I set the wall clock an hour ahead. Then, if the job has to be done by four o'clock, say, we've got an hour's cushion. Very psychological, but it works."

➜ HOW TO MAKE ROOM FOR A RUSH PROJECT

Every once in a while, an executive is asked by his superior to "drop everything and push through the X Project." The executive has an immediate problem of responding immediately to the request. Here are the three possible ways he can answer his boss:

O.K. This admittedly is boss-pleasing. But if it's done off the top of the head, the executive may not be able to deliver.

A flat no. If you have the status and the judgment to tell your superior you are not in the position to perform as requested, this may let you off the hook. However, it may also suggest that you don't understand certain business considerations or that you haven't recognized the exceptional case calling for special effort.

Maybe. That's the third possibility. It's safer all-around, but it can be too cautious in some instances and too promising in others. Any one of the three reactions may be correct, but the executive must choose the best one. There are no hard and fast rules, but the following checklists suggest guides.

Consider *okay* if . . .

- The boss is willing to accept delays in other work.
- All facts and information are readily available.
- Key employees are on the job or can be called in.
- All necessary supplies and materials are on hand.
- All necessary equipment is available and in good working order.
- You can depend on the group to "give a little extra."
- Your boss will go along with your decisions on overtime, additional expenses, etc.
- You have checked service departments—everything from Engineering to Safety—to make sure you'll get any service you need.
- You have checked other units that may be involved in helping process the work, to make sure they'll work with you on the emergency schedule.
- The company (and you) have a lot to gain by an affirmative answer— and delivering on your promise.

Consider *no* if . . .

You're sure that the priority of the rush job is less than work currently in the department.

You know it isn't humanly possible to do the job in the allotted time. (This usually means the person making the request doesn't understand as well as you do what's involved.)

There's a modified *no* answer that really amounts to *no, but.* . . . Here, if someone up the line can help eliminate an obstacle or qualify the request, you may be able to deliver some effective no, *but* answers that can make everybody happy, and you look good:

"No, I can't finish by five tomorrow, but I could give you X at that time, and Y by noon, next day."

"If you'd be willing to take the report as a rough draft and finish it. . . ." Or, "If they'd be willing to take them packed in bulk instead of individually. . . ." Or, "If they could use the order done with regular materials instead of the special formula on the specifications. . . ."

"No, we can't do it unless you can get Fred Bishop and his crew to assist me. . . ."

Consider *maybe* if . . .

In this situation, it's wise to use *maybe* only if you're pretty sure you can deliver as requested. The executive who says "maybe," and then comes through on schedule, rates a gold star. The one who falls down, hasn't added to his reputation for dependability or capability.

The fact is, almost every job can be done *if*—*if*—your boss or the front office is willing to go along with the extra costs, delays, or other inconveniences of making unexpected shifts in work schedules. The other part of the problem rests with the manager and the degree to which he has been able to build flexibility into his department. Essentially, this means making the entire work force understand that emergency jobs or rush orders aren't a headache, but a challenging part of the unit's responsibility that must be tackled when the heat's on.

➦ DEVELOP A SENSE OF TIME

We're notoriously subjective in our time estimates. To the man sitting on a hot stove, a second is an eternity. The amorous swain out with his girl will tell you an evening passes in a moment. Yet, it's important for us to be more objective about time, because the way we view it will affect what we do with it. These guides can help us develop a realistic and useful view of time:

Be a clock watcher.   Check for the correct time in the course of your daily routines. The more you do so, the better you will become at estimating time passage and expenditures. Remember that people tend to *underestimate* the time involved in what they *like* to do; *overestimate*, what they don't.

Watch out when time drags. This may be a signal of time waste and may call for your tackling another task that puts you under the pressure of immediate activity.

Come up for a breather. Absorption in a task *may* be fine. But when you're "lost in work," take time to ascertain that it's a job that deserves the time and concentration it's getting.

Avoid being "rushed to death." Being caught up in a sequence of tasks may mean you're very much with it, and swinging along at peak efficiency. But it may also mean that you're being pushed along by a series of "demand" tasks that have low priority—in which case, you may be wasting time.

Keep the end of the day in view. Knowing that you have "just one more hour to go" may suggest a rearrangement of tasks, so the essential ones that can't wait for tomorrow, get taken care of.

➲ **THE IMPORTANCE OF FLEXIBILITY IN EXECUTIVE TIME SCHEDULING**

Whether you use a highly systematic method of scheduling your workday—such as a self-time study—or develop a schedule on a practical, "demand" basis, there are overall considerations about executive time that suggest the need for *flexibility*. That is, you must be prepared to set aside one task for a more important one, or to drop everything for an emergency situation.

1. The executive job is essentially nonroutine. While every executive knows he has recurring tasks—he must cope with the in-box every day, for example—the crucial elements of the job generally do not fit into neat time compartments. A discussion with a group of key subordinates to plan a new project, a consultation with one's superior, may cut deeply into planned time expenditures.

2. Trouble shooting and fire fighting is a standard part of your job. Any difficulty that develops in the echelons below you tends to be kicked upstairs. It may be a personnel problem, or what to do about a plan gone awry. But you, as the court of last resort, are expected to take over if those below you are unable to cope.

3. Single time expenditures tend to be short. A time study of executive activity showed that few executives can spend more than twenty minutes on a single task. This fact probably accounts for executive "homework," at least as much as executive overload. The items tucked into executive briefcases for home attention are usually those that need hours of undivided attention.

The proper response to such considerations is to build time latitude into your time allotments. Be prepared to do a half-hour task in two fifteen minute takes. Be prepared to do a Monday task on Tuesday, if an unexpected conference with top priority completely shreds your Monday plans.

➲ HABITS CAN SAVE TIME

Some of your daily habits waste time, others save it. Psychologists make the point that habits are of two kinds:

Adaptive.   These are useful. For example: you develop the habit of checking the mail first thing in the morning, because it often contains orders or requests that influence the day's sequence of business.

Nonadaptive.   These are illogical, time-wasting. For example: an executive has developed the habit of going through his mail each morning. But since the correspondence only bears on routine matters that have to be taken up later in the day, he will have to reread it all.

Nonadaptive habits are usually adaptive habits that no longer have a useful purpose. For example, an executive reaches for a pencil in his vest pocket, only to recall he no longer wears a vest.

Getting habits to save instead of waste time means eliminating nonadaptive habits, developing adaptive ones. It isn't easy, but it's possible. Here are two ways to proceed:

Will power and won't power.   Take yourself in hand; be tough with yourself. Let's say, for instance, there's a tendency to bog down, become enmeshed in the unimportant. Force, persuade, teach yourself to pull out, get back onto a more productive track. The executive mentioned above, who needlessly goes through his mail, can force himself to give up the practice, with the realization that he'll be doing it later at a more propitious time.

The systematic approach.   Look at the problem in the way a time-study man approaches a work procedure: (a) size up what's to be done; (b) work out a series of movements that do the job; (c) whittle away at the procedure till it's efficient.

Accordingly, here's how you can substitute a timesaving for a time-wasting habit:

- Spot the habits that have outlived their usefulness.
- Work out a new habit to replace the old.
- Check the time and other efficiency factors involved; make sure it's really economical.
- Follow the sequence through.
- Repeat.
- Keep on repeating, till the new habit is established, the old one eliminated.

Finally, in getting rid of nonadaptive habits, remember that it's easier to substitute an action for a timewasting habit than to simply try to avoid it. For example, the executive who needlessly reads his mail will stop this time waste more effectively by filling the time by a desirable activity—contacts with subordinates, for example.

➲ SUITING TIME TO TASK

It's easy enough to say, "Give each task the time it deserves—no more, no less." But how to do it? These guides help:

1. Take time to take stock. Stop once or twice during the day to see how you're doing. Are you on schedule? Anything come up to throw you off the track? What can you do to get back, if you're off (delegate a task, reshuffle your task sequence, get help from colleagues, your superior)?

2. Watch out for time "hogs." A pet project, an intriguing but low-priority problem, the persuasiveness of a subordinate, may get you involved in disproportionate time allotments. Avoid such diversions.

3. Leave time for long-range elements of your job. Thomas Watson's admonition to his IBM managers, "Think," is not misplaced. It's amazing how seldom *thinking* appears in a listing of executive activity. Yet planning, problem-solving, and applying creativity to achieving objectives are often the most important, indeed, the payoff elements in your job. If these key items are missing from your workday, do what is necessary to include them, through delegation, etc.

4. Stay out front. In the race with time, you must lead, or you're in trouble. The executive who chases the clock, trying to catch up, is at a disadvantage. Again, if you find you're falling behind in meeting daily or weekly obligations, get out from under routines you can assign to others.

5. Review a sizable work period for overall stock-taking. You may have to be practical, and adopt the Casey Stengel view that, "You win a few, lose a few." Everyone has bad days, when the end of the work period finds one's schedule a shambles. O.K. But assess your performance over a week or a month. If from a longer-range perspective you're satisfied, forget the occasional "black rock" days. But if you're dissatisfied on looking back, tackle the problem of self-scheduling from scratch, as recommended on page 15.

➲ USE DEADLINES AND SUBGOALS

You can store up time just as electricity is stored in a battery. You do it by getting ahead.

Unfortunately, many executives do the opposite. They dig into their supply of time by transferring items from today's calendar to tomorrow's—when a phone call or a short memo could eliminate the items from both. Two devices help:

Deadlines.   A deadline puts you in a direct race against the clock. In many cases you find deadlines built into a task: "Let me know by three o'clock tomorrow whether we'll be able to handle the Johnson matter," your superior asks. When there is no deadline, you gain an advantage by creating your own. For example, you tell your secretary, "We want to get that report out by the last mail of the day."

Subgoals.   It's easier to keep track of progress with several sub-goals, rather than one long-term goal. And you have the added psychological spur of dealing with handleable, bite-size segments of time. For example: executive Jim Smith and his staff are starting a project that requires a week for completion. At the end of each day the group meets to evaluate progress, adjust methods of operation, solve problems that have appeared. The alternative, to work with only the final, distant goal in sight, fails to provide the incentive for daily accomplishment. Lacking also is the critique that helps keep them on top of the operation.

➲ TIME SALVAGING

"The moving finger writes; and, having writ, Moves on. . . ." said Omar Khayyam.

We tend to agree. We can't turn the clock back. *But,* the fact is, *time is salvageable.* Consider: when you use other people's ideas, you're using *their* time—the time they spent in developing the ideas. By checking other people's experiences you also save time. You avoid the necessity for repeating the time-consuming moves they had to make before they found the right answers.

At the top of the prospect list for time salvaging is your own past activity. Make it a practice to review your own past experience. For example: you spend time investigating the possibilities of a new office procedure, but end up in a blind alley. That time is not necessarily lost. At a later date you may get the additional information you need to round out the investigation satisfactorily.

To recap:

- Check back on your own past efforts, procedures, ideas. Ask yourself whether changed circumstances make it possible to apply them successfully *now*.
- Look for the products of time spent by others that you can adapt and apply.

➔ DO TWO THINGS AT ONCE

"You can't do two things at once," is an old saying that originated before carbon paper and the coaxial cable.

You *can* do two things at once—and save considerable time in the process. Just to convince yourself: Take a pencil and do a simple problem in arithmetic, say multiplying 916, 345 by 2. At the same time, recite a poem you know by heart.

A familiar illustration of multiple activity is the executive who (a) sits in his bathtub, (b) under a sunlamp, (c) reading a fistful of reports.

Here are some suggestions to help you get a double payoff from your time:

- Try to design dual-purpose activities. An executive, screening resumes for a stenographer, at the same time watches for the highly-qualified applicant who might be able to start as an executive secretary.
- Link activities that can be done simultaneously. Supervising a subordinate who is preparing a highly-detailed report, an executive catches up on his mail and discusses his plans for the week with his assistant.
- Lump together tasks that can be handled in the *same place*. An executive, flying across the continent, takes care of several contacts for the company. And bunching telephone calls is another application of the same principle.
- Start simultaneously different tasks that can proceed alongside one another. Where the jobs are to finish at the same time, you start the longer operation earlier.

➡ PUT TRAVEL TIME TO USE

The jet plane is a great time-saver—and a great time-consumer. More and more, executives are taking to the airways to conduct business in person, because it's now practical to get from New York to Boston, Washington, Los Angeles, London, Sydney, or Tokyo in a reasonably short time.

But whether a business trip takes an hour or a day, on train, plane, or boat, even an hour spent commuting can be a waste if it's spent staring at an unseen landscape, or doing a crossword puzzle (unless you're a puzzle fan, and you put crossword puzzling under the heading of Relaxation).

Fortunately, travel time can be put to productive use. Here are time-saving travel tips:

1. Avoid "jetophilia." Some executives seem to get caught up in a travel, do-it-in-person routine. The result: a certain percentage of their traveling is unnecessary. Benefit from their mistake and ask, before committing yourself to a personal appearance, "Is the trip necessary?" Don't travel if a letter or phone call will do. The personal touch may be just the factor needed to clinch a big deal. But if something less is involved, can you send a subordinate?

2. Schedule trips at low-pressure times.   In arranging for a personal appearance in another city, try to fit the trip into a day or week when you have the most time latitude.

3. Use a recording machine.   Many executives report successful conversion of hours spent on train and plane to productive time by dictating reports, memos, and letters. The newest recorders are small and lightweight. Mailing back the tape, sleeve, or cartridge to the office means the material can be typed and ready on your return. Double payoff: when a report is to be made on the outcome of the trip itself, executives say that dictating the report on the return trip gets it into permanent form while impressions are still fresh, and puts less of a burden on note-taking and memory.

4. Do brain work.   Armed with a pencil and a piece of paper—or pen and notebook, if your prefer—you can tackle problems, do planning, and develop projects, without threat of the usual office interruptions.

5. Do your "must" reading.   The normal reading load of managers has been rising steeply over the years. And some of it just can't be shunted off on subordinates, or neglected. Trade and industry information, new management methods, business developments, books on subjects relevant and helpful to your professional activities —all these require your attention to prevent gaps in your knowledge. Travel time is often made to order for this type of professional updating.

6. Transact your business at travel terminals.   A New York executive recruiter travels from city to city to interview prospects for placement. He saves himself hours of bucking downtown traffic by meeting the job applicants at air or train terminals. Sometimes lunch in a terminal restaurant gives him the "office" he needs. If more than one prospect is to be interviewed, he takes a room at an airport hotel or motel.

7. Bone up for a meeting.   Regardless of where the meeting is held, or for what purpose, going over relevant materials during your trip keeps the details fresh in your mind. Not only can you commit facts to memory, but you can plan your approach or strategy with the advantage of the imminence of the meeting as an aid to your mental operations.

8. Schedule visiting time as carefully as office time.   A frequent problem of efficient use of travel time is travel delay. Many an executive has experienced the frustration and time-waste of train schedule slippage, of being fogbound at an airport, or of being stacked up in an air traffic jam. But barring such efficiency destroyers, you can trim trips by some traditional means:

- Travel the most efficient way. If there is a cost differential, consider whether the fastest way may not be worth more to you in dollars and sense.
- Have your secretary or travel department check schedules, and put you on the most convenient runs or flights, both coming and going.
- Try to schedule the actual business contact so as to permit the best travel arrangements. If squeezing a meeting into two hours instead of three will save you several hours of waiting for transportation, let the others in on the meeting know of your time situation, and streamline the meeting.

9. Assess percentage of your time spent traveling.   Executives occasionally find that, without their being aware of it, more and more of their time is spent "on the road." It may, of course, be necessary, and time well spent. But it also may mean that an undesirable "travel habit" has been developed—where "I'll hop down tomorrow," gets to be the standard response for every minor crisis. Or an increasing travel schedule may mean that your responsibilities have been changing, and too much travel becomes a symptom of job content gotten out of hand. It's worth your time to conduct an overall review, if you are seeing too little of your office.

➲ TIME: QUANTITY VS QUALITY

Says an executive: "My time's my own. I get to my office any time I like before nine, and leave when I please after six."

But the **quantity** of time executives spend on the job is less important than its **quality**—that is, **how** it's spent. Hours devoted to routines better done by a subordinate may be profitless; one inspired thought developed in a few minutes may make your company rich.

Recommendation: in your time allocations, favor high-level elements like planning, analyzing, problem-solving, over routines which lend themselves to delegation.

➲ HOW TO MAKE A PERSONAL TIME STUDY

Usually, when a well-intentioned novice writes an article on executive time-saving, it usually starts by directing, "Make a self-time study. Keep a complete, accurate record of your time expenditures over a one or two month period. . . ."

There's a monumental task, tossed off in a sentence. If you attempted it, chances are you'd have to stop doing the very things you were trying to record, because you wouldn't have the time.

Nevertheless, it is possible to do a brief self-study that will yield helpful information. Three steps give you the data on which to base a weekly work schedule. If possible, get your secretary to work with you, both in keeping track of your time expenditures, and writing down the observations.

1. Keep a record. Select a normal work week. If unexpected developments disarrange a day, restudy this day during the following week.

Note the starting and stopping time of each activity. For example: "9:00 to 9:20—Reading incoming correspondence."

"9:21 to 9:40—Conferring with Smith about the new display project."

Keep your record sheets close at hand. Make your notations as soon as possible after a task is finished. Don't overlook small items.

A number of five-minute jobs can account for a major chunk of working time.

After you've kept the record for a week, or its equivalent, and you feel it's fairly representative of your schedule—

2. Analyze the data.   The next step requires sorting out your time expenditures. Here is a suggested set of headings. Add to it as your own data may indicate.

Contacts With Subordinates	Administrative Matters	Intracompany Contacts	Outside Contacts
Training and instruction	Correspondence	Reports	Customers
Work assignment and discussion	Departmental progress review	Interviews and conferences	Suppliers
General personnel matters	Planning	Contacting other departments	Service firms
"Social" contacts Other	Other	Other	Other

ANALYSIS SHEET

After you have distributed the items from your time record under the appropriate general headings, and indicated the time allotments, you're in a position to evaluate the results.

First question to ask as you look at the figures: is the time desirably balanced? Are your major time allocations going for top priority activities?

Additional questions:

- Am I devoting adequate time for communications with my staff, superior, other executives?
- Is sufficient time being allowed for planning, both short and long-range?
- Am I devoting sufficient time to the development of my staff, both as individuals and as a team?

Your analysis can help you remove some standard obstacles to executive efficiency. For example, wasted time may result from your duplicating the work of an assistant. Or, you may find that unscheduled items—that is, interruptions—consume sizable quantities of time. This may suggest possibilities for delegation or other means of shedding duties that consume disproportionate amounts of your time.

3. Restructure your time outlays. What you've learned in your analysis can be used to revise your schedule. But no radical change may be necessary. Rearranging a few key activities can make a great difference in your efficiency. Here are some possible steps:

Group similar items. You save time if you perform the same types of work in sequence. For example, handle all dictation at one time. Or, consider your contacts with a colleague: you avoid the need to walk back and forth between the same offices, and reduce starting and stopping by transacting all your business at one meeting. If routine matters of mutual interest arise, let them accumulate until you're ready for another session with him.

Change timing of key items. You may find it advantageous to re-schedule some activities from morning to afternoon, or vice versa. A daily progress check with your assistant, for example, might best take place at the end of the day, and should be rescheduled if it's been relegated to another less logical time.

Use for the miscellaneous items. Examine the items that don't fall neatly under any of the headings of your analysis sheet. For example, take a time expenditure like casual conversations with colleagues. If possible, shift these around so that they don't break up items that would be better uninterrupted. Your purpose is to enlarge as much as possible the time spans you devote to a given task. And don't overlook the possibility of shifting low-priority interruptions and so-called emergencies that can really wait to low-pressure hours of your workday.

2. Effective Communication

> *"Nobody ever tells me these things. . . ."*
> *"Why didn't you tell me sooner. . . ."*
> *"I guess I should have included you in the list of people getting my memos. . . ."*

The list of obstacles to good communication is almost endless. And each failure can mean serious losses—errors, delays, bottlenecks, misunderstandings. Accordingly, the executive who maintains effective communications up, down, and laterally has taken a giant step toward increasing his effectiveness. Points covered in the pages that follow are keys to greater communication effectiveness.

➲ **GETTING YOUR SECRETARY TO SCREEN CALLS**

It's up to you to tell your secretary how you want incoming phone calls handled. Calls can be broken down into general categories:

Business calls—urgent

Business calls—routine

Calls of solicitation (salesmen, for example)

Calls of inquiry

Calls from business friends that may be either business or personal

Personal calls

No general rules tell you how to handle calls in each of the above categories. But using the list as a basis for a discussion with your secretary you can tell her—

which calls come through immediately

which calls require taking a message for a call-back

which calls require a turn-down: "I'm sorry but I am quite sure Mr. Smith is not interested."

But it's important to realize that your secretary is a public relations operative in her position as call-screener. A secretary may make it all too clear that she's on the line to keep people away from the boss. The result can be cold, impersonal, and destructive of your executive image. The effective secretary is one who shows that she's not only serving her boss but is rendering a service to the caller.

➲ **HANDLING THE PAPER FLOOD**

The correspondence load tends to be a highly individualized problem. No two executives face the same situation. By the same token, no one employee can cover all aspects of the problem for everybody. Here are some basic methods that executives can use to individualize their handling of paperwork:

■ *The physical factor*   It's not unusual to find a lopsided pile of mail in an undersized in-box. Of course, a barrel-sized receptacle would *increase* rather than minimize the problem. But just check to make sure that you have an *adequate* container for incoming material.

■ *Pre-sort delivery*   One method of pre-sorting can be especially effective if you can get cooperation from your mail handlers. Here are two versions of such a plan:

Company I. A color system.   Rush interoffice memos are sent in red envelopes. Being easy to spot, they can be fished out of a pile of less pressing matters. Certain reports and other key material are distinguished in a similar manner.

Mailboy cooperation.   Mailboys are trained to do a rough sorting job, putting correspondence from the outside in one pile, company correspondence in another.

And here is a variation of some of the same elements:

Company II. Method of delivery.   "I ask the mail boy to hand me really important communications in person," reports an executive of his company. That's possible when you can tell him, "If it's from Mr. Smith, it's urgent."

In some cases, of course, you may want to arrange a special delivery for high priority items.

Size.   An executive had routine but *important* communication forms made up on eight-by-eleven cards. This card can be spotted in a stack of mail quickly.

Color.   Rush items from the front office are sent on colored stock—pink, yellow, buff, etc. Each color is keyed to a particular company function: pink for sales, yellow for purchasing, buff for personnel, and so on.

Once the difference among the items is made visual and obvious, pre-sorting can be carried out easily. The only prerequisites are that the system you use be *simple,* so that it doesn't overburden the intelligence of those using it, and it must be *consistent,* so that the chance of your color code getting mixed up is practically zero.

Receiving line.   To be effective, your plan for handling correspondence must include some kind of priority procedure.

What comes first? The executive who doesn't know the answer is liable to waste time on the unimportant, while the really critical matters go begging.

The priority problem is part of administrative detail that usually *cannot* be delegated. *Your* knowledge of your operation, *your* evaluation of what's important must underlie any priority system.

Priority "machine."   One executive uses what can be called the "three-box method" of assigning priority. In one box he puts the correspondence that requires immediate attention. The second compartment gets the letters, memos, etc. which have to be disposed of in a *week.* The third gets correspondence with *no special deadline.* This last accumulation is either discarded or acted upon periodically.

A variation of the same principle: the executive keeps his correspondence in a pile in the order in which it is to be handled. As new correspondence arrives, he sorts it into the proper place in the pile according to its comparative priority.

The one on top is always the most current piece of business. And, of course, he works from the top down.

➲ ONE EXECUTIVE'S MAIL-HANDLING TECHNIQUE

Andrew A. Lynn, President of Yardley of London, Inc., handles his morning paperwork as follows:

1. Read all mail.
2. Dictate replies to all letters requiring personal attention.
3. Instruct secretary on how to reply to routine letters.
4. Forward mail to be handled by others to the appropriate associate, with comments or instructions, as necessary.
5. File mail to be acted on at a future date in pending files, and instruct secretary to present them when they are due.
6. Sort out reading matter and periodicals, put those to be read in a briefcase for home or commuting perusal.

Even where secretaries are competent to reply to routine letters, Lynn feel the executive should sign them. He says, "You should know the contents of any letter that goes out over your name. You owe the recipient the courtesty of a *bona fide* signature."

You may agree with Lynn's statement. On the other hand, some executives use the time-saver of having their names signed by an assistant with the notation, "Per R.C." the initials of the assistant.

➲ SIX OBSTACLES TO COMMUNICATIONS WITH YOUR BOSS

Even the best of bosses may have qualities that may create communications problems. Here are the six major complaints executives make about their contacts up the lines and what can be done about them:

1. When He Won't Listen. Many top executives say they don't listen to communications from subordinates because information is presented in poorly organized form, or because opinions are brought in half-baked. Perhaps your boss *ought* to listen; but since he's human, you may have to encourage him to pay attention. Whenever you communicate with him—

- Be brief.
- Be clear on the purpose of your communication.
- Define the problem involved, so that he can see it—fast.

- Organize the relevant facts so that he can get a grip on them—fast.
- Map out possible alternatives, and give him your recommendations— clearly labeling what is opinion and what is fact.
- Appeal to your boss's special interests: do things his way, as far as possible.
- Sell the benefits of his paying attention.
- Present any recommendations you have in terms of what they will do for him and for the company.

2. When He Won't Talk. "Cancel all overtime starting today!" Nothing more—no further word of explanation to you.

You know your people have been counting on the extra pay. With no explanation to give them, you expect trouble. It's his mistake— but your problem.

Often a boss's failure to tell the whole story is simply due to the fact that he has overlooked it. In the press of business, the matter slips his mind. Here are arguments that make your case with him:

- Lack of information can foul up your handling of a situation for which *he* is ultimately responsible.
- Incomplete information may send you off in the wrong direction— causing delays in meeting deadlines and similar waste.
- You may know of a better alternative than one he suggests.

But, be specific. Talk about real cases and actual or potential consequences.

The most alarming aspect of this problem, though, occurs when the boss just hasn't given you any clue at all that something is in the wind.

You have to be on the alert, develop a nose for news, an eye for clues. If your boss has failed to schedule a regular period for getting together with you, make it a practice to keep in touch with him regularly on an informal basis, at a time when you know the pressure is off him.

3. When He Won't See You. The boss behind the Mahogany Curtain is certainly a most difficult problem for every executive. You may have to prove that time spent with you is beneficial to him.

How? The steps recommended above for the boss who won't listen apply to the boss who won't see you. Add one additional requirement: you may have to pave the way with a telephone call, a brief preliminary one-sentence remark to him personally, or a message relayed to him through his secretary. In any of those cases, your short message must be well thought out to:

- arouse his interest
- suggest benefits that can be derived
- indicate that you will not burden him

4. When He's Indecisive.   He's the kind of boss, who, for example, fails to give needed information. But later, when things turn out badly, he says: "You sure screwed up the works. . . ."

On the other hand, the error into which many people tend to fall is the belief that the top executive will be able to answer any question—whether it has to do with a purchase of a box of paper clips or the relocation of an entire factory—off the cuff.

If your superior is indecisive, first make sure that you're not expecting decision-making that would be as inadvisable as it would be impossible.

Let's assume, however, that the boss is, in fact, a Hamlet in executive clothing. Here are the moves to make in order to get a decision:

- First, try to find out what decisions he would like *you* to make. That in itself is a decision, of course, but it's one that would relieve him of a heavy burden.
- Second, when you do have a question for an indecisive boss, marshal all the facts he will need for a decision before you put the question to him.
- Third, spell out *why* a decision is needed and *when*.
- Fourth, if there is any chance of a kickback on the decision you ask for, spell it out. It's amazing how often we delay decisions because consciously or unconsciously we are trying to anticipate any trouble they may cause. If you spell out what such trouble may be, you save your boss the time it would take him to think these matters through for himself.

5. If He's a Bypasser.   He's the boss who steps right in and gives orders to your subordinates. It's safe to assume that there are reasons for the bypassing: the boss is in a hurry; he thinks he's helping you; he expects to get quicker or better results. In any case, steps like these can help:

- Don't show personal resentment. The important thing is not the damage done to your pride, but to the work and morale of the department. Keep it matter-of-fact; avoid accusations.
- Be specific about the harm done. Stay on a factual level. Don't suppose or guess. Show what actually happened in the past. (If nothing has happened, there may be no point in raising the question.)
- Watch for long-range effects. In some cases, bypassing may have no immediate consequences. But over a period of time, you may find your position with your people is weakened. They look elsewhere

for information and instructions, for example. Discipline itself may become a problem. In this case, your best bet is to sit down with your boss and give him the whole picture as you see it.

Your biggest problem will be to keep the issue from becoming *personal*. Don't let feelings and emotions complicate the situation.

6. If He's on Your Neck.   There are many possible reasons for the boss hanging around all the time. Maybe he's worried about the way things are going, wants to pitch in. In that case, accept his help.

Or maybe he feels uncertain about how well the job is being done. The remedy is to give him more information. Ask yourself:

- Are your reports too infrequent? Watch when he shows the greatest interest—if it's a couple of days before the regular report is due, volunteer the information earlier.
- Do your reports contain the type of information he wants? Pay particular attention to the kinds of questions he asks on his visits to your department. Make that information available to him regularly.
- Are your reports too detailed—or lacking in detail? Either may be wrong.

In any event, remember that your first communications duty to the boss is to give him all the information he wants.

And, of course, to your subordinates, *you're* the boss. Can you help *their* contacts with *you*?

➲ IMPROVING YOUR PUBLIC SPEAKING EFFECTIVENESS

"The executive who talks impressively in public may not be better than his tongue-tied opposite number, but he sure makes a better impression." That's a common opinion in top executive circles. The average executive has many opportunities for public speaking. Everything from the informal company meeting to an invitation to address an industry-wide convention may come your way. If you are less effective as a public speaker than you would like to be, consider first the three obstacles that act as deterrents:

- *Attitude.* "I can't give a speech," is a common excuse. In his book *People in Quandaries*, Wendell Johnson calls this defeatist attitude IFD disease—that is, idealization, frustration, demoralization. Many people set too high standards for themselves, are frustrated when they prove unreachable, and then consider themselves failures. If you have to coax yourself to accept speaking opportunities, remember that there are very few *great* speakers. Just set yourself a goal of a talk that is *adequate for the purpose*. (Obviously you will improve with practice.)

■ *Stage fright.* Everyone experiences it, from the high school vale-dictorian to the seasoned professional actor.

The fear of being "on stage" can be minimized. You may grope for a word; your voice may develop a quiver; your knees may feel shaky or—even actually quake. *So what.* If a man is realistic about his speaking abilities, expects to make mistakes and resolves to speak regardless of his fears, *generally he will do fine.* How often have you heard a speaker complimented enthusiastically respond by saying, "I was scared to death." He may have been. But chances are he was the only one who knew it.

■ *Opportunity.* Some executives don't consider speaking to groups important. "Why should I bother. It's a lot of trouble. . . ." Why should you bother? Because you want to be a leader, a motivator, and to grab a piece of the action.

In addition to minimizing the three mental blocks just described, there are three approaches that help you score: *Planning, Practice, Performance.*

1. Planning: the Preliminaries. In journalism school, aspiring reporters are taught to start out on each assignment with five questions in mind: why? who? what? where? when? Only when they have come up with the answers to all five will they be able to write the whole story.

The same technique can be used by aspiring speakers. When you are to give a talk begin your preparations by asking yourself:

Why are you giving the talk? To tell other executives about a pet project? To alert your men to new plans? To ask for help on a special project? The answer will put your purpose in clear perspective, help you get it across easily.

Who will you be talking to? Rank-and-file employees? Managers? Students? Industry businessmen? Will they be knowledgeable, sympathetic, resistant? The more you know about the audience, the less likely you will be to fail—with the words you use, the ideas you express, the way you present them. Knowing the audience and its areas of interest helps you decide what aspects of a subject to cover.

What do you want to say? What is the *one* major idea you want to put across? What points can you include to support it; what can you leave out? As we suggested, the subject must suit the capacity and interests of the audience.

Closely related to *what,* is the consideration of length—*how long* to make the talk. The answer to *how long* depends on the scope of your subject, as well as the actual amount of time allotted to you.

Where will you be speaking? In a conference room where there will be blackboards, tables, comfortable chairs available? In a TV studio? In a work area where you may have to contend with noise, interruptions, distractions? Your talk will have to be planned around the place—and its assets or liabilities.

When will you be speaking? Early morning or late evening? Is this to be a one-man show or will there be other speakers on the bill? Will you be the first speaker, or the last? Clearly, your position in the sequence of speakers will influence your approach; for example, you would want to put extra punch into a talk to rouse an audience wearied by a succession of previous speakers.

Once you have the five W's answered to your satisfaction, you can proceed to . . .

Planning: the Nitty-Gritty. An important factor in any successful speech is planning so that you know beforehand what you're going to say. This doesn't mean writing a talk out sentence by sentence. A person seldom writes as he talks, and what reads well on paper usually sounds stilted and dull when spoken. What you're after is a clear outline of your main ideas, plus brief notes, and key phrases to serve as an assist to your memory.

Organize the main part of the talk first.   Jot down the major theme of the talk and then decide on several key points to support it, shuffling and reshuffling until they're arranged in logical order, one leading naturally into the next. Add subordinate points, case histories, examples to back up each idea—but only those that actually help to clarify the idea. Don't try to include too much—it will only confuse your listeners. Better to say less, effectively, and have it remembered.

If you're going to want notes with you when you speak (and most people do), print each key idea at the top of a 3" x 5" or 4" x 6" card. Then under each heading list the necessary subordinate points, brief notes, or phrases that will serve as reminders.

Plan a "socko" opening . . . Start with something that will gain the immediate attention of your audience. It may be in the form of a question, a human interest story, a striking quotation, a statement of disturbing fact—but whatever your choice, it should be relevant to your topic. Keep it short, informal. And, unless you're an experienced raconteur, avoid humor—when it doesn't work it's embarrassing, to you and your audience. (Good idea: write out the actual opening sentences on a card—and memorize them.)

. . . *and a forceful, thoughtful closing.*   The close of a speech is a strategic element, since what is said last is likely to be remembered longest. Plan your ending carefully, know almost word for word what you are going to say. One of the best ways to end is to briefly summarize your main points. Telling your people what you said *after* you've already said it, really makes it stick. Or you may want to wind up with an appeal for action, or a sincere compliment for the audience. Your closing sentences should round out your talk, leaving no loose edges.

Keep your talk audience-centered.   People are much *less interested* in what's going on in Timbuktu than in what's happening in their own backyards. Talk in terms of the problems facing the people who will be listening to you—use illustrations and examples that they will recognize. Everything you say, and any visual aids you use, should relate to what they do, want, and worry about.

Plan for participation.   How will you know whether your audience has understood what you've been talking about? The best way to find out is to get them to tell it back to you. If appropriate, plan questions *now* that will promote discussions *then*. Don't leave this to chance. Add the questions to your notation cards—at the proper time use them to get the group started talking back.

2. Practice.   Once you know what you want to say, prepare for the big day. The only realistic way: get up on your feet and practice *out loud*. You may feel a bit silly at first, but keep at it. Make the first run-throughs in privacy, then move up to appearances before a mirror (where you can see yourself as the audience will see you) or before a sympathetic wife or friend (who may helpfully point out your goofs).

If you have a tape recorder available, of course, one or more run-throughs played back help polish rough spots, and give you an idea as to the overall effectiveness of your talk, as well as its length.

3. Performance.   You've done the planning, the practice—now you're on stage, ready to put yourself—and your talk—across. To succeed. . .

Dress neatly and to suit the occasion.   This may mean anything from khakis for the construction site to business suit with shirt and tie for the conference room.

Act confident—even if you're not.   A little nervousness is a good sign; it will give you the extra push you need to put yourself across. But don't let it show. Stand tall, steady down with a couple of deep breaths, glance around at the audience, and smile. You may be judged even before you speak, so make sure your attitude is a friendly one.

Talk naturally—and loud enough.   Today people don't dig the soapbox oration, four-syllable words, or "readings" from a manuscript.

They want you—your words, your ideas, your feelings. And, if you have any doubts about "projecting" to that guy in the last row, ask him if he can hear you, *before* you get into your talk.

Vary the tone and pitch of your voice, your rate of speaking, and the stress you put on words. You do this in everyday conversation— why not when talking to an audience? A monotonous, singsong approach doesn't win listeners. Prove the point now by noting the difference between. . .

We have the lowest accident rate in the industry. (Read in a monotone.) . . . and

We have the *lowest* accident rate in the *industry*. (Read with emphasis on the underlined words.)

If you find yourself running dull, running scared, or running down. . .

- Look at the blankest countenance in the room and direct your words to him. In trying to get him to respond, you'll perk up your way of speaking.
- Think of the audience as a group of people who owe you money. You could tell them what's what, couldn't you?
- Introduce a new point in the form of a question—then proceed to answer it. Makes it easier for you, more interesting for your listeners.
- Pause before and after important points. This puts added emphasis on them, gives you a chance to take another deep breath.

Avoid mannerisms.   Pounding fist in palm, pulling off and putting on glasses, clearing the throat, pointing. Any of these, *done once*, may be an effective attention-getter. Repeated, it takes away from your talk—the audience will be so busy wondering if you're going to do it again (and being irritated when you do) that they'll miss most of what you're saying.

End with a smile.   And that's all. No thank you's, no apologies for what you've said, why and how you said it. If you've done the best you could, your audience will know it and appreciate it.

A final thought. Don't worry about applause. There wasn't *any* after the Gettysburg Address.

➲ SELECTING THE BEST MEDIA

Executives have five general methods for communicating both up and down the line. None of these is inherently better or worse than others. Each has advantages and disadvantages. You may have to compare two or more to select the most effective. Here are the media available to you and their respective pros and cons:

ADVANTAGES	DISADVANTAGES
MEETINGS	
You can develop a two-way flow; also permits use of visuals—charts, films, etc.—you can show and explain. Permits discussion and better meeting of the minds. And you reach several minds at once.	Time-consuming, possibly inconvenient, and sometimes difficult to keep a meeting on track. Can be a field day for the long-winded individual.
PHONE	
Speed. Permits questions and answers. Can be done from your desk.	Man at the other end might be interrupted with something more important. Also, generally there is no record of the conversation.
FACE TO FACE	
Personal contact. You can set a mood by a show of friendliness and relaxation. You can show, discuss visual material. Conversation is two-way.	One or the other individual may be subject to pressure by a powerful personality or other persons of high status. May not be easy to terminate.
NOTE OR MEMO	
Brief. A tangible record can be filed. You can prethink your message.	One way. No control over its respondent at the other end. A rigid form, limited by permanent words on paper.
FORMAL REPORT	
Can be comprehensive. Material may be organized at your leisure. Can be disseminated widely by means of copying. Provides you or a subordinate with an opportunity to show his stuff. Indexing and other summary devices help reader grasp scope of piece, locate specific subsections.	May require considerable time in reading. Problem of actual writing may be discouraging to a time-hungry executive.

The five methods above are not mutually exclusive. For special purposes, executives may use two or more methods to get a reinforcement effect.

➲ EVALUATING YOUR OUTGOING COMMUNICATIONS

All the material in an executive's out-box represents an investment of thought, time, and energy. It is an investment that requires periodic evaluation. One way of evaluating your adequacy as a communicator is to test key memos, reports, letters by questions such as these:

> Does this communication have a purpose?
> Is the purpose well-served?
> Is the communication needed and used by the person receiving it?
> If the communication is a request for information—
>> is it going to the right person?
>> does it ask the right questions?
>> have you clearly indicated what you are asking for?
>> have you set a time limitation, that is, when you need what you asked for?

Are you communicating too frequently about the same things? (If the answer is yes, face to face meetings may be indicated.)

Could a form—for example, a checklist form—simplify a message or report?

Would you understand the communication if you received it? (As a matter of fact, put yourself in the place of the respondent. How do you feel about your communication now?)

➲ EVALUATING YOUR INCOMING COMMUNICATIONS

For many executives, their in-box is a terminal of a lifeline essential to keep them functioning effectively in their organizations. An occasional review of the communications that are dropped into your in-box can both improve your contacts and save you time. Questions like these should be raised about your mail:

If you tend to receive any amount of unnecessary or junk mail, should your secretary or assistant be screening your in-box?

With reference to material received periodically, do you really need it?

Do items with "perishable" material get to you on time?

Do regular communications contain all the information you need?

If a periodic report contains more material than you need, can you have the sender streamline it?

Should you pass a particular report on to others?

Generally you will find that your information needs tend to change. Responsibilities and job content tend to vary even when job title or status do not. Accordingly, it is a good idea to make an assessment of your in-box a periodic affair to maintain a maximum level of effectiveness

➲ SHOULD YOU TELL IT LIKE IT IS?

Executives sometimes have a basic communications question to answer: is it always best to level with your subordinates—to tell it like it is, regardless of consequences? The problem arises in situations like these:

- The truth is unpleasant and telling it isn't going to be easy. For example, there may be traumatic consequences. Some people are going to be fired, a restrictive policy is going to be instituted, and so on.
- The truth—good or bad—is something management is not ready to reveal as yet.

It's difficult to set down exact guidelines in this explosive communications area. But here are some preliminary considerations that can shape what you eventually say:

Your own sense of integrity.   Do you believe that you must always tell the truth, even when it hurts? Or do you think that conditions sometimes justify the "little white lie," modifying the truth? (Would you tell your Aunt Tillie that her new living room rug makes you seasick—or, that you'd never seen such an unusual pattern? If you'd spare Aunt Tillie's feelings, why not spare a subordinate's feelings?)

Your reputation.   If you stretch the truth often, and without good reason, your employees will learn that they can't rely on you as a source of information.

Where your loyalties lie.   There is to be a personnel cutback but management is keeping quiet: it doesn't want to cause wholesale upsets, and to have people quitting before they're ready to lose them. Do you say something or don't you? You have been entrusted with a certain amount of responsibility and are expected to handle that responsibility wisely. What do you do?

To the question, "Should you tell it like it is?" there are three possible answers: "Yes." "No." "Partially." And here's how executives arrive at each of these decisions:

Yes   You *should* tell it like it is if you have nothing to gain by concealing the facts, or by evading the question, or by putting off the answer. For example:

A subordinate asks if he's going to get the promotion he's been working for. You know he isn't. If you tell him you won't know for a while, and someone else tells him no that very afternoon, you haven't really spared Ernie's feelings. But you have lowered his opinion to you.

It would have been better to tell it to him straight: "Sorry, Ernie, Phil's getting the promotion. I know you've been breaking your back for this one, but Phil's experience is more in line with what's needed. However, there's going to be another spot opening up. If you keep going the way you have been, you'll have the jump on all the other guys. . . ."

No   You *shouldn't* tell it like it is if the truth will be destructive, and there is some way to avoid it; *or* if you have been specifically asked to say nothing.

A subordinate asks you how he's been doing. You know he's looking for a compliment, for reassurance. But he's *not* doing very well, and you suspect it's because he can't. It seems to you that he's accomplishing almost all he's capable of. You certainly aren't going to tell him you don't think he'll ever be able to do any better than he is now. You might tell him that he's making some progress, a white lie that is justified and that you can state with a clear conscience. And since you know motivation is probably the crucial factor in achievement, you are hoping that encouragement may help him in the future.

Partially   There are times when you *do* gain something by concealing some facts, giving an evasive answer, putting off the answer, or cushioning impact.

A subordinate wants to know if there's any truth to a rumor he's heard around the office, and you tell him, "A decision has been made on that, but we won't know the decision until Monday." The subordinate assumes that you know something he doesn't—as well you should, in your position—but you're respecting management's request that you say nothing.

But—when an employee comes to you asking your opinion of his work and you know there's room for improvement, the "little white lie" won't help him and putting off the answer won't help you. This could actually be a good opportunity to give some criticism, since he came to you. Tell him you've noticed how much effort he's putting in and you're really pleased. Then, suggest an area where he might work harder so that he'll keep on moving forward.

➲ BYPASSING

Bypassing is a traditional communications problem in which a manager is, in effect, dropped out of a communications chain. It can happen in one or two ways:

■ **Contacting your subordinate without going through you.** Example: Your boss, or another manager, may take up some business matter directly with one of your subordinates, without your knowledge or permission. In other words, someone from up the line, or at your level, goes "behind your back" on some business matter with one of your people.

■ **Contacting your boss without your knowledge or permission.** Here, one of your subordinates undertakes direct communication up the line, or with your superior, without your knowledge or consent.

Bypassing represents an undesirable shortcutting of channels because it has destructive consequences: it weakens the bypassed manager's authority; it deprives him of information that sometimes he should have; if procedures or operations are started as a result of the bypassing, the manager many remain in ignorance of operations which he should be controlling.

To handle this problem, you should first know some of its possible causes. Here they are.

■ The authority of the manager is either being questioned or flouted.
■ Subordinates feel that they can get a better response which somehow favors them, by going "directly to the top."
■ When someone up the line bypasses you to get to your subordinate, it may be because he's under time pressure, or you're not around at the moment when the upper echelon executive wants to get some information or action from one of your people.

If you're a victim of bypassing, the first thing to remember is, don't show resentment, particularly if it's a first. Constructive action is much more possible if it begins on a factual, rather than emotional basis.

The manager who is bypassed must consider some tough questions. Here they are; first, if it's a subordinate who goes over your head:

1. Are you too slow?   In some cases, a failure to respond quickly to an employee's request prompts him to think of going directly up the line. If you can't act fast, tell the person why and how soon you

think you can move. If your communications up the line are at fault, see if there isn't some way you can improve them.

2. Are you using the "back of your hand"? A manager with so many other items to demand his attention, may not give as much weight to a request as the employee does. The manager may show this by the way he handles the problem. You have to take pains to let the employee feel that you share his concern with the question.

3. Are you failing to "listen"? The specific matter the employee wants you to take up the ladder may not actually be his real interest.

You have to listen carefully to tell whether an employee is bypassing you because you have failed to understand what it is he *really* wants.

4. Do you use your influence with your boss? This may be the toughest aspect of all. But when a manager doesn't swing his weight with a superior, the employee may feel he can get more consideration directly from the boss.

Don't dismiss the possibility that an employee may be expecting more of you than he should. Within the limits of a normal relationship with your superior, you may be going at full power. If that's the case, explain the facts to your subordinate.

But where there's definitely something lacking, you'll have to look for an opportunity to discuss it with your boss. You should have specific information to pass along to him rather than a vague feeling that you need "more authority." Go into the facts of the matter with him.

Next, if the bypassing is by a superior who goes to one of your subordinates without your knowledge:

1. Is it just a one-time emergency occurrence? For example, your boss needs some information which your subordinate has and you're not around. In this type of situation, the only requirement is that either your boss or the subordinate lets you know what has happened after the fact.

2. Have there been instances where you've failed to respond to a superior's request for information? For the forgetful manager, or the one who procrastinates, the answer to this question must be, "Yes, I've been guilty in the past, but it won't happen again."

3. Is the boss at fault? It may be an unpleasant fact to face up to, but in some cases, bypassing from the top down is the failure of disinclination by the superior to recognize the authority of the manager. In this case, what's called for is a tactful discussion with a superior that emphasizes: a. the manager's willingness to act as a communi-

cations link—get the desired information, or convey it; b. emphasis by the manager that his authority role, vis-a-vis the employee, will be undermined if the bypassing continues.

Bypassing situations sometimes are complicated. You might be involved in one for which none of the above points is the sole answer. But you'll be able to uncover the reasons and be guided accordingly if you ask yourself:

- *Why* does the man bypass me?
- Is his reason an indication that I'm not running my job properly?
- What must I do to prevent recurrences?

➲ MEETINGS—HOW TO MASTER THEM

Contrary to what many people say and others may privately believe, meetings are one of the most effective group communications systems available to managers. However, meetings have acquired a bad name for two reasons:

- *They may be badly run.*   Irritations and frustrations arise when a group of people, usually with heavy work schedules set aside, discover that due to poor planning or other reasons, every moment in the conference room is being wasted.
- *"He's at a meeting."*   It's an excuse many executives encourage their secretaries to use with unwanted callers or visitors. This practice has helped create the impression of scores of managers cooped up in the meeting rooms of the nation while important work goes undone.

But in fact, for certain types of communication, there's no other medium as effective as the meeting. Nothing else approaches the total effectiveness of a group gathering where questions can be raised and answered. Here are some guides for increasing meeting effectiveness:

➲ **Key Checkpoints for Your Meeting**   When the new Treasury building in Washington, D.C. was dedicated, goofs occurred during the ceremony that represented an excellent how-*not*-to-do-it example for managers. Everything from Freud to the weather seemed to conspire against the event. For example:

- The first speaker began by welcoming everyone to the "historic equation."
- Another speaker introduced the Secretary of the Interior as "Secretary Rogers." His name: Rogers Morton.

- Flags, provided to brighten the occasion, fell like autumn leaves due to brisk winds.

Meetings, large and small, will benefit from a checklist of key points which can prevent similar fiascos. This checklist applies to the meeting in which a large group is addressed by one or more speakers, as well as to the small "work" meeting where the reins are in the hands of a conference leader:

- *Meeting place preparations.* An individual or team must be given the responsibility for having the meeting room in readiness. Everything from temperature and ventilation, to lighting and acoustics should be checked.
- *Rehearsal.* Your chairman or other individual must make sure that whoever will be called on to speak knows in general what he or she is to say and how much time is available to say it. The conference leader should have a final version of the program, including all the notes needed to introduce the speakers by name, title, qualification, personal background and so on, as called for.
- *Substitutes.* If this is a meeting at which important matters of policy are to be discussed, it's desirable to have substitutes ready to pinch-hit for key people who may be unavailable at the last moment.
- *Muscle men.* If there's any moving of furniture or equipment involved, don't depend on volunteers. Appoint a group of people who will know in advance what they're supposed to do, and can plan how to do it with a minimum of fuss.
- *Prop control.* If your program calls for equipment of any kind— lecterns, easels, projection equipment, sound equipment, pencils, blank paper for the audience, and so on—put someone in charge of procuring and properly deploying such items.
- *Flexible crowd size.* In some situations, you may not know in advance how many people will turn up. It is wise to have alternative plans in case a substantially larger—or smaller—number of people appear. You don't want to use a 500-seat auditorium for 50 people; and you don't want to crowd 150 people into a small conference room.
- *Agenda.* Finally, of course, the conference leader should be prepared with a list of discussion points. In an informal meeting, just a few notes will suffice. But if crucial matters are to be dealt with, meeting notes should be more complete, and in some cases, copies of the agenda should be sent to the conferees in advance.

➜   **Six Kinds of Meetings Managers Should** *Not* **Hold**   "Meetings waste my time," groans one conference-fatigued manager. He is not necessarily wrong. Meetings *can* be misused. To reap meeting benefits and avoid pitfalls, avoid conferences like these:

1. *Mystery agenda.*   You are invited to a meeting but not given the slightest hint of what you are going to discuss. Result: Everyone comes unprepared. The meeting disintegrates into a discussion of what participants will have to study up on for a subsequent meeting to discuss the *real* topic.
2. *The misidentified problem.*   "We will meet to discuss how to increase interdepartmental cooperation." There's a problem of some kind; nobody knows what it is, and no one really wants to find out because it might put somebody on the spot. Yes, cooperation may be a problem. But *the* problem may be poor discipline, or carelessness about deadlines. Still, everybody knows that you can get a glow of accomplishment by discussing interdepartmental cooperation; and everybody knows nobody will be blamed for anything. None of the plans made will be carried out—as they are not responsive to any problem.
3. *The avoid-a-direct-confrontation meeting.*   For example, one or two people violate the dress code, so everybody is bidden to a meeting to discuss the rules of dress. This gives the manager the illusion that he has done something about the problem without suffering the embarrassment of having to speak to offenders directly. Actually, all it does is waste time and insult those who are *not* breaking the rules. Offenders are usually immune to group pressures, or they would not be nonconformists to begin with. Placing more group pressure on them will not cause them to conform. The innocent ones naturally resent this waste of their time.
4. *Inappropriate attendees.*   This is a favorite in government and overly-rigid companies. Whatever the problem may be, the attendance list is determined by *status*, not by involvement in the issue. Thus, the meeting is characterized by a preponderance of people who do not understand the issue at stake but feel no reluctance to give advice. They naturally assume that if they are invited to the meeting, their views must be relevant. The people who are there legitimately are out-talked and end up thinking meetings are no damned good.
5. *"Put the blame on Mame."*   This gathering, ostensibly called to determine "how we can set up a liaison with Department A," is really designed to give everybody a chance to see what stinkers

the Department A people are. But the meeting reinforces hostile attitudes both by making people believe that their partisanship is acceptable and by pooling all grievances against Department A. Department A's problems then begin to look insurmountable.

6. *Illusory information.*   Top management gets everybody together ostensibly to describe past accomplishments and future objectives. In fact, it's a snow job no more believable than a typical annual report. But management kids itself into believing that morale has been raised. In fact, all that's been done is to raise expectations falsely and give many people a feeling there must be something bad going on they don't know about. At lower echelons, managers misuse the forum format to propound their pet beliefs or gripes.

These six items are not a complete catalog of nonproductive meetings. But they do underscore the point that while the meeting is absolutely unmatched as a means of achieving specific communications objectives, it can be a time-waster unless:

- Participants come well prepared and have a legitimate stake in the outcome of the deliberations.
- Objectives are clearly defined and are of a kind that can profit from group discussion.
- The meeting is not used as a substitute for direct confrontation with unpleasant subjects.

Running a Problem-Solving Meeting   There are eight agenda points considered essential to the success of a meeting called to probe a problem:

1. *State the problem.*   The problem should be defined in terms understandable to all the participants. Discipline yourself to be as objective as possible so that you do not reveal which direction you would like the discussion to take. If the group has a goal that is larger or more far-reaching than the objective of this meeting, then you should explicitly relate today's subgoal to the overall goal, show where it fits, and how it works toward the achievement of the larger objective.

2. *Clarify the problem.*   This involves restating the problem from time to time during the meeting. Do all participants know the meaning of each contribution of each member, in terms of what is to be accomplished by the group as a whole? Do they understand clearly what is being proposed at any one time by any member?

3. *Develop alternatives.*   This is one of the most critical leadership functions, especially if the group is charged with refining ideas

or making decisions. Bear in mind that groups often tend to select one solution early in their discussion and ride with it to the exclusion of possible alternatives. It is up to the leader to be sure that no possible solution or factor is stifled—that no participant is "going along," because of a hesitation to express disagreement.

4. *Keep the discussion on the beam.* Nothing can kill the effectiveness of a meeting more than the leader's willingness to let the discussion wander. You must know when to channel the talk back to the subject. But be careful not to shut off a member of the group who may take a somewhat unorthodox approach to the purpose of the meeting, and actually has something constructive to contribute.

5. *Summarize.* This is a matter of timing—too early, and it may forestall further helpful discussion; too late, and the discussion may already have become unfocused or chaotic (and unsummarizable). It's up to you to decide when it's time for a summary, but you may find it helpful to get the group's agreement that you've covered the necessary ground in your summary. Furthermore, you should be sure they agree that the data you've rejected in the summary are as irrelevant or unconstructive as you judge them to be.

6. *Test the consequence of the group's tentative choice.* As leader, you have to satisfy yourself that the group understands the significance of the solution or action they have chosen. How does it relate to the larger goals? What are the possible consequences, direct and indirect? Have they considered such essentials as cost, time involved, human resources, and facilities required?

7. *Test the members' commitment.* How involved and responsible do the participants feel in what has been decided upon? You have to assure yourself that each member is willing to take responsibility for the group's action and is available to help carry it out if necessary.

8. *Get a consensus.* Push for a firm statement: "This is what we are going to do." Or, "This is the action we've all agreed on." Make sure it is a true consensus, not just "going along" on the part of some members. Also make sure that all members are truly willing to subscribe to the action, and that they are all willing to see it carried out.

These formal functions work only if the leader or chairman does not let his personal vested interest undermine his objectivity. If he favors one idea or one member's contributions above others, then he can manipulate the meeting to see that his own choice is presented in a better light than any other contributions. If you are aware of your partiality, your best bet is to encourage others in the group to perform these functions, confining your leadership to making sure they are done.

➲ **What's the Best Size for a Meeting?**   The effectiveness of a meeting can be affected by its size and by the purposes it is expected to achieve. Therefore, take the limitations imposed by size and task into account when deciding whom you should invite and what you should ask them to do.

There is growing evidence that the most creative *problem-solving* or *decision-making* will occur in small, odd-numbered groups (5, 7, 9). The probable reason is that a majority is possible, which undoubtedly explains why such groups seem to be more relaxed and efficient.

If you want originality and creative contributions, psychologists recommend that you keep the group small. Five people is the number many researchers suggest for optimum efficiency, freedom of exchange and cooperation. As the group gets larger, the chance for individual participation becomes smaller.

➲ **How to Avoid Quiz Trouble in Your Meetings**   You've described a new program to the group. "Any questions?" you ask. A few minutes later, maybe you wish you hadn't.

- Charley Dolan wonders what you mean by something you've already explained six ways from Thursday.
- Sam Wright, who occasionally drives a Volkswagen on company business, wants to know when mileage allowances will be increased. The meeting has nothing to do with same, but Sam's in a hurry to amortize his beetle.
- Phyllis Lombardi throws you a curve . . . a complex question you're not sure how to answer.

Yet, as an experienced meeting leader, you know that anything which can be misunderstood will be misunderstood, and must be clarified. How do you give full explanation and still keep the session in bounds? Use these guidelines:

1. *Even if the question seems "dumb," answer it seriously.*   Some learn fast, others slow. A person who asks a question you've already answered at length is undoubtedly sincere. Odds are, he is asking what others—people with less guts and sincerity—would also be asking. So reply carefully, patiently, and fully. This person may not be the biggest brain in the world, but he is insurance that everyone understands what you're saying.
2. *When a "dumb" question is repeated, assume it's still sincere.*

But don't answer it yourself; direct it to someone else. "Charley, maybe I wasn't completely clear." (Now turn to another person.) "Phyllis, how would you answer Charley's question?" This may help Charley and will surely provide a change of pace for everyone else.

3. *Answer the individual—and the group.* There's a fine line to tread here. The question was asked by, say, Ed Farron. Ed's a man you know. You naturally answer him in particular.

At the same time, you don't want to lose the group. A lengthy dialogue between you and Ed may bore the rest, especially if his question isn't universally interesting. So you don't look only at Ed. Your gaze travels around the room. You catch a few eyes. The answer is addressed to all. But end up with Ed and make sure he and the others are satisfied with the solution.

4. *Try to summarize your answers.* Since your answers are ad lib it's not always easy. But you can double the probability of the group's understanding and remembering by ending the answer session with your major points. "So, there are three major items. First . . ." And so on.

5. *Don't be led down bypaths.* Back in school there were specialists in getting the teacher to ride his favorite hobby horse. Instead of mathematics, the students would get the instructor to talk about geography. Instead of geography, they would get the geography teacher to discuss the binomial theorem.

Avoid such bypaths. Whether a deliberate attempt to get away from the subject at hand or the result of one person's wandering mind, just don't answer. Instead say, "I'd rather not discuss that security question now, Francis. The new procedure is still up in the air . . . Any more questions on the topic we're discussing?"

6. *If you don't know, admit it.* Promise to find out. A well-known teacher once put it this way: "When I'm asked a question I can't answer, I'm glad. What better proof is there that I have stimulated the thinking processes of at least one student?" If you're well prepared for your meeting, you can find the same satisfaction in being buffaloed by a tough question. So thank that person for asking, explain that you'll find out and report either to the individual or to the group as a whole.

Be sure your people ask the questions on their minds. Don't be satisfied merely to say, "Any questions?" and, if there's no reply, to close up shop. Ask questions of your own that will stimulate people. Get them talking . . . and asking. That way, you'll be sure your meeting is making the intended points.

➜   **Getting the Maximum Payoff from Seminars**   Seminars, or other types of information meetings you attend, can pay off better or worse—depending on how you deal with them. Here are five ways to stretch seminar participation benefits once you are back at your desk:

1. *Share your learning.*   Either formally or informally, it's good to report back what you have learned to others in your department or in the organization. For one thing, what may not be applicable for you may be just the idea someone else has been looking for. In addition, making the effort to report helps you organize and remember what you learned.

    One department head believes in getting his reactions down in writing within the first day or two back at work while the session is still fresh in his mind. Others advocate a short staff-meeting playback or informal conversations with other managers.

2. *Circulate the list of attendees.*   Seminar participants generally receive a list of names and company affiliations of others present. If you don't get one, ask for such a list. Circulate this to anyone who might be interested. For instance, the sales department might want to see the names for sales leads.

3. *Continue your seminar frame of mind.*   Back on home ground, don't let an idea you wanted to try out get lost in the shuffle. Consider following the lead of an engineering department head. A week after he returns, this engineering manager sets aside time to sit back and see what changes he might make as a result of his seminar participation. During this time, he also reviews the seminar material that he brought back.

3. *Keep in touch with other participants.*   Soon after you return, send letters to the people you want to keep in touch with. And let them know you enjoyed meeting them. That paves the way for another contact any time you want to compare notes or get information. One manager makes a point of jotting down brief comments next to the names, noting who was interested in what, and who might be helpful in what areas.

5. *Give colleagues a verdict on the seminar.*   Be honest in identifying strengths and weaknesses. This will be particularly helpful for anyone thinking of attending the same seminar or sending a subordinate. Also, if the seminar organizers run a poor session, the odds are good that their other seminars—even if the subject matter is different—won't be any better.

    Finally, try to get people who report to you to follow this post-seminar game plan, too. If they don't, follow up until it becomes a department habit. Otherwise, you'll miss getting top value out of the dollars budgeted for training, and won't get a payoff from the time investment.

⮕ **Two General Approaches to Avoid**   The success of meetings depends in large part on your leadership role. Managers who are successful usually avoid these two common traps:

- *Don't lean over backward to be democratic.*   The result can be a leadership vacuum. Once the manager has stated the objectives of the meeting, he may mistakenly relinquish control. That abdication may cause meetings to stretch interminably. Decisions become compromises because of the fatigue or desperation of the conferees. Issues turn into personality conflicts, and struggles for leadership begin among those who aspire to fill the vacuum created by the formal leader.
- *Avoid rigidity.*   Don't keep the discussion firmly on a predetermined track to reach a predetermined objective in a predetermined period of time. While this approach *may* help the group achieve an immediate objective, the leader is likely to stifle the initiative that could find a better way to get the job done. He or she will probably not achieve either the full utilization of the group's resources, or the commitment of everyone around the table to the desired goal.

  Furthermore, autocratic or manipulative methods may produce resentment that may undermine the success not only of the present project but of future group efforts as well.

There is a leadership role between these two extremes: to understand the forces that are at work within the group and use them constructively. Call on people for their opinions, reactions. Permit a certain amount of digression—as long as it's helpful. This middle way, for short-range and long-range benefits is the best leadership role.

⮕ **How to Make an Effective Presentation**   Presentations by individuals—who basically are either selling an idea, viewpoint or making a report—play a key role in determining a group decision or action that follows. When a speaker's presentation doesn't win points with the audience, oversights are frequently to blame. A short review of often-overlooked considerations can help you score more effectively next time you make a presentation:

- *Be your own worst critic.*   Challenge every assertion or proposal you make for accuracy or practicability; and, of course, discard any that flunk the exam.

Ask yourself: "Has anything important been omitted?" Say you're offering a report on the test-marketing of a new product. You've carefully checked to see that it contains all the pertinent data. But have you analyzed the bugs in the tests? What may be learned from the negative information?

- *Visualize and dramatize.* Where possible, particularly at key points, use audio-visual helps. Charts, graphs, slides that clarify or compress data, add visual confirmation to what the audience hears. One manager, reporting on a field trip to visit customers, dramatized his verbal findings by playing tapes of his interviews with key people. These days the range of audio-visual aids is broad, including everything from flannel board to videotape, from sound-slide projectors to the hand-drawn chart. Your presentation will be more vivid and interesting with devices like these.
- *Level about the minuses.* When you're trying to sell an idea, level about the proposal's disadvantages. It is far better than having someone else bring them up and giving the impression you haven't seen the whole picture. Instead, be candid about flaws and then demonstrate how the idea's merits overweigh them.
- *Don't underplay your enthusiasm.* As any good salesman will attest, enthusiasm is contagious. Yet many people are so shy about showing how they feel that they wind up giving a bland and ultimately ineffectual pitch.

    "Emotion," says one executive, "has a place in planning the strategy of all presentations."
- *Know your audience.* How well informed are they? Explaining the obvious often irritates people; conversely, insufficient explanation can lead to confusion. Could anything in your presentation place one of the participants in a bad light and thereby trigger hostility? Are there antagonisms in the group that you will have to be wary of?
- *Capitalize on stage fright.* A well-known producer and director observes: "Practically everyone feels the familiar symptoms of stage fright—the wet palms, dry lips, parched throat." Far from detracting from a performance, such upset can add to the speaker's effectiveness—providing he channels it properly. How? By letting the excitement come through. "Show it, don't stifle it," is the idea.

    If your heart is pounding 10 minutes before your presentation, take a tip from actors: repeatedly inhale and exhale as much fresh air as you can; then expel it until your chest feels like a deflated balloon. The replacement of oxygen in your lungs helps relax tense chest muscles and recharges your energy.

➔   **Building a Climate of Trust**   Most people find it risky to express feelings openly in meetings. Their wariness can mean hesitation to reveal themselves. Or, they may fear that to express emotion—anger, for example—may create some kind of crisis. As leader of a meeting, it is your responsibility to reduce this I'm-sticking-my-neck-out feeling. Here are some of the things you can do:

- Avoid even the suggestion of reprisals on your part, and discourage reprisals by any member of the group who feels criticized or embarrassed by feedback. Honesty, even when it hurts, should be encouraged.
- Convey your conviction that a group cannot hope to approach optimum effectiveness until its members can honestly express their feelings, can openly describe the impact of others' behavior on them, and can develop a deep-seated desire to collaborate with their colleagues instead of competing with them, to the detriment of all.

➔   **Who Said What? Let Good Note-takers Provide the Answer**   All too often those asked to take notes at a meeting wind up missing important points. Before leaving on an extended vacation, for example, a manager held a lengthy departmental briefing session. He asked two people to take notes.

"I was floored when their notes were typed up," he reports. "Not only did each person leave out items of obvious importance, but each left out something different. Their reports also varied considerably on a number of key points."

Putting the meeting on tape or having a stenographer take everything down, of course, is the answer when managers want verbatim reports. For most purposes, however, this is unwieldy and inefficient. So the problem becomes: How do you choose the right person to make a selective record? Here's how to pick good note-takers:

- *Reconsider the "obvious" choice.* Many select someone with shorthand skills. But this person may be least qualified. Note-taking at a meeting involves value judgment, and making such judgments is often "trained out" of people in shorthand courses. They are taught to listen for words without necessarily making any distinction as to their importance.

  Nor is the executive's key subordinate always ideal for a meeting at which others may make significant contributions. Any assistant that is close to the boss is attuned to him and can easily miss the significance of others' comments.

A note of caution: this does not mean you should rule out everyone with shorthand, or any close subordinate. The main point is not to assume that rapid note-taking automatically yields properly selected material.

- *Key qualifications.*   Four types of experience equip people to function as effective note-takers:
  1. *A good academic record.*   This information can be obtained from employment records. It matters less how far the person went in school, more as to how he or she did. Learning tends to be highly selective. Good students know what is important to retain.
  2. *Experience as a reporter on a school or college paper.*   Journalistic training is useful—knowing what's noteworthy as well as listening for the who, what, when, where, why and how.
  3. *Interest or familiarity with the subject.*   A subordinate who knows the ground to be covered and is familiar with the conferees, is likely to see things in better perspective.
  4. *A club secretary background.*   A personnel executive says, "This may sound oddball, but I find it works—picking a person who has been a club secretary where rules of order are observed. It doesn't matter if it was a high school fraternity or sorority, the PTA, whatever. Organizational secretaries are used to taking minutes and *having them reviewed by everyone present* before they're accepted."

  It's a good idea to have note-takers transcribe notes while the memory of the meeting is still fresh. They should also be encouraged to ask questions at the meeting to clarify points or unclear statements—i.e., "Is that a final decision or just temporary?"

How to Keep People Listening When You Talk   Many a manager has realized with a sinking feeling that as he speaks the audience's attention is wandering. According to seasoned speakers, there are warning signs indicating listeners are drifting away from the speaker's wavelength—and there are ways to get them back on the right channel. Here are some symptoms of inattention and what to do about them:

STATIC.   To stop people who are whispering together:
- *Glance pointedly at the culprits.*   If they don't stop yakking on their own, the nudge of some neighboring person should most certainly put an end to the chinning.

- *Stop talking.* When a speaker stops and just looks at the audience, it generally brings everyone back to attention. People are curious to find out just what the speaker is going to say to break the silence.
- *Single out one of the distractors with a comment.* For instance: "By the way, John, I'm coming to an aspect of the problem on which I particularly want your views."

PUZZLED EXPRESSIONS. If people look perplexed, the chances are good they don't understand what the speaker is saying. The language may be too technical or obtuse for them. Here are some countermeasures:

- *Recap in simpler terms.* Raise a rhetorical question such as: "Now, what does all that mean?" Then you can proceed to answer in simpler terms; if possible, try to amplify with an analogy.
- *Get an "interpreter."* Ask someone else to explain in his or her own words what you've just said. This change of focus should get people's attention and vary the pace.
- *Use props.* Improvise a flip chart—or use a blackboard, if available—to put down in outline form the points you're making, thus clarifying what you're saying.

DOZERS. Are one or two in the audience nodding? Then you might:

- *Change the decibel count.* Maybe you are speaking too softly. Interrupt yourself to inquire, in a stronger voice, "CAN YOU ALL HEAR ME?" Thereafter, try to vary your pitch. It is just as effective after speaking loudly for a time to suddenly talk in a soft voice.
- *Have someone open a window or adjust a shade.* The problem may be lack of fresh air or light glare.
- *Try humor.* Not everyone has the knack for telling a joke, but if you do, use it. There's nothing like laughter for waking others up.

POKER FACES. Although those with the power of decision (not to say their satellites) often prefer to appear inscrutable, impassive expressions may suggest that people are gathering wool. To regain their attention:

- *Toss out a general question.* It could be of the SOS variety: "I'm sorry, I've forgotten the bottom line of our first-quarter budget. Can any of you help me out?" Or try a pocketbook-type query: "Okay, how's that likely to affect our take-home pay? Or the cost of medical care? Or the price of steak?
- *Use down-to-earth English.* Deliberately interlace your formal language with informal terms. After a few sentences containing

polysyllabic, Latin-root words, some short, down-to-earth English (including a mild—or strong—expletive or two) will usually galvanize your audience.

- *Talk eyeball-to-eyeball.* To stimulate attention, look directly at individuals as you talk. Deliver one remark to one person, your next comment to someone else, making a round of the audience as much as possible.

WRIST-WATCHING. If people are glancing sidelong at their watches, time may be running out; they may be tired of sitting, etc. Some attention-winning tactics:

- *Telescope the balance of your talk.* You might remark briskly, "I see that it's almost noon. So, if you'll forgive me, I'll run rapidly through the remaining key points." They'll forgive you—and most likely hang onto your words until you complete your presentation.
- *Call a break.* Giving people five or ten minutes to stretch and walk around should bring them back refreshed and more attentive.
- *Do the unexpected.* Jolt your audience to attention with the unexpected—tear up your notes, clap your hands, drop a book on the floor, toss a coin in the air, etc.

Keeping a Brief Meeting Brief Many executives schedule "brief" staff meetings. But though they adhere to the effective-meeting basics—having an agenda, holding down the number of participants, etc., they find these sessions rarely wind up on time. If this is a familiar problem, you may want to consider these proven techniques for keeping brief meetings on target:

- *Schedule a collision.* In setting up meetings, managers usually try to avoid possible conflicts with appointments or lunch hours. But the *opposite* tack is one way to keep it brief. In other words, schedule the session to end at lunch or quitting time. When it is their own time that will be taken up, participants generally learn to keep things short and to the point.
- *Use a "time" signal.* At the start of short meetings, one purchasing director takes off her watch and puts it down in front of her. If anybody monopolizes the conversation or goes off on a tangent, she makes a point of picking up her watch and looking at it, without saying a word. This cue gets others back on the beam.
  Another executive uses a buzz-alarm wrist watch to go off at the meeting's midpoint. This signal helps people stick to the business at hand and brings the session to an on-time finish.

- *Keep them on their feet.* If the meeting is going to be a real "shorty," one can avoid the overtime pitfall by making it a stand-up get-together. When people are seated—particularly if the chairs are comfortable—there's a tendency to become long-winded. On the other hand, at an on-your-feet meeting, everyone tends to come to the point faster, without needless emphasis on fringe details or issues.
- *Accent the positive.* The airing of trivial department complaints can easily knock brief meetings off their time course. One manager enforces these ground rules: Each person who brings a problem up must also provide a specific recommendation. In addition, if the matter doesn't concern any of the others, it's considered "off limits"—to be discussed on a one-to-one basis with the boss. The results he reports: "Little opportunity for any griping or pointless talk that runs on and on."
- *Don't worry about loose ends.* Sometimes sessions go overtime because managers are preoccupied with winding up loose ends. They feel nothing should be left dangling. The important thing: accept the fact that nine out of ten times there *will* be some unfinished business—which may well be the reason for the next meeting. You can avoid the appearance of things left hanging simply by specifying the loose ends—"We'll get to that supply question tomorrow"—as you conclude.

➲ **When You're a Participant** In some meetings you will be just another member of the group. Here's the kind of participant behavior that you—and others—can perform to help keep the meeting productive:

- When you talk, try to avoid "locking in" on one person. It's natural to note someone in the group who is more sympathetic than others. But you may be undermining his or her power to help you by being labeled as your ally. More important, by seeming to exclude others, you risk alienating them.
- Don't rush to answer a question or defend your position against attack. Pause to make sure you really have all the information about the other person's view that you need. Sometimes your silence will lead him or her to amplify a statement, and so help to clarify the issue.
- If a colleague openly or even hostilely objects to what you are saying, listen carefully and look at him while he speaks. You are getting important feedback that tells you where you may not have performed effectively. If he becomes patently unfair, you may

well find yourself defended by others—which is often much more effective than taking up the cudgels in your own behalf.

- Look for areas of agreement that you can call to the attention of the group. Even if these are minor matters, the group will develop a sense that it is getting on with the job. This will help a resolution of the large issues more readily.
- If you feel hemmed in by challenges and objections, get help from others. For example, "I guess I haven't done justice to this, or "I guess I haven't made this clear. Can someone else here help me out?" The point is, place the blame for the lack of understanding (if that's what it is) on yourself. You may be surprised to find how much help in clarifying or in closing gaps you'll get.
- Be realistic about the concessions you can afford to make. Sometimes your willingness to give up a minor point—"Of course, we can see that you get copies of the requisitions"—can make all the difference in getting acceptance of your major proposition. Know what you can afford—and cannot afford—to yield.
- Don't hesitate to ask for action on a proposal or a decision. This is one of the best ways to smoke out any hidden objectives or reservations which otherwise might not appear until after the meeting, if at all.

Disruptive Behavior   As a leader, it is important to be alert to behavior that is disruptive. Chances are you have seen such behavior in meetings you've attended. Most people are guilty of obstructive tactics once in a while—often without realizing it. But as leader, you have to be prepared to take countermeasures:

- *Shutting off.* B responds to something that A has just said: "That's the most ridiculous thing I've ever heard." Or, "Your facts are all wrong." These are merely two of an infinite number of ways to put someone down. Of course, there are more subtle ways—humor, for example; take some aspect of a conferee's point and turn it into a joke. By the time everyone gets through laughing, what was said loses impact.

  To offset the damage, ask the man who has been a shut-off victim a question: "Did you get a chance to finish? Was there anything you wanted to add?" You may even wish to let him know you think he was shut off by saying, for example, "I have a feeling we didn't give A chance to finish his point. I'd like to hear him out." You can water down the effect of this kind of attack by a simple, "No personal references, please. Let's talk about the subject, not one another." Putting a label on another man's behavior, such as "You're defensive," or "You're not being honest," often results in sidetracking the group's business while the labeled one tries to purge himself of the charge.

■ *Analyzing.* "You're projecting," or "You sound as if you're being threatened." It seems as if everyone today is tempted to play amateur analyst, to tell his colleagues not only what they are doing but why they are doing it. One person's diagnosis of another may be true, but he can't really know for sure. It's a trap—and one to avoid.

Be especially on guard for this sidetracking technique. Sometimes it is necessary to be quite blunt to forestall it: "Let's listen to what A has to say. I think we're really more interested in what he is saying than in guessing why he is saying it. In fact, suppose we let him tell us why he is saying it, *if he wants to.*"

■ *Not listening.* Actually, much of the misunderstanding that is evident in any meeting is a result of poor listening. Many people do not listen well. One reason is that our personal biases get in the way of our analyzing objectively what is being said. That's why so much time is spent by people rebutting things that were never really said.

If you encounter much of this during your conference, suggest that, to save time and increase understanding, each person, before commenting on another's point, repeat the latter's point in essence and get his agreement that that is actually what he meant. Then, at least, the rebuttal or analysis has a better chance of being on target.

The Hidden Agenda A good deal of what happens in any meeting is rooted in attitudes people bring into the meeting but may not openly express. Psychologists call it the *hidden agenda*—those conflicting motives, emotional reactions, prejudices, leadership aspirations, etc., that some of the conferees bring to the table. Hidden agendas are not always easy to spot. However, there are certain clues. For example:

When two or more conferees engage in an emotional interchange that seems out of proportion to differences they have on the stated agenda, or when they begin to debate points that are tangential to the main subject, or when a person gets hung up on what seems to be a trivial matter, then very likely these members are working on a problem they have brought into the room rather than getting on with the subject of the meeting.

There are several steps you can take to help work out these hidden agendas so that progress toward the stated objectives can be made:

- *Look for the hidden agendas.* Don't try to pretend they don't exist. You won't get rid of their influence by rigidly insisting that the group stick to the stated agenda.
- *Bring them up?* One way to bring the hidden agenda to the surface is to say something like this: "I wonder whether we've really said all that we feel about this matter. Why don't we take more time to satisfy ourselves that there aren't any more thoughts on this." Perhaps call on the person you suspect is holding something back: "Amy, is there anything you'd like to say" or "to add"?
- *But don't force them up.* Some agendas *are* better left under the table. Sometimes they can be better worked out by the people involved without bringing the rest of the group into it.
- *Don't embarrass anyone.* Don't chide any members of the group about their hidden agendas. In one meeting, a manager listened to a prolonged but cautious exchange between two colleagues, then announced, "All I can hear is someone grinding an axe." Not only did progress stop on working out the hidden agendas, but those who had been talking fell silent on the stated agenda as well.

    People have a natural way of working out what's on their minds and it may often sound diversionary and even annoying. If you truly don't want an off-track subject aired, remind the conferees of the subject at hand, or say, "Terry, I'll discuss that with you privately."

Two Problem Conferees Few people ever develop perfect meeting manners. From time to time, almost anyone will be argumentative, stubborn, discursive, inattentive, hostile, etc. It is usually possible for the group to work out these problems and get on with the business at hand. But there are two conferee attitudes which can torpedo the meeting unless the leader takes firm action:

The clam. He sits at meetings week after week and never opens his mouth. Yet he may be one of your vital sources. Here are some techniques to help the stage-shy, intimidated or nonparticipating individual:

- Call on him for his experience or specialty. "This is something that Jim has had a lot of experience with; let's hear from him."
- Tell him in advance that a certain topic is going to come up. Ask him to prepare a comment. Then at the appropriate moment in the meeting, feed him a cue line.
- Pose questions he can handle: "How does this breakdown procedure on this equipment look to you?" or "Did you ever run into this kind of situation when you were out in the field?"

- Give him time to compose what he is going to say. Try calling on one or two others in the group before calling on the clam. That way you can tip him off and give him time to prepare an answer.

  However, never cut off or put down another conference member to protect or favor your reticent subordinate; and don't wrench the conversation around to set things up for him.

The hog. He talks and talks and talks. It isn't that he has nothing to say. More often, it's just that he takes so long to say it. In the process he prevents others from making their contributions.

To control the monopolizer:

- When he has made a point, and is rambling on to another, interrupt to reinforce the one point he has made so far and suggest that it ought to be discussed. Then ask others for their reactions to the point he has made. Or explain to him that you want to go around the table to insure that everyone else gets an equal chance.
- Once he has begun to ramble or become disorganized, stop him. Explain that you are not certain you understand what he has been saying. Ask him to clarify. If he persists in digressing, cut him off and call on someone else.
- Make him write down his ideas. Explain the scope of the meeting to him before it is called, and ask him either to write down what he considers the main points or to make an outline. Then during the meeting ask him to refer to his outline as he talks.

➔ MEETING RATER

You may want to get a line on how well your meetings have been going, as a help to reslanting those in the future. The points below cover key aspects of meeting excellence.

1. How effective was the meeting? (An effective meeting develops when every member pushes for the most proficient resolution, when each member responsibly contributes his resources to the achievement of group goals.)
- ☐ Most effective possible
- ☐ Quite effective
- ☐ Moderately effective
- ☐ Moderately ineffective
- ☐ Quite ineffective
- ☐ Worst possible

2. How clear were the meeting goals?
- ☐ Completely clear, and explicitly stated, and agreed upon by all members
- ☐ Almost completely clear
- ☐ Moderately clear
- ☐ Moderately unclear
- ☐ Almost completely unclear
- ☐ Completely unclear. Everyone was making assumptions about everyone else's intentions and we didn't know whether we were working toward the same goal or not

3. To what extent did we deal honestly with the meeting's purposes and avoid outside, extraneous issues?
- ☐ Completely on target
- ☐ Pretty much on target
- ☐ More on target than off
- ☐ Somewhat extraneous and off target
- ☐ Quite extraneous and off target
- ☐ Completely extraneous and off target

4. To what degree were my views considered for obtaining understanding between me and the rest of the group?
- ☐ They were completely considered, examined, evaluated and discussed in an effort to gain understanding
- ☐ Almost completely considered
- ☐ Considered quite a lot
- ☐ Considered and disregarded equally
- ☐ Disregarded more than considered
- ☐ Largely disregarded
- ☐ Almost completely disregarded

5. Was I leveling with the group? That is, did I say what I really thought or did I find it difficult to express such ideas and feelings?
- ☐ Completely free to express any or all feelings and ideas
- ☐ Almost completely open
- ☐ Somewhat open
- ☐ Slightly more open than closed
- ☐ Somewhat closed
- ☐ Almost completely closed
- ☐ Completely under wraps, closed and hidden

6. To what degree have my expectations been achieved in this meeting?
- ☐ Expectations have been completely achieved or satisfied
- ☐ Expectations only partially met
- ☐ Expectations completely neglected

7. Group Atmosphere. (Check as many words as needed to describe the meeting)

☐ Productive	☐ Avoided issues
☐ Rewarding	☐ Tackled problems
☐ Opinionated	☐ Contentious
☐ Ineffective	☐ Tense
☐ Competitive	☐ Enjoyable

Reprinted with permission of the Research Institute of America.

➲ ART AND CRAFT OF THE MEMO

Everybody in business and organizational life writes and receives memos. From executives down to the lowest echelons there is a more or less continuing flow of messages. Subject matter may range from a simple announcement—"There will be a meeting of the Order Department at 11 o'clock in Mr. Smith's office."—a report on an intricate problem. Length may vary from effective one-word statements— "Thanks!", "Yes!", "No!"—to those which run to many pages.

The memo plays a vital function. It's a flexible communications medium that reflects the complexity of organizational life—its conflict, its harmony, its humanity, and even its politics. The ability to write an effective memo is an essential skill. The person who becomes adept at handling the memo not only increases his effectiveness, but also improves his chances for recognition and advancement within his organization.

In short, the memo gives you an opportunity to participate directly in the give-and-take of communication. The person who masters this medium is vastly strengthened in his quest for status and achievement. The aspects treated below can assist you toward these important goals.

The Memo as a Personal Showcase   When you write a memo, you're doing at least three things:

- You're moving ahead on the subject of the communication itself.
- You're showing your degree of mastery of one of the most important management skills—the ability to put thoughts in writing.
- You're exposing your personality—the kind of person you are. To put it another way, you're using an everyday business tool and—for better or for worse—trumpeting your skill before your associates.

Since the memo can be highly personal, your own output adds to your personal portrait. Reputations are not made—or lost—on the basis of a single communication, as a rule. *They can be.* But usually, it's over a period of time that the accumulative effect of your memo-writing helps form a part of your image for associates and colleagues.

Two Basic Forms   Many forms and conventions have been developed that aim for convenience, quick comprehension, and fewer errors. Case in point: the physical form of the memo, of which there are many versions. Basically, however, there are two. One is the *organization's* own interoffice form. Here's a sample:

<u>ACME COMPANY</u>

INTEROFFICE MEMO

To _____

From _____

Date _____

Subject _____

The other form is an *individual* one, which some companies provide, or which the manager gets for himself from a local printer. This form tends to be quite simple and may bear some printed legend, such as "From the Desk of..." and the name of the manager, or simply the word "Memo." This is an area where some managers give their imaginations free rein.

Accordingly, you sometimes see memo forms with busy little figures rushing around smoking at the heels, flying Mercurys, sheets of paper being propelled by beating wings, and so on. Each to his own taste.

Another variation is the company name with the suffix *-gram* added; for example, the Ray-o-gram (for the Ray Company). The company's interoffice memo is usually typed by a secretary or typist, whereas the personal memo (From the Desk of...) is more often handwritten by the manager or executive.

The "Self-Mailer"   In some cases the efficiency of the memo exchange is helped by write-in answers tailored into the original form. Note one executive's memo to his staff:

Dear _____:

Frank Amster, vice-president of Kayline Products, will be paying us a visit on Friday, January 21. He would like to meet the key people in engineering and production. Please indicate below what time period would suit your schedule best:

( ) between 11 A.M. and 12 noon
( ) lunch
( ) between 1:30 P.M. and 2:30 P.M.
( ) between 2:30 and 3:30 P.M.

Other?_____

Soon as possible, please.

Pat Masters

This "self-mailer" technique is particularly useful when:

- You want to obtain fast replies from others within the department or within the company.
- You need 100 percent response. Most people tend to complete a fast check-off form more easily than one that involves the time and thought that goes into an open-ended reply.
- You are asking a number of people the same question. It then becomes easier to tabulate the responses, or plan a schedule, as shown in the example above.
- The answers you're looking for can be *categorized* ("Yes," "No," for example) or put in *numerical form* (0–25, 26–50, 51–75, and so on).

Memo Language That Soothes   The experienced memoist tends to write tactfully in touching on certain sensitive situations. One can use tactful language to protect a friend or deal wisely with a foe. The language we are talking about is a euphemistic way of expression, a way of hiding the seamy side of things—if that seems desirable. It often does; here is an example:

A secretary who hasn't been getting along well with her boss is leaving for another job. She writes him a memo that will give him no reason to blame himself for her departure:

> Dear Mr. _____
>
> I have just been offered a position which includes special writing assignments, increased responsibility and a chance to advance to a managerial job.
>
> I hope you will understand my eagerness to accept this challenge. Accordingly, I will expect to be leaving in two weeks. Please be assured I'll do my part during this period to break in your new secretary, to the best of my ability.

Here are some other common usages:

"I have been asked by our President, Mr. Tom Cowley..." Tom Cowley has ordered.

"Paul Barba has resigned..." Paul Barba has been fired.

"You are invited to attend..." It's a command you'd better heed.

"My assistant has requested a two-month leave of absence to give him an opportunity to recoup his health. . ." An employee with a severe alcohol problem is being given a chance to resolve his difficulty.

Ordinarily, openness and honesty are virtues in communication. But in some touchy and even explosive situations, it can be the height of wisdom to use indirectness and the euphemistic phrasing.

When Not to Write a Memo   Usually there's no problem about when to write a memo. You want some information, you answer a question, and so on. But there are times when memos should *not* be written because of unpleasant consequences: you might lose face because of a memo written in the heat of anger; you might take a stand based on incomplete information; you needlessly put yourself on record in a controversial matter.

Here's a rundown of the situations in which the manager should sit on his hands until his memo-writing impulse disappears (of course, you can *write* it, just don't *send* it):

When they are setting you up.   "A colleague sent me an inquiry asking for my thinking on our new sales presentation. He knew I had negative views, and wanted me to put them on paper. I wasn't sure how he'd use my memo, but I knew it wouldn't be helping me any. I conveniently 'lost' his request. After a second attempt, which I countered by saying I'd be glad to 'share my thinking when I could get around to it,' he gave up. I never regretted not writing that memo. I know I'd have regretted writing it."

When passions muddy the mind.   "If I'd written my boss about what I *really* thought of his hiring a man for a job that I wanted, I'd have been through in this company," confesses a new company president. "I was burnt up by what I considered an injustice. But soon I found myself working with the new man. We proved to be a terrific two-man team—and I soon sent my boss a memo to that effect. A few years later I was made vice-president, and just recently president, of the firm. And my 'rival' is now my general manager—a great asset."

When one is angry, scared, hurt—in short, suffering from any of the negative emotions—interoffice communications on the upsetting subject should be postponed. It is inevitable that one's thinking is being influenced, and that afterward, when emotional balance stabilizes, the message will be different, and that usually means better.

When you have nothing to say. Sometimes this is a matter of quantity. It may be okay to write a brief say-nothing memo. But occasionally a gremlin takes over and the executive finds himself turning out page after page of nonsense, when a one-sentence rejoinder would do.

"Our president asked the heads of operating departments, of which I am one, to send along ideas for new products," says a production manager. "I dictated a five-page memo summing up a number of third-rate ideas, and even as I was dictating it I knew it was a lot of hooey. Fortunately, I tore up the memo after it was transcribed, and simply sent a note saying I would give the matter some thought. The following week I had a really good idea, and sent that along. It started a whole new profitable line for us."

To paraphrase a great truth related to another medium, "The absence of memos can be golden."

When face-to-face is better.   "My boss asked me to send him my reactions to a lengthy report. Ordinarily, there'd have been no problem. But I hesitated because I wasn't clear on a couple of points, including the basic purpose of the report. So instead of writing, I called and suggested that we discuss the matter over the lunch table. It made all the difference. He was able to clarify some key aspects. I understood what he was driving at, and in the exchange I was able to make some useful suggestions. None of that would have been possible without the advantage of the give-and-take conversation."

In addition to the situations already described, there are others that do not suggest complete suspension of the memo-writing impulse, but *do* suggest either hesitation or some other modification of memo-writing procedures:

When your secretary can do it.   There are many memo's that one's assistant can handle. For the executive to get involved with these is a waste of time. For the routine message, the executive's great contribution should simply be signing it.

When the timing is wrong.   There may be nothing wrong with the communication being sent. However, there may be something in the situation that makes for poor timing:

Manager Bill Tompkins comes to work one morning and has a difficult time getting his car placed in the company parking lot. He rushes into his office and gets off a big blast to the personnel director asserting that the new parking rules that have just been put into operation are "useless, stupid, unacceptable, ill-advised," and so on. He shortly gets a response saying, "Dear Bill: Still too early to tell." Sure enough, in a few days, the new arrangement works out well. Understandably, this leaves Bill Tompkins feeling like the rear end of a common domesticated animal.

➲   **Editing Your Memo**   For a longer memo you may want to take special pains. This means essentially writing your memo in two phases: First, a rough draft in which you've said everything you want to but without paying too much attention to exact wording and other niceties of writing. Second, you edit the draft, ending up with a finished, ready-to-go version. This is the professional writer's way. It's a process that may almost be called secret, it's so little known to nonprofessionals. As a matter of fact, the nonpro thinks that the skill of writing lies in having such a great command of language that you start with the first sentence and go, chugging flamboyantly along to the end, without a pause, and end up with a finished piece.

The opposite is true.   The very best writers—like De Maupassant, Tolstoy, Hemingway, and Faulkner—would do a second, third, and fourth draft before they were satisfied. "I'm not a writer, I'm a rewriter," says one author with many books to his credit.

To start your rewrite, you change your viewpoint. Now you assume the role of reader instead of author. You are about to pass judgment on *what you have actually said*, and you don't want to be confused by any recollection of *what you intended to say*.

First, read it for the overall effect. If you run into a point that is unclear or badly worded, don't stop to change it—just put a mark in the margin. Similarly, if there is something omitted, note it briefly on the side, and then go right on reading your draft.

As you read, you'll find a word that doesn't sound right; too strong, too weak, not clear enough, not really what you had in mind, or not sufficiently arresting. Change these. Eliminate unnecessary verbiage (called "cutting" by the writing pros). Eliminate a statement you feel is inadequate. Correct the grammar.

Also, look for repetitions. Don't assume the repetition must *auto-matically* be eliminated. Sometimes there is a good reason for repeating yourself. But if you are doing so, be sure you know why:

For emphasis.   To make an important point stand out, you may be perfectly justified in repeating. Only, be sure it is really important.

For clarity.   You may want to repeat an old point in a new context in order to make sure your reader will understand. You can't risk the possibility that he has forgotten the point, or that he may fail to make the connection. So it may be wise to do your reader the courtesy of saying, "As I pointed out before..." But if you find too many "as I mentioned earlier's," it may signal the need for reorganization.

One word is usually better than two. Extra words are excess baggage. In business especially, it's best to "travel light." When you read over your first draft, concentrate on eliminating heavy phrases. Here are some of the worst offenders:

Heavy	Light
accompanied by	with
afford an opportunity	allow
at all times	always
at this point in time	now
due to the fact that	because
experience has indicated that	we learned
in the near future	soon
in regard to	about
meets with our approval	we approve
prior to	before
subsequent to	after

Here's how one manager was able to edit a paragraph in a memo. First version:

> Please afford my secretary an opportunity to check the Jones file. Since you at all times have cooperated with such requests, I hope you will ac-quiesce once more. Due to the fact that this information must be forth-coming in the near future, I trust you will be able to grant permission at your earliest convenience.

Here's a streamlined version:

> Do you mind letting my secretary check the Jones file? We need some information urgently and your help would be greatly appreciated.

If you think the first version of the paragraph above is exaggerated, of course, you're right. But the sad fact is that it is representative of much business writing, even today.

➡ **Six Key Memos—and How to Write Them**   The need to write some types of memos recurs frequently. Their subject or theme is such that you are often called on to put words on paper to express these particular sentiments. Here are a group of sample memos under six headings that can guide your thinking—and writing:

Admonition.   A subordinate is undertaking a risky course of action; a colleague invades an area that is not his responsibility. One wants to voice concern, to warn, advise, caution, suggest alternatives. Another purpose of the admonitory memo: to put one's views on record, in case later developments raise questions of one's judgment, attitude, or alertness.

This sample is from a division manager to the company's purchasing chief. A few facts and for-instances would have helped make a stronger, more persuasive message.

To H.B:
   I understand you're considering placing my order for desks with the XYZ Furniture Company. I have it on good authority that they're an unreliable source. You may not want to take my word for it, but I hope you'll at least check this out before placing the order.

This message was posted on company bulletin boards. The message wisely avoids the angry reprimand for wrong-doing, yet makes a strong and reasoned case.

To All Employees:
   It's been noticed that some employees have been parking in the executive area. This misuse of our available space is causing problems with our overall parking plan.
   The new area just completed provides convenient parking for everybody. To the few who are failing to comply: please don't create needless difficulties. Anyone parked improperly from now on wil be asked to re-park during the lunch hour.

From one production manager to the head of a neighboring department. Somewhat sharp, but to the point.

To A.R.:
   Pete Jones tells me you've given him an assignment to do "on the side." Since Pete is in my department, taking such a step without consulting me is most ob-

jectionable. I've told him to disregard your request. And, in the future, if you want to take up work matters with my subordinates, please check with me first.

Condolences.   A misfortune, failure, or bereavement may call for an expression of sympathy. What you say and how you say it is a function of your actual feelings, your relationship to the individual, and so on. This is one area of communication where the error of omission is most undesirable. Even a brief message shows thoughtfulness. Silence is likely to be interpreted as indifference.

Message to a colleague before an operation. Maybe hospitals aren't fun, but the writer does a good job of projecting a cheerful front.

Dear _____:
   I hear you're about to join that small and select group known as the No Gall-bladder Club. As a member myself, I can tell you that you're going to a hospital that has the prettiest nurses and the best meals in the world. And your convalescence will at last give you a good excuse to do what we all yearn to do, but can't because of guilt—be lazy!
   Good luck. It'll all be here when you get back!

A colleague writes to one of his group whose wife has died after a long illness.

Dear _____:
   We all share your grief. Mae was a good friend to many of us and admired by all. Please take comfort in the thought that her pain is over, something that she herself wanted. And certainly, her last months of life were brightened by your endless hours of care and attention at her bedside. She couldn't have had a more loving or devoted husband.

A manager writes to the wife of a deceased colleague.

Dear Mrs. _____,
   It is with a feeling of shock and deep loss that we hear of George's demise. He was a most popular and well-liked friend and colleague. In the eight years of our close association, I got to know and enjoy George's wit, his good humor, and unfailing friendliness. His accomplishments were many, and his quick creative mind was a major company asset. Things won't be the same around here without him. We miss him, and I can appreciate your own great sense of loss. Please know that you are not alone in your mourning.

Gratitude.   Appreciation falls as the gentle rain from heaven on the parched place beneath. Recognition is one of the holy grails of corporate life, more sought after than found. Any time you have the chance to express thanks to someone, you can be sure, whether the message is aimed at your boss or a subordinate, it will be taken as an indication of your thoughtfulness and sound character.

A subordinate voices gratitude for off-the-job consideration from a boss.

Dear Ben:

Now that I'm back at work, after three weeks of hospital incarceration, I want to tell you how grateful I am for your visits. They certainly brightened the days. And the plant you sent is adorning my desk this very moment, a permanent reminder of your thoughtfulness. I would say the fringe benefits in this company are tremendous!

Thanks for an assist in winning advancement.

Dear Mr. Henley:

We both know that promotions in ths company are earned. And I'd have to agree that when the news came through today, my satisfaction included a certain amount of feeling that justice was being done. But I'd have to be both stupid and ungrateful if I failed to recognize the full extent of your contribution. Starting from that day three years ago, when you sat me down and gave me a picture of what the possibilities were for me, and the countless times since that you helped with sound advice and encouragement, your efforts on my behalf made all the difference.

I'll never forget your kindness, your friendship, and your wisdom.

Appreciation to a boss for praise in an especially important circumstance.

Dear Mr. Miller:

That was certainly a great buildup you gave me in the board meeting this morning. I want you to know that my hat still fits—for two reasons:

Only a great boss can have great subordinates.

We both know that it has been your help and encouragement that moved me along every step of the way.

As the song goes, you made me what I am today, I hope you're satisfied. I am—and very grateful as well.

"I told you so." Every once in a while an executive gets lucky: Something has happened that he predicted, or an action was taken that he warned against and, happy day, he was right!

It's always nice to have one's views reinforced. But the "I-told-you-so" memo is usually written by that not altogether admirable person, the poor winner. However, in certain situations the "I-told-you-so" memo can avoid the crowing and the implied rebuke it suggests. Here are some samples that almost make the message palatable:

A superior to a subordinate; the moderate tone and constructive conclusion take the curse off the fault-finding.

Dear Pete:

Just got the production figures for last month, and although they're better than the previous period, they fall substantially short of target.

Now I'm sure there was no lack of effort. More than ever, I'm convinced that what's needed is an overhaul of the entire operation—everything from more careful work planning to better utilization of your people.

I realize it's a big job, but when the old ways don't work, new methods must be developed. I'll be glad to sit down with you and map out an approach that could brighten up the production picture for the future.

When this type of message goes from a subordinate to his boss, the writing problem becomes more ticklish. Here a head-on but humorous approach may just do it.

Dear Boss:

Hear that Steve Avery quit last week. I hate to say, "I told you so," but I did, didn't I? You'll never get me to admit that I'm smarter than you are, but I did have a chance to see Avery operate at a closer vantage point. If you promise not to hold it against me, I'll try to continue to be right in the future, particularly when you ask for my opinion.

Here the writer and recipient are at the same organizational level. "Y-ness" refers to industrial psychologist Douglas McGregor's idea that most people are willing to accept responsibility and work on their own initiative when given the chance.

Dear Hank:

Never mind the ten bucks you owe me. If your conscience hurts, you can buy me lunch some day. Bet aside, the important thing is that my faith in the Smith-Calvison team paid off. Actually, I was betting on the ability of those two people to respond to a clear-cut challenge, on their own. Everything I believe about the "Y-ness" of human beings was at stake. I'm hoping that aside from a temporary partisanship, you're as pleased as I am at the successful outcome.

Orders and Instructions. "Do this," "Do that," "Come here," "Go there," "See X," "See Y"—on the workscene there is almost no end to instructions. To a large extent orders are verbal. But there are often good reasons for orders and instructions to take the written form to avoid misunderstanding, for the record, etc. Here are some examples:

The request form of order written to a subordinate.

Dear Jane:

Don't you think it would be a good idea for you to stay close to the new expediter, especially for the first two weeks, until he gets the hang of things? Remember, his experience isn't too heavy, and he seems to have enough on the ball to warrant the investment of time.

Velvet glove, iron hand.

Gerry:
I'd like to see the corridor in your department cleaned up by next Frday and kept free of litter and mess thereafter.

Flat order.

To all supervisors:
I expect all departmental production reports on my desk each morning before noon. Thank you.

This memo makes the point that when one speaks with authority, an order can be low pressured indeed. This top executive is saying, "Be there!" The quiet tone doesn't belie the order's need to obey.

Dear Harry:
Will you, and your staff meet with me briefly in the conference room at 9 A.M. on Wednesday to discuss our compliance with the antidiscrimination laws?

Praise. Someone has done something, achieved something, been honored. You want to state your pleasure, possibly adding your own congratulations. A complementary memo is a good way of cementing an old relationship or strengthening a new one. It's your chance to make someone feel good and show that you appreciate an effort. It's the business equivalent of the naval "Well done."

An executive writes to a member of his staff on the occasion of his twenty-fifth anniversary with the company.

Dear Jack:
Twenty-five years—twenty-five great years of creative accomplishment! I've had the benefit of working with you for the last ten years of that period and I want you to know that our association has always been one of the big pluses in my job. So, here's wishing you many more years with a company that has every reason to appreciate your contribution.

From a top executive to another who does considerable public speaking and has just addressed a national businessmen's conference.

Dear David:
"Another superb achievement" is the comment one always would like to make of an admired colleague. You create an instance where it applies perfectly. I enjoyed being a witness.

An executive writes to the editor of the company's house organ.

Wendy:
  I particularly liked the last issue of the company monthly newspaper. The lead article, on the customer use of our service, was lively and made me feel awfully good about us. And the tribute to George Planter on his retirement said the right things in the right way—real feeling without getting sloppy.
  Keep up the good work!

Note written on a report which a boss returns to his subordinate.

To: Avery Grant:
  Sharp and analytical, bright and imaginative. Damn fine job!

3. Decision-Making and Problem-Solving

> *"I can't decide. . . ."*
> *"If we could only lick that problem. . . ."*

Hang-ups in operations often result from weaknesses in making decisions and solving problems. Although the two subjects are related, they are different in key respects. Compare these two examples:

Problem: How can I get my salesmen to make calls on one more prospect a day? Or—how can I produce 100 more widgets from our new equipment?

Problems require a method, an idea, a principle to eliminate a difficulty. In developing a solution, the objective is to eliminate undesirable aspects of the situation.

Decision: Which of the three applicants I interviewed shall I hire as my secretary?

Decisions usually require a weighing of two or more alternative moves and the selection of one or a combination of two or more. Decisions don't promise the same 100% satisfaction that a perfect solution does. Decision-making always involves a certain amount of risk, and the objective is to minimize the amount of risk as far as possible.

DECISION-MAKING: A HISTORICAL MODEL

A critical incident in history provides a model of decision-making that dramatizes the cardinal aspects of the process:

In August, 1492 a soon-to-be-famous "executive" left Spain with eighty-seven men and three small ships. Day after day the ocean slipped behind to the east. Eventually, the men lost heart. Hope gove way to alarm, to be replaced in turn by panic and festering mutiny. Even his officers pleaded with Columbus to turn back.

The chief executive considered the situation, and decided to remain on the set course. The three ships continued westward. On October 12, land was sighted.

This encapsulated moment of history illustrates the essential elements of decision-making:

- a situation that demands, or seems to demand, action
- time pressure, created by a degenerating of circumstances
- lack of complete information
- uncertainty, suggesting a risk for *any* decision made
- likelihood of costly consequences if the decision is wrong
- likelihood of benefits of an effective decision
- the existence of two or more alternative actions

To clarify a decision-requiring situation in which you may find yourself, compare it to the Columbus model. Pinpointing the elements, may assist your decision-making.

PSYCHOLOGICAL HURDLES TO DECISION-MAKING

More than almost any other executive process, decision-making is ringed about with mental blocks. Here are four basic ones:

- *Hamlet's disease.* For some individuals, committing themselves to a course of action goes against the grain of their personalities. They are men of thought rather than action, and taking action of a decisive kind is difficult for them.
- *Compulsion.* Some individuals suffer from the opposite of the Hamlet syndrome. They feel compelled to make decisions, to take action, often premature and just as often, ill-considered.
- *Consequence anxiety.* For some, the decision-making situation is fraught with mental discomfort. They have an excessive fear of "guessing wrong," and tend to distort the consequences of a less-than-perfect decision.
- *Do-nothingism.* This is a subtle variant of some of the hurdles listed above. It shows up as a disinclination to act, a tendency to procrastinate. But unlike *consequence anxiety*, the individual who suffers from this difficulty doesn't seem excessively anxiety ridden.

And unlike *Hamlet's disease,* the deterrent to action seems to be unawareness, rather than a personal antipathy to action.

As opposed to all these ailments, the "mentally healthy" executive finds a certain amount of excitement in decision-making, and approaches the process with zest and the feeling that *his* decisions are likely to be as good as anyone else's.

THE ABC'S OF DECISION-MAKING

The basic method for making a decision involves a sequence of six steps:

1. Analyze and identify the situation.   You first clarify the situation you're trying to resolve. Sometimes this step is simple. For example, there may be a vacancy on your staff. You want to promote one of several possible subordinates into the spot. You have to make a decision; choose among them.

However, some situations may not be clear-cut: a department in your jurisdiction is doing poorly. Before you can make a remedial decision, you have to take into consideration the circumstances, find out *what's* wrong, and *why* it's wrong, in order to proceed.

2. Develop alternatives.   In every decision-requiring circumstance, there are at least two possible actions, for example, taking action or not taking action. In most cases there are more. For instance: in filling a vacancy in an executive staff one might—

- Leave it unfilled.
- Hire from the outside.
- Promote the person who is most familiar with the duties of the open job.
- Set up some kind of test which will make it possible for you to grade the qualifications of applicants for the job.
- Ask for volunteers.

3. Compare alternatives.   There are few cases where the executive is lucky enough to have one alternative that represents the likelihood of 100% satisfaction. Usually each alternative has advantages and disadvantages. An alternative that you might prefer may be too costly; or you may lack the manpower to carry it out. Where the decision is crucial, take the time to actually write out the advantages and disadvantages of each alternative.

4. Rate the risk.   You remember that one of the differences between decision-making and problem-solving is that a proper solution to a problem is sure-fire, if it is indeed the right solution. You're practically sure of getting the results desired.

But in decision-making, the usual situation is one in which every alternative you're considering includes an uncertainty factor. Since you seldom have total information about the situation you are dealing with, you can never be sure that the decision you make will be completely satisfactory.

Accordingly, in considering alternatives, it is important to rate the degree of risk each one involves. Obviously, this must be an estimate. Yet this approximation should be a part of the considerations that lead you to select the most desirable alternative.

In rating the risk, you may use percentages or any other rating system you prefer: grading from 1-10, using the academic A-F rating, and so on.

5. Select the best alternative.   If the previous steps have been done carefully, it is possible that the most likely alternative becomes self-evident. But there are other possibilities:

- No alternative is desirable. The riskiness of all alternatives for example, may properly persuade you not to take any action because no move you can think of at the time promises to be successful.
- Merge two or more alternatives. In some cases you may find that while no single alternative provides the averages you want, combining elements of two or more provides you with the most likely plan.
- The "resources factor" may swing your decision. Alternative A may have more advantages than Alternative B. However, in carrying out Alternative B, you may have a piece of equipment that promises to save the day. Or, and this element is often crucial, you may have a subordinate of outstanding skill that will make Alternative B a much better bet because of his availability for this move.

While it's wise to gather information and check facts, get expert opinion and project the possibilities into the future. There will still remain some uncertainty in your attempt to pinpoint the best move. This uncertainty element can never be completely eliminated and the usual practice is for the executive to select between two otherwise "even" alternatives by hunch or intuition. Don't underestimate the importance of your feeling. Veteran executives consider intuition a standard part of decision-making and use it when facts, logic, or systematic considerations are unavailable.

6. Getting into gear.   After a decision has been made, it must be made operative. You, or a subordinate, must take on the assignment of getting the people, resources, and so on, involved in putting the decision to work.

It may seem like an unnecessary emphasis to make this final point at all. But the fact is that many a decision, made even after days or weeks of effort, fails to produce results; or the decision is followed up in such a weak fashion that despite its many excellences only mediocre results are achieved.

In short, a decision implemented with energy and conviction can make a sizable difference in the outcome. For example, the manner in which a decision is communicated to the people who will be affected by it is, in itself, an important factor. And the manner in which the assignments represented by the decision are given to the people that are to carry out the plan is a major aspect of its effectiveness.

⊃ THE UNCERTAINTY FACTOR

In many decision-making approaches, an early directive is: get the facts. Unfortunately, there are very few situations requiring a decision in which the executive can have all the facts he needs or would like to have. For example, you have to make a decision about marketing a new product. It would be extremely helpful if you knew a competitor's plans for marketing a similar item. Yet you will have to make your decision without this vital piece of information.

The effective decision-maker learns to operate in the face of this information gap. He will do the best he can with available facts; or allow a given period of time for fact gathering: a day, a week, a month, and then set about making his decision on the basis of the data available.

Recognizing uncertainty.   The executive has two recourses after he has made his decision.

- *Test run.* In some cases it's possible to try out the decision short of full implementation. For example, an executive has decided to adopt a particular kind of package for one of his products. He makes up a trial run of the packaged item and tests it out in a limited market. If he's satisfied with the results, he goes all out. If not, he can rethink his decision.
- *Flexibility.* It is possible to develop a decision with "branching" steps. For example: An executive says, "Let's use training method

A with a group of 10 people, and training method B with another 10. Then we can compare results, and adopt the method that works best for all our trainees."

◑ IMPLEMENTATION: KEY TO DECISION-MAKING SUCCESS

"Not *what* you do, but the *way* that you do it," holds the secret of a successful outcome in decision-making. This is the opinion of a veteran executive decision-maker who has seen both in his own experience and that of colleagues the crucial role played by implementation in determining the outcome of decisions.

There are several basic considerations to be made in implementing a decision:

Commitment.   Once a course of action has been decided, others involved must be willing to put aside all hesitations, partial commitments to other courses of action, and so on. You have made a decision. You must move ahead on the decided course without further hesitations or doubts.

Announcement.   In some cases this element is minor. But in others the way in which a decision is revealed to a staff or an entire company roster can make a difference in its acceptance and its viability. When a decision is stated with resolution, confidence, and optimism, its chances of success are considerably increased, as compared to a reaction of doubt, hesitation, gloom, and pessimism.

Personnel.   Who gets to do what in putting a decision to work is often a crucial factor. Some alternatives can simply not be adopted because the people to develop it are not available. Consider the historical incident of the message to Garcia in the War with Spain. It was only when the officers of the United States Military Intelligence were able to find a man sufficiently qualified for the task, Lieutenant Andrew Somers Rowan, that the decision to contact General Clixto Garcia could be implemented.

In considering the personnel aspect of implementing a decision, think of it not only in terms of quantity, but quality. You may have enough people to do a job but ascertain that they have the skills, experience, initiative, and so on to achieve assigned objectives.

And more and more, executives are learning to use small groups rather than individuals in personnel assignment in some situations. Ask yourself "Would a two or three man team be better for a given assignment than a single individual?"

Facilities.   Everything from raw materials to production equipment may have to figure in your implementation. Like the personnel factor, every one of the facilities require hardheaded detailed thinking:

Do we have enough machines for the job?

Are they in satisfactory condition?

Must we rent or buy?

Can we subcontract?

Are present maintenance arrangements satisfactory or will they have to be changed for this particular job?

In the same way, you may have to go through considerations of space, transportation, materials-handling equipment, and so on.

Time.   Exactly when to start a plan, what deadlines to set, what pace to adopt, must be clearly spelled out. An undertaking started prematurely may suffer just as much as one started too late. On the question of pace, you must consider whether a particular project should get "crash" treatment or may be spaced over time. Considerations may involve the state of mind of a work group. For example: you may want to announce an exciting new program in the fall when people are psychologically "ready to buckle down," rather than during the summer doldrums.

Responsibility.   You may want to stand at the helm to make sure that the implementation of the decision remains on course. Or you may want to delegate this responsibility. If you make the latter move, the individual you select and the manner in which you hand out the assignment may be crucial.

There's a big difference in the motivating effect of "Jim, there's a little project I'd like you to take over for a few weeks," and "Jim, there's an important responsibility I've decided to turn over to you, and the outcome of it so important that it can make a considerable difference in the futures of both of us."

➜ WHEN DECISIONS GO SOUR

Executives—using one method or another—somehow manage to make decisions. But only a small percentage of decision-makers know how to proceed when a decision goes wrong. And remember, even the most carefully considered, well-planned decision can turn sour. Five positive moves may save the day:

Recognizing.   This move is a "must" prelude to all the others. Clear-headed, honest recognition of the fact that, on this particular decision, you have come up with a clinker. It may not be your fault at all. Other people, other forces, other events may be wholly or partially responsible. But whatever the cause, there is nothing to be gained by clinging to a losing situation. Executives who don't—or won't—recognize the inevitable, who are determined to make a decision work, to stick it out come what may, are only compounding wrong. *Your* lead: to accept the losses, analyze the causes, try to recoup what you can.

Reversing.   Many a decision is the result of a multi-step process. From Step A to Step B to Step C . . . and on and on till the final stage is reached. Somewhere along the line you may have tripped. Can you, after thinking things out, retrace your steps to the point where the misstep occurred? Backtrack from E to B, for instance? Then revising B, begin a subsequent series of steps, this time in the right direction? If so, you're halfway home.

Replacing.   There will be times when you have a decision that looks great—on paper. You've followed all the proper procedures, made all the right moves, said all the right things. Then, in execution, up pops a weak link. And trouble. Does this mean that your idea is not workable? Not at all.

Take the case of the executive who decides to set up a permanent team to handle the selling of a new product, Tom, Seth, and Gene, his three best producers. But it turns out that their sales go down, not up. Why? Analysis of the situation shows that Seth is the culprit, missing orders that he should land. Does the executive scrap the team idea? Indeed not. His original decision is still a good one; only the weak link needs replacing. Seth goes back to his old selling assignment. Jack joins the team on the new.

The weak link replaced, the decision can look good again—on paper and in execution.

Revising.   In some instances, of course, a decision-turned-bad can't be remedied by simply replacing or retracing. Accordingly, major surgery is called for, a complete revision of the original plan. Now's the time to ask yourself, "Do I have an alternative? Is there a workable Plan B that I can substitute for unworkable Plan A?" Undoubtedly, in arriving at Plan A you had considered other ways, other means of achieving your objective. Can one, or a combination of these, with additions, subtractions, amendments, successfully serve your purpose? Possibly it can.

This stage, incidentally, may call for consultations up, down, and along the line.

Reviewing.   Results are the proof of the decision-making pudding. When they go wrong, analyzing when, why, how can teach you a great deal. About your own decision-making ability. About techniques that need sharpening. About pitfalls to be avoided. About planning, performance, people. Failure often triggers more knowledge than success.

➜ A DECISIONLESS DECISION

Is it possible to "make a decision" without making one? In a sense, yes. Company president William Mott is fed up with his assistant. The young man seems to have lost the interest he originally had in his job. His performance is sloppy, even careless.

Repeatedly, Mott has tried to face up to the situation and make the decision to fire his subordinate; but somehow, although he has marched up to the hurdle repeatedly, he can't bring himself to take the jump.

Then one day his subordinate comes in late; he fails to do an important job that Mott has assigned, and takes a coffee break that stretches to a full hour. When the young man reappears, Mott, carefully restraining his irritation, calls the young man and suggests that he find a job better suited to his abilities and interests. After it is all over, Mott feels greatly relieved. Actually, the young man takes the firing so agreeably, the company president realizes the assistant also was in favor of the move.

"Why didn't I make that decision months ago?" Mott asks himself. Under the pressures of the moment, he had *acted* without the considered thinking we call decision-making.

The Mott case indicates an interesting aspect of decision-making. Essentially, a decision is a resolve to take action, and from time to time situations may arise where the executive takes decisive action without necessarily thinking of the move as a decision. However, such actions obviously are decisions, or rather are prompted by a decision made unconsciously and spontaneously.

So it seems that in some situations you can "decide" without consciously making a decision. Just beware of the pitfall to such executive action: sometimes the spontaneous decision can kick back. For example, executives have fired subordinates on the spur of a moment's anger or irritation—and regretted the act.

➲ A GENERAL APPROACH TO HANDLING PROBLEMS

Your personal attitude can help build a strong approach to dealing with problems. Here are the key elements that make for effectiveness:

1. Develop a "can-do" attitude. There is more to this concept than meets the eye. Psychologists have proved again and again that the individual who is optimistic about his ability to solve problems has a much greater chance of doing so than his pessimistic opposite number. In the area of practical problem-solving, the manager who goes on the assumption that a problem *can* and *will* be solved, is halfway to his goal.

2. Mobilize the creativity of your people. It has been proved repeatedly: we all have unplumbed depths of imagination and ingenuity. Develop the practice of posing challenging assignments and problems to your people to stimulate their creativity. They're not likely to let you down.

Most of us respond favorably to the excitement of a challenge. Many of us will work our fingers to the bone to come up with an answer to a difficult problem because we hunger for the feeling of self-esteem and the increased respect of colleagues and co-workers when we score a breakthrough. Your subordinates' "need to achieve" can supplement your own.

3. Break problems down to bite-size. Some work situations cannot be coped with because they're too vast or complex. For example, one manager was told by his boss, "In the next year, we're going to be replacing every piece of equipment in your department. Your employees are all going to have to relearn their jobs, develop new skills."

The problem of retraining about 40 people in a dozen different skills, and still keep things running on a regular basis is clearly tremendous. But the department head made his first step an effective one. He got down to cases. He spelled out what each employee needed in order to handle new assignments. Once he had done this he was able to set up schedules that permitted each employee to get the training that was needed to make the transition.

4. Make the distinction between "gradual" and "crash" solutions. Some of the problems executives face can be solved over a long period of time. When the problem you face is of this character, a policy of "gradualism"—that is, piecemeal and consistent planning—gets you off the hook.

However, some management problems are "emergency" or "rush." Here's where you're under deadline pressure and simply can't stretch out your thinking about the problem, or take your time developing solutions to fit problem situations.

You strengthen your approach by using "crash" tactics. Whether you use a brain-trust or maintain close contacts up the line and with staff experts, give yourself the advantage of *multiple brainpower.* Don't hesitate to draw on the mental resources and experience of other people in your company—subordinates, specialists, colleagues, and so on.

➲ IDENTIFYING THE PROBLEM

It has been said that a problem identified is half solved. An incident in an engineering class makes the point:

An engineering instructor tells a group of beginning students, "Here's a problem. Make up a sketch for a bridge to cross a river a mile wide."

The solutions come in describing suspension, cantilever, and viaduct designs.

The instructor gives all the papers but one a failing mark.

"Only one student is on the right track." He reads from the winning paper: "No solution is possible unless we know more about the problem." Some of the missing elements: how wide a channel must be allowed for navigation? How high must the span be above the channel? How much traffic is the bridge to bear?

Each one of these factors is a part of the problem. Each one must play a part in the solution.

In thinking about a problem situation, these steps keep you on track:

1. Don't assume you know the problem. You can't come to grips with a difficulty unless you know—

- the background—how long has it existed? How bad is it? And so on.
- the causes of the problem—what factors have brought it about? Why does it persist? What factors intensify the difficulty? What factors alleviate it? And so on.

2. Avoid the brass-tacks urge. Many executives like to strike directly at the heart of the matter. In some cases that's commendable.

But in dealing with problems it may lead to "solutions" that solve nothing. Particularly, when dealing with a difficult problem, make sure you know the one-eighth that shows above the surface, with as much as possible of the seven-eighths that may not readily meet the eye. The importance of identifying a problem is that you force yourself to consider its different aspects and details.

A comedian once boasted that he discovered a cure for a disease that didn't even exist. It happens in executive suites every day—we solve problems that don't exist, because we haven't properly identified them.

➲ PRACTICAL TIPS ON SOLVING PROBLEMS

International Management, a business journal headquartered in London, offers a series of practical points in the problem-solving process:

Is there a solution to this problem?   Not all problems can be solved.

Say it or write it down.   Lay it out so that you can analyze its complications.

Define the problem positively.   The optimistic outlook inspires a positive solution both in yourself and others.

Have you forgotten anything?   Don't let the omission of important data fog your focus on the problem.

Get additional information.   Research may bring out facts you've overlooked or simply don't know about.

Look for more than one solution.   Are there alternative solutions? If so, which is best? Can you combine?

Welcome new ideas.   And give a new idea the opportunity to prove itself.

Check your solution and check yourself.   Evaluate your answers. Since you can't foresee precisely how a solution will work, changes and corrections may be necessary.

Don't look for a perfect solution.   Aim for the best you can get under the circumstances.

Rest your ego.   Insistence on being right all the time only alienates others. If your problem involves other people, give them the chance to be right once in a while.

⮕ WHEN THERE'S NO SOLUTION

You sometimes tackle a problem to which you can find no answer. Should you go on plugging away seeking the key? Or, should you give up? When you face this dilemma—

1. Assess the importance of the problem. Stick with it if it's a major obstacle. There's no point, for example, in conducting business as usual if a bottleneck is obviously going to wreck chances of filling a major commitment.

On the other hand, don't tie yourself up over a minor matter while regular operations go to pot.

2. Consult. You can't get away from sound arithmetic: two heads *are* better than one. And three are better than two. Take up the problem with your boss, the people in your group who are directly concerned, specialists in your staff departments who might be able to help.

They may or may not be able to provide immediate assistance. But it's not unusual for your own thoughts and ideas to become clarified in the process of discussion. Even if you draw blanks, you have at least multiplied your chances of success.

3. Can you ease up? If you have a little elbow room in terms of time, let the teaser rest a while. Give your mind a chance to cool off. Relaxation can renew your mental vigor, may give you a new approach and new understanding.

In some cases, time may work for you. For example, an executive found himself with the standard problem of two subordinates who couldn't get along. They were both key people; shifting either would have meant further complications. After days of futile thinking, he decided there was nothing he could do. Six months later, he observed the problem no longer existed. The two individuals had little by little ironed out their own differences.

4. Review. If the problem is important, you'll probably be forced to reconsider it from time to time. Do so in the light of changes that have taken place since you last considered the matter. A change may suggest a solution.

➲ WHEN IT'S RIGHT TO BE WRONG

Occasionally a problem presents itself in which all the "right" solutions have failed to work. In such a situation, the "wrong" way may prove effective. In a sense, Solomon's dealing with the Case of the Disputing Mothers applied a "wrong" solution. When he suggested that the child both women claimed be cut in two, it clearly was not a good solution. But it caused one woman to agree to give up the child; the other perfectly willing to abide the ruling made it easy to decide who the real mother was.

Here are some situations in which you might want to consider doing the "wrong" thing:

1. When the "right" way doesn't work.   Sometimes you just have to throw the rule book out of the window to save the situation.

2. When the "right' way won't end well enough.   In some cases, the quality of the result you want may persuade you that the "right" track isn't getting you where you want to go.

3. When there's doubt as to what the "right' way really is.   This development may turn up in connection with work methods. One experienced executive says:

"Sometimes in order to solve a problem of technique, I have to go as far off the deep end as I can. That helps me find limits within which a sound solution may be developed."

➲ SOLVING UNSOLVABLE PROBLEMS

"Reaching for the moon" is a phrase that denotes trying to achieve the impossible. But now in our lifetime comes the achievement that gives lie to the old phrase. Our national heroes, Neil Armstrong, Michael Collins, and Edwin Aldrin, did the undoable by achieving the objectives of *Apollo Eleven* and being the first men on the moon.

The feat made the whole world proud—and thoughtful. Perhaps other "undoable" tasks are within our reach. At the very least, there's a tremendous lesson to be learned from the moon-conquering accomplishment of the first man-on-the-moon rocket.

Analyzing the steps by which we forged our triumph, key points emerge that may be applied to "unsolvable" problems on the job:

1. Commitment.   In 1961, President John F. Kennedy made a rousing, determined statement that committed the nation to landing men on the moon "before this decade is out." When starting any ambitious project we must resolve to put into the task the effort required. This act of will provides us with the drive and the emotional strength to start and sustain the energies needed for success.

2. Deadline.   In President Kennedy's statement, the words, "before the decade is out," created a sense of time pressure. Compare the effect of Kennedy's statement *without* the time deadline What if he had merely said, "We must go to the moon." It *may* have been as exciting a declaration. But without the deadline, we would not have had the same feeling of urgency, a highly motivating factor.

3. Resources.   Thousands of companies, hundreds of thousands of people became involved in producing the ideas, the planning, the hardware, and the techniques that eventually landed us on our satellite. In the same way, the manager who is undertaking "mission impossible" must have resources available. Part of the solution is the assessment and gathering of resources, manpower, materials, equipment, and so on.

4. Piecemeal victories.   We didn't get to the moon in a single jump. As a matter of fact, a succession of ambitious projects starting with *Pioneer I* in 1957, and including Ranger, Mariner, Surveyor, Explorer, and Gemini, preceded *Apollo 11*. Each added to our knowledge and refinement of techniques. Within the framework of each of these major projects were thousands of piecemeal accomplishments—the improvement of a valve, the redesign of an electrical system, the continuing modernization of vital parts and instruments, such as the on-board computer.

In the same way, the executive should strive to break down his long-range goal into subelements and subgoals. These bite-size tasks or goals *are* attainable. And reaching the overall goal, in a sense, is the sum of many small successes.

5. Refinement and improvement.   A large part of the scientific and engineering talent in our space effort was devoted to continuing improvements in design methods and standards of quality. Accordingly, the executive who may be trying to drastically reduce overall production time on a major item may find that he moves towards his objective when, under his direction, a subordinate comes up with an idea for a special bit for a drilling operation, or a more efficient jig for an assembly operation.

6. Consolidate learning.   As advances were made, the benefits were quickly incorporated into the overall activity. Accordingly, each project benefited by what had been learned in previous ones. For example, the know-how for building bigger, better, and more reliable rockets advanced steadily from 1958 on. The same is true of the improvements in design and application of computers used in the space conquest.

7. Communications.   A part of the space effort that seldom made the headlines: the countless hours of meetings, conferences, discussions; the exchange of memos and reports among the various groups and individuals involved in the space project.

It's both stimulating and helpful to let the left hand know what the right hand is doing. Employee A who has solved a problem in his part of the project may be able to help Employee B solve one in his area. Or, Employee C, struggling with difficulties, may receive an idea from Employee D that will ease the bind.

8. Leadership.   An essential ingredient is continuing direction from the top. With a project involving even a few people—and certainly where larger numbers are involved—a single "command center" must supervise the effort, keep it moving along, and keep the parts of the project effectively related to one another. *This is the ultimate contribution of an executive.* And, as some experts see it, *Apollo 11* may be said to be a triumph of American management know-how as well as of "technology."

An "unsolvable" problem? *Apollo 11* proves that *if* there is such a thing, the number of items in this category are fewer than we think. *Apollo 11* is an inspiration to the entire planet, but to American management, it's a stimulating reminder that any goal we set ourselves is possible—if we work toward that goal and believe in our ability to achieve it.

In World War II, maangement developed the saying: "The difficult we can do at once, the impossible takes a little longer." Our moon triumph suggests that the "impossible" may not take that much longer.

⬦ QUANTIFICATION, AN ASSIST IN PROBLEM-SOLVING

Roger Bacon said that knowledge wasn't scientific until it used numbers. Sir Francis Galton, who launched the modern theory of statistics suggested, "Whenever you can, count."

For executives, numbers are an important tool of thinking and problem-solving. Problems that seem vague and unmanageable come into sharper focus when you *count* and *compare*.

Clearly, when a problem naturally involves quantities, they become a key aspect of the solution. For example, you have a problem of moving 10 pounds of material across the continent. The solution is likely to be quite different from a similar problem involving 1,000 pounds.

But you are faced with many problems in which the quantification isn't built in. In this case there are two possible approaches:

- *Assignment of values.* Let's say you have a problem of evaluating the performance of an employee. His job involves three different elements, each of which is of different importance. You represent this difference by "weighting": element A, the most important, is assigned a value of 50%, elements B and C given values of 25% each. Now, as you go about evaluating the quality of his performance in these three areas, the quantification step gives you a continuing reminder that his accomplishments in element A, or his failings, are twice as important as those in B or C.

- *Rating scale.* Instead of numbers, it's also possible to make helpful comparisons by use of a graded scale such as Excellent, Good, Fair, Poor, Unsatisfactory. Another common method is the old school grading method: A, B, C, D, E, and F.

In each of the above cases the objective is to make your thinking more specific. In avoiding vagueness, you sharpen the facts and make possible comparisons that are helpful in problem-solving.

4. Planning

"What isn't planned today, won't be done tomorrow," says the experienced executive. Thinking and arranging for future activities— everything from routines like a staff meeting to a major project, such as the launching of a new product or the building of a new plant— is one of the strengths of the effective executive.

Planning failures are of two kinds:

Neglect. "Tomorrow will take care of itself," says the self-deluded manager, and counts on improvisation and fast reflexes to make up for planning deficiencies. But time and tide often find him high and dry, and his failures become legion.

Flubbing. Some executives go through the motions of planning, but inadequate methods don't do the trick and too often consequences are dire.

Suggestions in the following section help review and improve planning methods, stacking the cards heavily in favor of job achievement.

→ WHEN TO PLAN

Planning becomes appropriate when a *special activity is* contemplated that must be prepared for, organized, and scheduled; or, at *periodic* times dictated by the calendar. Here then are three planning occasions:

- The beginning of a new year with its newly set objectives.
- The quarterly intervals that give you the opportunity for appraising achievements and resetting your sights.
- Any new undertaking or project.

In addition, there are the tasks that may confront you at any time; the need, for example, to cut costs, revise operations, improve quality of output, increase the level of performance of personnel.

→ TYPES OF PLANS

The list below can help clarify your approach to planning:

One-time plans.   Some situations you plan for are one-shot. They will be used once and may never again be repeated. Involved in this kind of planning, executives will often improvise. Cost considerations may suggest planning for achievement at a get-by level, the lowest possible acceptable standard.

Standby plans.   Executive sometimes develop a plan for handling a situation that *may* develop. Such contingency planning must be done with as much care and detail as a plan you will be putting to work tomorrow. Too often a standby plan has been developed with the feeling that the contigency, although possible, is not likely. And when the situation does arise, the standby plans are found to be impractical, incomplete, or unrealistic.

Standby planning may require more imagination and ability to visualize than ordinary planning. You may have to depend heavily on your own abilities or those of others to foresee possible situations in order to plan for them realistically.

Short-range plans.   Short-range planning has the value of imme-diacy, and can depend heavily on informal and direct communication. When you are going to start a project that can be completed in a few days, the amount of paper work can be minimal. Face-to-face commu-nication can usually get across the exchange of ideas and information required.

Long-range plans.   Unlike short-range planning, projects that ex-tend over months or years must have three built in characteristics:

1. *Continuity.*   You must put down on paper and build in controls that will keep the project moving in the desired direction and at the pace originally planned.
2. *Review.*   Periodic considerations must be made of progress in order to make sure that original objectives will be achieved.
3. *Goal reconsideration.*   Factors which have helped determine the purposes or goals of a plan may change. Sights may have to be raised or lowered. Along with reviews of progress, the executive may also want to assess original objectives to see if they are still valid or whether they must be modified.

Back-up plan.   No matter how carefully planning is done, intro-duction of new factors or performance failures in some areas may bring a project to a point of crisis or failure. In this case, it is desirable to have "Plan B," a back-up plan which can be substituted for the original one.

⮕ PLANNING FOR PLANNING

Management authority Peter Drucker has commented that work plan-ning must be planned for just like any other aspect of management. He recommends five steps required by "planning for planning":

Establishment of objectives. What are the things my company and my department wish to achieve—and when?

Determining priority of objectives. If all the objectives cannot be achieved at once, which are the most important?

Identifying resources. What will it take to achieve the objectives set forth? What are the resources of the department, and the company, available to help achieve the objectives?

Executing action programs. What will it take to move the plan off paper? Who must issue what instructions and to whom?

Maintaining control. Are follow-up procedures used effectively and thoroughly? Does the department head know what the score is, on a continuing, up-to-the-minute basis?

➔ GIVE YOUR PROJECT A NAME

Manhattan Project (atom bomb); Operation Overlord (Invasion of Normandy). You'll generally find that every big project is given a name. It's not an affectation. It's an effective idea for projects, large or small, for two reasons:

- The name acts as a convenient handle. When you discuss the matter with other people you then have a simple means by which to refer to it. You develop a common understanding of what it is you're talking about.
- Less tangible but possibly even more vital, the project in your own mind becomes more specific, more concrete.

➔ PINPOINT THE PURPOSES OF YOUR PLANNING

In your planning, it is highly desirable to state goals in terms of specific quantities. In some areas there is no problem. When, for example, you are setting production goals or sales quotas, it is perfectly natural to state these in specific terms: January quota, 10,000; February, 12,000, and so on.

But even with less clear-cut objectives, it is sometimes possible to reduce your aims to numbers. Take the matter of quality, for example. In the average office the quality of the work cannot, as in the industrial scene, be expressed in terms of tolerances, types of finish, color range, and so on. But let's say you're out to improve the quality of the typing done by members of your staff. This goal might very well be put in terms of the numbers of typos or erasures that mean a given piece of correspondence must be discarded.

A threat to achieving planning objectives lies in an unexpected direction:

A department head, alarmed by the figures that jump out at him from a cost of operating report, decides he'd better bear down, fast and hard. He plans an impressive program: close check on every expense item, from stationery to overtime; conferences with his subordinates to sell them on the need to keep a tight rein on expenditures; an intensive probing into current work methods to see where they can be made more efficient.

He gets his assistant and the entire work group to cooperate. They go along, and he's pleased as punch the way the plan is clicking. He considers the matter finished, turns his attention elsewhere. But, unfortunately, he has forgotten his original purpose. *He never bothers to find out whether he's chopped one penny off operating costs.*

Write your purpose down in black and white. Be as specific as possible: "To cut $500 off monthly expenses." "To get dealers to take 10 per cent more of our product." And so on. And, check to ascertain to what extent goals have been met.

➲ MANNING THE PLAN

List all the people who should be involved in furthering a plan. Conceivably, this might include everyone on your staff. More generally, there are one or two key people through whom you will work directly.

This helps in two ways:

(a) You may sometimes discover that you lack one or more other people needed to implement the plan.

(b) In listing the people, you may discover that although you have the man, he will require further instruction before being able successfully to tackle the task for which he has been selected.

Once you have spotted this need for training, you will find it becomes one of the subgoals which the plan must take into account.

➲ CHECK OUT AVAILABLE FACILITIES

Planning requires review of resources available. You may need new facilities, or you may have to revamp those on hand in order to be able to implement the plan.

Make your facilities list as complete as possible. Remember the old story of the kingdom that was lost for want of a nail. Facilities lists will vary, depending on the nature of the project involved. For a plan of production, for example, you might list available resources under headings like these:

Raw materials
Fittings and supplies
Production equipment
Auxiliary equipment
Standby equipment
Handling equipment
Packing materials

The problem of human resources, of course, is an essential and related part of your planning, covered in the previous page.

Another approach to assessing facilities is shown in the chart below:

Have on Hand	Modifications, Repairs?	Additional Facilities Required	Date	Sources & Remarks

◆ DEVELOP AND CHECK METHODS

Where tried and true methods have been satisfactory, you may merely have to state briefly the means you intend to use to achieve your goals. But in other cases, this may become the key item of the plan.

Let's say, for example, that the purpose of your plan is to cut down on absenteeism in your company. When you come to methods, your first inclination may be merely to jot down the means that have been used in the past: the record keeping by supervisors, the occasional warnings backed up by a severance of the really extreme case.

But writing down the method gives you an opportunity to reassess its potential effectiveness. In your plans to combat absenteeism, you may be moved to seek additional methods: development of an absentee record form that will go more fully into the reasons for the absence; or follow-up by a personnel officer of the reasons that have been contributory to absenteeism, such as poor transportation facilities, and so on.

◆ ESTIMATE COSTS

The wise executive keeps the cost consideration in mind in every planning move he makes.

You may say to yourself: "Sure, I did a good job on that project. But I wonder whether it couldn't have been done at half the cost."

You're always working within a cost limit. Putting it in other words: if money were no object, almost any plan could be brought to a satisfactory conclusion. But the executive who can do it well and do it cheaply, achieves a double success from his planning.

➲ SCHEDULE PLANNING ELEMENTS

Draw up the timetable of the planned operation. Set specific dates for the various phases of your plan:

Preparation.   Under this subheading, for example, you may want to indicate training steps required to equip your personnel for the tasks you intend to give them. You may have to go out into the market to secure additional equipment, more space, and so on. Many of the items here will have been turned up in your filling out of the earlier parts of the guide.

Sequence.   Your plan will be advanced by specific people assigned to definite parts of the total effort. Your usual assignment procedure will figure here. You'll select your people according to their suitability for the tasks you want performed. You'll set up deadlines, subgoals, and so on.

Time targets.   Be specific "Noon, May 20," or "End of business, Friday, June 17." Build a tradition in which meeting deadlines becomes a matter of professional pride. Alter time targets only when unavoidable.

➲ BUILD IN CONTROLS

Whether you call it progress review, follow-up, or checking on assignments, set up some means of reviewing the progress of the plan and of readjusting to unexpected developments. If one subordinate is lagging behind, you may have to put an additional man on the job. If another subordinate is getting ahead faster than you anticipated, you may have to stop him and put him on another job if his completion must coincide with the work being done by a second individual.

The controls you use will depend, of course, on the nature of the effort. You may want to set up a system of written reports by which your subordinates keep you informed of how they're making out. Or where cost is critical and must be checked with a sensitive hand, you may want to have all bills for the project collected in a central agency so that you can be kept continually informed of how fast the money is going out.

If you have been successful in quantifying your objectives, it may be helpful to keep track of progress by means of a visual chart or graph. Whether you chart your progress daily, weekly, or monthly depends again on the nature of the project. But you'll find such visual aids particularly effective in the conferences you may want to hold with your subordinates to discuss the rate of progress and the need to alter methods to changing conditions as the program progresses.

➲ EVALUATE RESULTS

A progress review is, in a sense, a running evaluation of the plan. in many cases, you and your people have much to gain by taking a retrospective view.

Discuss Project X in terms of the *original objectives* as compared with objectives accomplished. You can survey the methods used, starting from the methods you had intended to employ and ending up with any changes and the reasons for changes that may have been necessary.

The other items mentioned in previous pages—purposes; man-power; facilities; methods; costs; timing and scheduling; controls— similarly suggest points of departure and specific areas that can be covered in your evaluation sessions.

➲ DEVELOP A PLAN B

When large sums of money or other vital consequences are involved, consider having an alternative plan available if the preferred Plan A fails. In preparing Plan B, keep in mind these two questions:

■ *Can Plan B produce what Plan A was meant to achieve?* Many executives tend to be meticulous about Plan A, but give Plan B a once-over-lightly. Plan B deserves just as much consideration as Plan A, for a state of emergency *already* exists when Plan B is brought in.

■ *Is Plan B free from Plan A's weaknesses?* Plan B will, of course, be inferior to Plan A, or it would have been your first choice. But even though Plan B has more serious faults than Plan A, they should be *different* faults. If the two plans have similar weak spots, they may be no better than one plan. Actually, *Plan B is an added danger* in this case, since its very presence may lend a false sense of security.

The classic case is the driver who never travels without a spare, but whose spare wont' hold air.

⮊ BUDGETS AS A TOOL

Usually, executives think of budgets as a financial fence. While in a sense, budgetary limits are meant to deter excessive or misdirected expenditure, budgets also have strong additional advantages:

- *More complete planning.* A budget may be viewed as a scheme of operations converted into dollars and cents. As such, it forces executive planning and provides a stable financial framework that can help insure performance. A budget can be especially helpful in times of change, as many companies have learned after living through the turbulence of significantly fluctuating economic conditions.

- *Measure of performance.* A budget kept up to date gives ·the executive a continuous view of how well he is progressing. Top management, too, is provided with a check on total company performance. Any significant variations from budget allocations signal the need for investigation.

- *Control over spending.* A good budget allows managers to maintain close control over expenditures. Sophisticated executives have learned that properly viewed, budgets can encourage spending where it will clearly improve net profit.

- *Better coordination.* The financial controls provide the mechanism for improved coordination between various parts of a business, or between departments. Financial controls may help correct such problems as poor communication between production and sales, faulty timing in the introduction of new products, and improper staffing of operations such as order, service, warehousing, and so on, in the light of projected sales volume. Finally, for many executives, a well-drawn budget is a helpful measure of his performance. It tells the executive who reaches his goals and remains within budgetary limits that he has probably done a satisfactory job. For the executive who has done violence to budgetary limitations, no matter what his accomplishment, there is the need to backtrack to learn whether performance, no matter how outstanding, has been really profitable.

⮊ A CONTINUATION PLAN—KEEPING THINGS ROLLING IN YOUR ABSENCE

Details of a continuation plan will vary from executive to executive, depending on the nature of his job responsibilities, the length of time he'll be away, who will be left in charge, and so on. Any plan for continuation involves two factors: people and paper. Here are tips for making your continuation plan work in both areas:

1. Always keep your superior and subordinates reasonably well informed about what is going on.

2. Train one particular person to take over your job in emergency absences.

3. Make your assistant privy to as many of your current problems and concerns as possible.

4. Use short absences and your vacation as training periods for both plan and personnel.

5. Prepare a continuation folder to include key job descriptions, an outline of your own duties, whom you report to on what, who reports to you, where key items are located, who can answer questions, etc.

6. Have job descriptions written by key personnel, outlining their areas of responsibility and detailing their duties and the names of all subordinates.

7. Make sure your folder includes a plan of action for continuing present projects, for deciding about upcoming matters of major significance, plus a review of proposals for change, an outline of future projects, and any other helpful information.

8. Revise and update these reports as often as advisable, but at least semiannually.

9. Keep your continuation folder constantly up to date by filing recent correspondence, memoranda dealing with current problems, etc. in it. Weed these out from time to time.

10. Go over this folder with the man you have picked to take over in your absence, and let him know where it is kept.

11. The typical executive's secretary becomes a key source of information and opinion: "I believe Mr. Jones would handle that situation this way. . . ." Let your secretary know your expectations in this regard.

12. Should you leave word as to where you can be reached in case of emergency? That's a highly personal decision. Just be sure to give the question some thought, and act on the decision, whichever way you decide.

5. Delegation and Assignment

"Executives work through others. . . ."

That principle of executive action is generally accepted, even self-evident.

It is true that the executive satisfies his responsibilities by using the manpower at his command, from his secretary to his staff and other subordinates. It likewise follows that many executives operate on marginal levels because they have not mastered the methods by which their manpower can be utilized to best advantage.

The techniques of delegation and assignment are major keys *to* effective utilization of your subordinates. Suggestions for these crucial procedures are detailed in the pages that follow.

➲ WHY YOU MUST DELEGATE

Delegation has been called "the secret of executive sanity." No matter how good an executive you are, your responsibilities will always be greater than your personal capacity to carry them out. For example, no one expects the company president to personally purchase, package and sell his product. The diagram below graphically represents the situation:

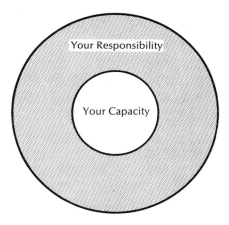

The Area of Delegation   In the diagram the outer circle represents the limit of your responsibilities. The inner circle marks the boundaries of your human capacity. The shaded ring is the area that you must delegate to others; your secretary, your subordinates, and so on. Note that the tasks you delegate are not parts of their job—they have their own areas of responsibility. What you delegate are tasks that definitely fall within your job responsibility, but which, for one of several reasons which will be described later on, you prefer to pass along to others.

There are two general problems in this area:

Under-delegation. The executive tries to push the inner ring (his capacity) outward in an attempt to make the two circles correspond. Then he complains—"I have to be in three places at once."

"I don't dare take a day off."

. . . of ulcers.

Over-delegation. The executive who suffers from this misjudgment has so many tasks delegated that he loses control. His cry: "Why doesn't someone tell me these things!"

The skill of delegation is to know how to concentrate those matters that are most important within the circle of the things you handle yourself. Less important tasks can be passed along to others.

➲ SIX STEPS TO SUCCESSFUL DELEGATION

A sequence of six moves helps insure the favorable outcome of delegation:

1. Pinpoint the task. Delineate in your own mind the limits of the responsibility you want to pass along. It may be to do research for a report. Or it may be to do the research and the actual writing. Or it may be the research, writing, and overseeing of the production of the report. Whatever the dimensions of the assignments, clarify it as your first step.

2. Select the person. The individual you choose as your delegate may vary considerably:

- If time is short, and you must have acceptable results, select the most capable person.
- If your delegation has as a primary purpose to train or challenge an individual, delegate to the employee requiring this type of attention.
- You may rotate your delegation to broaden the base of trained, flexible people on your staff.

3. Make the assignment. Let the delegate know *what* you want him to do. How much more you tell him depends on individual circumstances. For example—

- You may want to put on paper the details of the assignment, wholly or in part.
- You may want to tell him why he was selected.

In any event, you will probably want to explain why the job is important and the results that are expected.

And finally, you will want to check his understanding to make sure that he is perfectly clear on all aspects of the assignment.

4. Supply supports.   Occasionally your delegation can be made on a minimal basis: simply tell a capable subordinate what you want and leave the rest to him. But in other cases, it may be necessary for you to provide additional help:

- Clarify his authority.
- Tell others about his assignment so that they will be aware of your backing his efforts.
- Tell the subordinate of any danger points in the assignment, or what to do if emergencies develop.
- Let him know of your availability in case he runs into trouble.

5. Check his progress.   If the task isn't simple and clear-cut, it may be desirable for you to keep in touch with developments. This gives your continuing control and prevents undesirable complications. Checking on progress may involve anything from a casual, "How are things going," to reports at key points of the project.

6. Evaluate achievement.   If the delegation is something other than routine, you may want to review your subordinate's progress. There are several purposes: you may want to reward his achievement or to pin down the learning aspect of the delegation; you might want to go over with him aspects of the job that have been well done, areas in which he might have performed better. In any event, your subordinate will undoubtedly want the recognition that such a review represents. It can be demotivating for an individual to put effort into an assignment and get no response from his superior for what's been accomplished.

FIVE BASIC DELEGATION SITUATIONS

Here are five basic delegatables:

1. Routine tasks.   Screening your mail, preliminary interviewing of job applicants, discussion of minor maintenance needs—activities like these may be parceled out to subordinates when you're not inclined to do them yourself.

2. Tasks for which you don't have time.   There's another group of activities, not necessarily routine, but of comparatively low priority. When you have time for these, you prefer to do them yourself. But when more urgent matters occupy your attention, these may be passed along to a capable subordinate.

3. Problem-solving. Some executives properly turn over a problem situation to a subordinate. This is usually of a low or medium priority area; and actually there may be one or more of your subordinates with a particular knowledge or skill in the area that qualifies him to take on the task. In addition, he will be motivated to give it special attention, since it will represent a challenge for him.

4. Changes in your own job emphasis. For the average executive, job content changes over the years, slowly in some cases, rapidly in others. As executives become aware of these changes in emphasis, they understand that new elements in their activity require more of their time. To "make" the time, the executive must, as a practical matter, delegate "old" aspects of his responsibility to subordinates.

5. Capability building. Last but not least, delegation may be used to increase the capability of individual subordinates and your staff as a group. Properly managed, delegation becomes the means by which you train and develop both the skills and horizons of subordinates. In the item that follows, "Delegation as a Man Builder," you will find more on this vital point.

DELEGATION AS A MAN BUILDER

Greater efficiency isn't the only motive for delegating a part of your job. Enlargement of a subordinate's job can give three other important results:

Developing his sense of responsibility. You may wish to make an assignment purely in the interest of increasing his ability and value to your activity as a whole.

Enlarge his general understanding. For instance, the best way to stress the importance of customer relations for one of your assignments might be to ask him to take over answering customers' complaints.

Increasing his job satisfaction. Some subordinates thrive on varied assignments; their interest in the job increases along with its responsibility. Delegation of challenging projects helps maintain a subordinate's effectiveness as a team member.

Used in these ways, delegation is another means of getting cooperation, of increasing ability and motivation.

Properly handled, delegation guarantees that your overall job will remain in control, and that the people working under you will keep moving in the right direction. But there are hazards.

You'd be wrong to assume, for example, that delegation is a one-shot affair. Your responsibilities tend to change; new problems come up and make new demands on your time. You must be ready to review past delegations. You may have to make corresponding changes in the tasks that you've assigned to others.

➲ THE PSYCHOLOGY OF DELEGATION

The process of delegation poses some psychological difficulties for the average executive:

Decision.   For the manager who has difficulty making up his mind, the simple process of deciding which tasks to delegate and which to retain poses a mental hurdle.

Standards.   No two people are likely to perform a task in the same way or to achieve exactly the same end results. Therefore, for some executives it becomes painful to look on while a subordinate goes about performing a delegated task in a manner the executive himself would not use, or about which he may even have doubts.

Control.   For some executives, this is the toughest hurdle of all. To these managers, handing over to another a task for which they are directly responsible causes grave concern: "If the job is badly done, it may reflect adversely on me." "If the job is done differently from the way I would do it, I may not be satisfied with the outcome."

Or this possibility must be confronted: "If a subordinate does the job better than I could do it, it may make me look bad."

The solutions to the problems suggested above lie in mastering the technique of delegation, knowing when to delegate, what to delegate, and how to delegate. And it is precisely this information you will find in the following pages.

➲ WHEN TO DELEGATE

There are specific occasions in the course of your work when delegation is called for. Here, for example, are three instances:

When you're overburdened.   It's a safe general rule that you simply can't handle *all* your responsibilities and still do a good job on the important ones.

In emergencies.   Your first thought may be to let everything else drop. Yet the temporary suspension of even a routine matter, may leave you with too big a backlog when the crisis is over.

When you have to be absent.   It might be a two-week vacation— or a series of conferences. But someone will have to provide a *minimum* amount of authority while you're gone.

As a starter, check up on the time you spend now in:

- Filling out routine reports, requisitions, etc.
- Making calculations and entries.
- Checking materials and supplies.
- Running your own errands.
- Engaging repeatedly in certain simple, mechanical tasks.

If you can reduce any of these to a matter of a final O.K., signature, or dispatch of a messenger, consider handing them over to a subordinate. These are the easiest duties to delegate.

➲ WHEN NOT TO DELEGATE

Just as there are situations for which delegation is a solution, there are circumstances which make it inadvisable.

Delegation can cause trouble if the wrong duties are handed over. Some of your responsibilities are yours for keeps:

The power to discipline.   This is the backbone of executive authority.

Responsibility for maintaining morale.   You may call upon others to help carry out assignments that will improve morale. You cannot ask anybody else to maintain it.

Overall control.   No matter how extensive are the delegations, ultimate responsibility for final performance rests on your shoulders.

The hot potato.   Don't ever make the mistake of passing one along, just to take yourself off the spot.

Some jobs must be retained. It's best to hang on to them, if:

They are too technical.   Computing a floor load or projecting a cost estimate may be routine for you—but completely beyond a subordinate's skill.

The duty involves a trust or confidence.   For instance, handling confidential cost data, dealing with the personal affairs of one of your people, and so on.

To keep things moving at full blast, you may find it necessary at times to delegate duties involving initiative, judgment, and decision. But consider these factors:

- the duty to be delegated
- the ability of the person it will go to
- your ability to keep control—that is, to keep posted on progress

➲ HOW TO DELEGATE AND KEEP CONTROL

When you delegate responsibility, you don't really get rid of it. You must still exercise control.

You *need* control in order to achieve coordination—to see that the assigned task works in with other objectives—and to achieve satisfactory results.

Your instructions must include a standard operating procedure, a list of rules by which the subordinate can handle the situations your own experience has shown constantly recur.

Examination of results. This is the easiest kind of control you can exercise. You simply look at the completed performance. It's sort of "hands-off—men working" policy, used where your assistant is highly capable or where the task is largely mechanical.

Control by follow-up. In many cases, it isn't wise to wait until the performance is complete. Errors may simply be too expensive, too hard to correct. You may want to check progress by inspecting, sampling, or spot-checking. This approach is particularly good where the responsibility is new, large, or difficult to handle.

Progress reports. For a variety of reasons—time element, location, etc.—you may prefer to have your subordinate report on how he is making out. Such a report may be frequent or infrequent, written or oral, by personal contact or telephone. You must decide what is adequate under the circumstances.

➲ HOW TO PREPARE THE DELEGATE

To get the subordinate off on the right foot, consider these four points:

Give him the facts about the job. Give your delegate a clear picture of what he's to do, how he's to do it, and the *degree of authority* he has with which to get it done. "You never told me," is the sorry epitaph on many a well-meant delegation.

Explain the relative importance of the job. You know to what degree it's important, because you see it in the setting of your whole responsibility. He will be able to make the necessary adjustments when he runs into trouble only if you have given him the background.

Tell him with whom he's to deal. If the assignment will bring him into contact with new people—for instance, men in other departments—take care of the introduction yourself. Be sure you let everybody involved know that they're to deal with your subordinate.

Prepare him psychologically. He may feel an excessive weight of responsibility. Lessen the tension by removing his sense of crisis. Indicate: (a) your confidence in his ability—that's why you picked him; (b) reassurance from time to time; and (c) emphasis on your availability whenever he's in doubt.

➲ GETTING COOPERATION FOR THE DELEGATE

The responsibility you assign may require a certain amount of authority over others. It may be minor, but, even in the case of a clerk trying to collect figures for a report, you're apt to find people with their backs up, slow to cooperate.

To avoid conflict—

Define scope. Specify the exact nature of the *responsibilities* that you are delegating. That's essential to keep the delegate on track. He *may* think you're handing over your job, unless you tell him what's what.

Tell the others. Define clearly and *publicly* the limits of the authority you delegate. And take care of complaints about overstepped boundaries promptly. Make cooperation attractive.

Set harmony as a goal. Reserve the right to discipline. Don't let your delegate try to enforce cooperation. Impress your delegate with the importance of working harmoniously with the other members of your team. Sell your people on the need for your delegating the job.

➲ DELEGATION CHECKLIST

Face it. The man you delegate won't do the job the way you would do it. Even if you have given instructions, even relatively complete ones, don't be surprised if a delegated assignment ends up in a somewhat unexpected fashion. However, if you are inclined to throw up your hands and renounce delegation as an executive technique—*don't*. Use the checklist questions below to see if you can strengthen your technique. Ask yourself:

Have I delegated duties I can more efficiently handle myself? When you have to follow up with constant observation, the game of delegation isn't worth a candle.

Are my delegations boomeranging?   When you pass along a sizable task to a worker, you may have to provide him with a substitute or understudy. Otherwise, as soon as he's absent, you'll have the delegated duty back in your lap.

Are you picking the delegate properly?   Don't mistake a failure in delegation that results from an employee's inability to handle a task with a failure of the delegation technique. Whether it's delegation or just job instruction, an unqualified, insufficiently skilled subordinate won't be able to do a job beyond his capabilities.

Have I provided all the help he needs?   Generally, in delegation, you want to give your subordinate a free hand. But don't give him freedom when what he needs is your assistance or continuing supervision. Checking on his progress from time to time tells you how much autonomy the delegate requires.

Have I set up the right controls?   The ability to make controls work, and work effectively, is a true test of executive leadership. Measure any questionable control by these tests:

- *Duplication.* Is this control necessary? Do you get the same information elsewhere?
- *Reports.* Are you getting long, rambling reports that consume too much time?
- *Delayed control.* Are you using "control by result" in a case where too much damage can be done before you can act?
- *Frequency.* Are you checking up too often on unimportant matters—facing a pile of progress reports you simply can't read? Or, are you failing to get reports often enough to give you the true picture?

WHEN TO DELEGATE UPWARD

According to the dictionary, delegation is "the act of empowering an individual to act for another." This definition, as well as common practice, suggests that delegation takes place downward, between an executive and his subordinates. But there are situations in which an executive might justifiably *ask* or *suggest* that his superior take over an action within the executive's bailiwick:

Praise or reward.   An honor won by a subordinate that, ordinarily, the executive might bestow, can have even greater weight if given or announced by the executive's boss.

Approval or backing.   "I know that hiring the promotion man is entirely my responsibility," an executive tells his superior, "but since he will be working with you to some extent, I'd like you to interview the final two candidates, and we'll make the final selection a joint decision."

Supercritical decisions.   "Frankly, J.B., there's so much riding on the outcome, I'd prefer you to make the decision as to the final design of the product." Where the superior is especially capable in the area involving the decision, this approach has much to recommend it.

The full weight of authority.   "I'd rather you announce the new policy," an executive tells his boss, "to make clear its importance."

The obvious hazard of upward delegation is that it suggests dependency or hesitation in making decisions. Make sure that this type of delegation is undertaken sparingly, and only after one's reasons for the move have been thought through.

THE DIFFERENCE BETWEEN DELEGATION AND ASSIGNMENT

There is a tendency to use the words *delegation* and *assignment* interchangeably. Actually they represent two different things:

Delegation.   Here you pass along to a subordinate a task that is essentially within the area of *your* job content.

Assignment.   Here you tell him of a task you want him to undertake which is within *his* area of responsibility.

BUILDING INCENTIVES INTO WORK ASSIGNMENTS

In most cases, assignments to subordinates are made matter-of-factly. They are routine, part of the individual's daily job. However, there are some occasions when an appropriate motivating note can make substantial improvements in the level of employee achievement.

Here, for example, are a number of benefits a particular assignment may win for subordinates:

- Increase in value to the organization and to himself.
- Gain more responsibility, training, and an increase of skill.
- Practice in connection with any job weakness.
- An opportunity to make suggestions or contribute ideas.
- A chance to make decisions and develop self-leadership.
- An opportunity to demonstrate his abilities.
- Psychic reward—the satisfaction of successfully meeting a challenge, accomplishing a difficult task.
- Material reward—special privileges, promotion, or an increase in salary.

➲ WHEN TO USE THE DIRECT ORDER

Assignments can be made in various ways. A direct order lays it on the line for an employee and is an approach to use when—

- There's an emergency.
- You need results fast.
- There's no time for discussion or argument.
- An assignment is simple and its urgency is obvious.
- Earlier instructions have been understood, but not followed.
- The employee doesn't fare well acting on his own, but does best under authoritarian leadership.

➲ WHEN TO DETAIL YOUR INSTRUCTIONS

In giving a subordinate an assignment, it's desirable to spell out directions—

- on large-scale, complex assignments
- on tasks that must meet definite standards
- with uneasy employees or those starting important, but unfamiliar projects
- to keep close control

➲ WHEN TO USE THE "REQUEST" APPROACH

Occasionally you hear an executive say, "Bill, do you think you can handle the Jones matter?" It may mean, "Bill, I want you to handle the Jones matter," but worded as a request, the assignment takes on a slightly different character. This approach is effective—

- when you really want to know if it's possible to comply
- to build cooperation and rapport
- to encourage volunteers
- when time permits discussion of pros and cons
- when you are dealing with a fully capable old timer who "doesn't like to be told"
- when you are unsure of the means by which a task is to be accomplished
- when you're asking for extraordinary effort or contribution

➡ WHEN TO USE THE "END-RESULT-WANTED" APPPROACH

Under some circumstances, you get the best results from your assignments if you simply state the result you want, and leave everything else to your subordinate. This approach is preferred—

- to give an individual the opportunity to show his initiative
- when you want the individual to show his own capabilities
- where the uncertainty of the *modus operandi* precludes definite instructions
- when you know less about the matter than the person you are directing

➡ ASSIGNING THE UNPLEASANT TASK

From time to time the executive is confronted by the problem of making an assignment that may be tedious, boring, or undesirable for other reasons. A negative reaction from a subordinate in such a situation is understandable: no one likes to take on a job that may be physically or mentally taxing or distasteful. When you face such a situation—

1. Review your approach. One Philadelphia executive says, "I was making trouble for myself by giving the desirable assignments as though they were Christmas presents. Naturally, when the lemons came along, the difference in my manner was all too obvious. . . ."

It pays to be matter-of-fact about assignments in general. If you overplay your hand with the popular tasks, by implication, you build up resistance against the less popular ones.

2. Don't call a spade a rose. If climbing into the bottom of the dye vat is a grimy, nasty chore, say so. No point in telling Harry this is his lucky day if he's tapped for the honor. He knows better; kidding him is likely to have a painful payoff.

3. Be fair, but firm.   You want to be certain that you assign the messy jobs on a fair basis. No one wants to be the fall guy.

Once you make the assignment, expect and insist upon acceptance. If you can point out the basis on which the choice was made, you should have no trouble.

4. Make no apologies.   You can be honest and sympathetic. But your attitude should never be apologetic. Make it clear that work is work—not fun and games. When it's pleasant, then so much the better. When it's unpleasant, the only thing to do is get it over with, and on to the next task.

Odds are that you'll not only eliminate a needless wrangle, but your people will respect you for taking a realistic stand. In this connection, you'll be interested in a jingle by a nameless, but poetic, executive:

> Work is work,
> And can be fun.
> But when it's not,
> Must still be done.

6. Building Group Effectiveness

Most executives have a group of subordinates for whose activities they are responsible. The number and makeup of this group varies broadly. Staff executives may have a secretary and one or two assistants. A production executive—a plant manager, for example— may consider all plant personnel as his "team."

It's clearly in the general interest—the employees', the company's, and the responsible executive's—for his group to function at the highest possible level of effectiveness. In the pages ahead, you'll find a number of specific ideas and methods for improving the capability and performance of your group.

➲ HOW TO CREATE A CREATIVE CLIMATE

Occasionally, when companies wish to place the accolade of achievement on an executive's brow, they say, "He builds a climate that promotes high achievement among his people. . . ."

When we speak of a "good climate," we're talking about a quality in a company or department that is conducive to some desirable activity. A climate may help good attendance, make people safety-minded, or stimulate employees to offer suggestions and ideas.

Here are some suggestions aimed at developing a climate that will foster creativity among employees and encourage them to develop and submit their ideas to you.

1. Set a value on ideas. Start by creating a feeling of excitement and involvement about the whole matter of idea production. You do this by making it clear to your people that ideas have great importance:

"All we need is one good idea," says an executive, "and we'll be able to get this safety program off to a flying start."

Managers who are able to sell their people on the value of ideas, generally do it by stressing exactly what it is a good idea can accomplish. It can solve a nagging problem, get a crucial project off to a good start, cut costs, and so on.

2. Spotlight the areas of challenge. Almost any idea has *some value*. However, the ideas that are of particular value to a department are those which eliminate *key* difficulties or increase capability in vital areas.

Whether you talk to your people individually or as a group, let them know the kinds of ideas you're most anxious to get. Do this by focusing on the problem or the activity you are trying to treat. Avoid the abstract. Show them what you're talking about. Demonstrate the operation, let them observe the condition for which you need ideas.

3. Show your willingness to help develop their ideas. Seldom do ideas spring full blown from an individual's mind. More frequently, a glimmer, a wispy thought emerges. If properly coddled and developed, it can take on sufficient substance to be considered as an idea with potential application.

Let your people know that you're interested in their ideas at whatever stage they maybe. If you're presented with an idea that is at the "gleam-in-the-eye" stage, deal with it with the same interest as you would a fully ripened one.

The experienced manager, the one with an outstanding record for getting ideas from his people, is the one who wins the confidence of his people in one major respect—he *never* reacts negatively to an idea however simple, stale, or inappropriate it may seem.

4. Don't freeze anybody out. "George is our best idea man," a manager confides to his colleague. Perhaps George is the major contributor of ideas. But it may very well be that the reason George's fellow employees fail to submit ideas is that they've already been ruled out.

Accordingly, they "let George do it." He has the name. He might as well have the game.

"Ideas don't care who gets them," says one veteran manager. Favoring the bright employee will probably increase his motivation, but you are liable to lose out with everyone else. The greater your efforts to enlist all your people in the production of ideas, the more ideas you will get.

5. Reward the successful ones, but encourage the others, too. It's an axiom of the game that those who have come up with good ideas be rewarded for their contributions, whether the reward be a pat on the back, or fat in the pocketbook.

But while giving full credit to those who have been successful, make clear your gratitude to the "almosts." Employees who have worked hard to develop an idea that never quite panned out may have labored above and beyond the call of duty. Let the others in the department know how much you appreciate what has been done even though there may have been no final payoff.

6. Emphasize the benefits. When an idea has been implemented, generally there is a payoff. The company has gained, the department has gained, and in most instances the contributor of the idea has been rewarded either by tangible or intangible means.

You provide a highly motivational goal to your people when you point out the advantages of an applied idea:

"With the new setup Hank designed, we've been able to cut the cost of these units by ten percent. As a result, Sales has just been able to bring in one of the biggest orders we've ever had. . . . "

Make your idea-building climate a permanent part of the department's life rather than an occasional one-shot subject. When you talk about the department's work to individuals or the entire group, fit in the suggestions described above. The thing about ideas is that almost anyone can have them—when you create the appropriate climate.

➲ STIMULATING CREATIVITY IN YOUR PEOPLE

"It's ideas that make the world go round—the management world, that is," says one business expert. Executives, well aware of the need for more and better ideas, realize that their subordinates are a key source. Steps like these can encourage your people to contribute solutions to problems, ideas for improvement, in short, mobilize their brainpower:

1. Pinpoint the problems. Make the problems specific. *General* difficulties are not enough to get your people moving in original lines of thought. "Things around here are in a mess," doesn't give your people anything tangible to wrestle with.

Use your detailed knowledge of the department's functioning to break down a problem and point out the crucial difficulties, the particular bottlenecks.

Here are typical examples:

- how to cut down on telephone interruptions
- how to increase working space without cutting down on equipment
- how to centralize mail pickup and delivery without tying up rush material
- how to assign the work so as to avoid individual dissatisfactions

2. Personalize the problems. Describe the difficulty in practical and immediate terms. Get it out of the realm of abstract. Don't just present it as a "problem," suspended in midair. Instead, talk of it as the problem of (a) the organization; or (b) specific people in the organization. "We're all being slowed up by. . . . " It's emphasis on this aspect that builds team responsibility, and helps each person understand that his job is part of the organization's total effort. A problem solved helps that entire department.

Refer to the individual involved: the bottleneck that "makes Joe and Steve rush like the devil every afternoon" or "makes Helen stay overtime at least twice a week."

And let everybody know about it—not just the people who are directly affected. People who are too close to a situation may lack the perspective to think of doing things in a new way.

3. Suggest a line of attack. Help your people get started on the problem. That means two things: (a) Make sure they understand the present procedure. They're not likely to improve it unless they're thoroughly familiar with it; (b) Put your finger on the exact troublespots in the procedure. "This is the point where we're apparently going wrong." Or: "If we only could figure out some way of rearranging allocation of sales areas. . . ."

Where possible, discuss with your people promising points of departure: "An article I read last week had some good ideas about job enlargement. . . . "

4. Keep in touch. Possibly the most constructive move the manager can make to keep the creativity ball rolling, is to maintain contact. Asking for progress reports, checking back from time to time to see how your subordinates are doing, is concrete evidence of continuing interest in the project.

During these contacts you have the chance to help with any obstacles that may arise. Also, you can watch for the discouragement that traditionally haunts the creative effort. When things aren't working out or a promising development falls flat, encouraging and helpful words can make all the difference.

5. Time to succeed. Executives who have the greatest success in stimulating their people to creative effort find there is a big variation in the *time element*. Some individuals work quickly, seem to be "action oriented." These people develop numerous possibilities, test them out one by one, until they hit.

Others tend to be "thought oriented." These individuals will spend more time assessing alternatives, and will try to come up with a single one that promises success.

Both approaches work, and it is important that the manager avoid trying to rush the thoughtful subordinate into premature action, or to become impatient with the activist's trial-and-error testing.

➲ GETTING THE MOST OUT OF EMPLOYEE IDEAS

Even in the absence of suggestion systems, subordinates will make suggestions or offer ideas that they think bring about desirable improvements on the work scene. When an employee offers an idea, how do you push for a payoff? Consider these moves:

1. Develop and refine. Often when an employee brings you an idea, it's half-baked. You have to help him develop the idea to where it is usable. You and he—and others who can contribute—put your heads together, eliminate the undesirable aspects, and add the elements that make the idea usable.

2. Prepare. Few ideas can be put to work immediately. Some ideas may have to lie fallow for weeks or months until the proper opportunity for a trial presents itself. In this preliminary period, you may have to figure such things as costs, people, equipment and facilities, and the situation to which it applies. This is the time to acquire whatever missing elements you may need—anything from a special machine to an employee of particular skill—to test the idea.

3. Arrange for a trial.   Some ideas promise advantages that may or may not result. Make sure that a test of an idea is fair and appropriate. For example, you may prove nothing if you take an idea that has been suggested for improving an assembly operation and have the test performed by an inexperienced employee in your group.

Also, for some trials, you may want to have more than one observer. "The results were great," says an employee, following a test of a jig he suggested. "A waste of time," is the opinion of another employee. Of course, your own presence is advisable to evaluate both the trial and the other opinions you get.

4. Don't shortcut on final evaluations.   Time and time again it happens that a new method or system passes a preliminary, limited test with flying colors. Then the idea is adopted generally—and the trouble starts. Unexpected developments that didn't turn up in the trial may develop in widespread applications. For example, a new system that was tested successfully by one of your skilled workers gives other employees trouble in full-scale use.

In short, it's wise to stick with the implementation of an idea until it is really proved out in a "production run" or full-scale application.

5. Reward the Idea Man.   One way to assure a continuing flow of ideas is to reward those you get. The rewards may range from a simple statement of appreciation to cash payments, bonuses, promotions, and so on.

Assuming that the reward, whether of the psychic variety—that is, a statement of appreciation—or a more material kind—such as a salary increase—is being made appropriately, there is one more move to make. It is desirable both from the point of view of the individual who has been rewarded, and your own interest in getting additional ideas, that the group learn of the return your subordinate has been able to get for his efforts.

➔ CAN YOU UNBRAINWASH YOUR SUBORDINATES?

"I try to get as many original ideas as possible out of a new employee before he gets brainwashed—that is, settles down into a rut like most old-timers do."

The implication of the above statement is that a "company way of doing things" eventually erodes originality. After a man's been on the post for a while he gets "brainwashed" in the sense that he adopts the views, values, and behavior of those around him.

Where creative thinking is necessary for performance, the executive may consider steps like these to stimulate a subordinate:

1. Tell him the wraps are off. In giving the assignment or instructions, make it clear that you want your subordinate to strike out in new directions. You may have to say it in so many words: "I'm giving you a completely free hand on this assignment. . . . "

2. Applaud originality; downgrade mediocrity. As the subordinate goes about the assignment, let him know that you are pleased by any novel turn his efforts are taking: Frank," says one executive, "I'm pleased to see you get away from that old form. I've always suspected it was a major cause of our paper work problem." Not all original ideas are good—but your reactions can make it clear that you favor the effort towards freshness.

3. Make the "new way" a continuing goal. It's not enough to limit your approval of originality to special assignments. Make it clear to your group, in the course of work discussions, conferences on departmental problems, and so on, that you're always on the lookout for breakthroughs, innovations, new and better ways of doing things.

Of course, managers aren't exempt from the inhibiting influence of company brainwashing. On the contrary, top executives point out that often the supervisor or department head not only puts restrictions on the thinking of his people, but also keeps his own thinking in a rut.

According to the president of a chemical company, "Ideally, we must walk two paths at once: try to capitalize on the good aspects of conformity: acceptance of company standards, general behavior, and so on. At the same time, we must strive for the benefits of untrammeled thinking, keep vision free, and reward originality whenever it appears constructively on the work scene."

HANDLING EMPLOYEE COMPLAINTS

Justifiably or otherwise, your people may complain. It may be about anything from the air conditioning to dissatisfaction with career prospects.

Your handling of complaints is an important key to the morale of your group. Consider these guidelines, when you get complaints from employees—

1. Check actual conditions. Some complaints may be founded in fact; others may represent disguised gripes about anything else. Avoid leaping to conclusions about the justness of the matter. Make actual checks and comparisons: take a thermometer reading, use the flow of cigarette smoke to check complaints about a draft, for example.

2. Check consequences. After you've looked into the objective facts, examine the results. Consider taking a "poll" of group opinion on the complaint. This information not only helps you verify the objective situation, but also may represent a measure of the gripe— whether it's appropriate or an overreaction—and how widespread it may be.

3. Suit relief to the problem. If the complaint is justified, move as quickly as you can to remedy the situation. This may mean changing the directions of vanes in a heating system, or having Maintenance put weather stripping on a loose window. For some situations, you might ask the complainer for suggestions.

On the other hand, if you find the complaint unjustified, present the facts to the employee, or employees involved. Be matter-of-fact. Your people will be much more likely to accept your findings, if you avoid the "you're-all-wrong" approach.

As veteran executives know, unfounded complaints may be an individual's bid for attention, or his way of saying, "Show me that you're interested in my welfare." This is a possibility when the gripe is baseless. Then your move must be to review your relations with the employee, to see how you can give the reassurance he wants—that he's recognized and needed as part of the team.

4. Follow up. Don't assume that the action you have taken will solve the matter. Chances are, it will. But avoid complications by checking back on the condition, as well as the attitude of the person who made the original complaint. When both show improvement, you've got the problem licked.

◆ WHEN ASSIGNMENTS TAKE SUBORDINATES OFF THE PREMISES

From time to time you may have to send an employee on an assignment out of your immediate personal jurisdiction. It may be an assistant, who must do some research for you in the library, or a subordinate to dig into an operating problem in a distant plant.

When these people are new to this type of assignment, working outside the range of your personal supervision may pose problems. You don't want to lose control.

Here are seven steps that can help them perform more effectively:

1. Encourage employees to accept responsibility. Impress your people with the opportunity to show their self-reliance and reliability. "You're going to be on your own. . . . "

2. Appoint a leader, if it's more than a one-man job. Here's where you have to judge the caliber of your people. If you have two people who you know will work together, it may be best to give them equal status. But sometimes, even with just two on the job, you'll have discord. Giving primary responsibility to one may be the most desirable solution.

3. Spell out your instructions. It's even more important than usual to be clear and concise as to what you want done. Be sure you cover two points: (a) the overall objective, (b) the immediate goal.

If necessary, provide written instructions. Where the job can be broken down, write out the steps.

4. Have a send-off inspection. "We forgot to take along the inventory cards. . . . " Forestall loss of time and effort by making sure all necessary materials go out with the employee.

If there's a question of appearance or condition of equipment they're taking with them, set up a regular inspection that will catch any oversights.

5. Make sure of what they'll find. "Mr. Smith," telephones an employee from a distant suburb, "I got to the address you gave me, but the supply company moved away three months ago." Obviously a phone call would have prevented a wild-goose chase.

To repeat: check out the situation before sending your man into it.

6. Arrange for a check-back during the job. Tell the individuals or leader how to communicate with you if any trouble develops. It may be clear *to you* that the obvious thing is to send a message back with one of the men if anything unforeseen arises. But sometimes the on-the-spot leader's solution is to call a halt and wait for you to show up. Be sure to spell out how and where they can contact you. If the job's a long one, you may want regular progress reports.

If you have the time, it may be best to visit the scene and check the operation personally. In that case, deal with the appointed leader first, and get his version of how things are going.

7. Ask for a report at the end of the job. You may want to make this report written or oral. Use it not only as a check on the satisfactory conclusion of the work, but as a cue for the next job.

➔ **THE NEW LOYALTY**

The kind of company loyalty inspired by the old paternalism is fast fading from the business scene. To put it another way, paternalism as an effective management technique is dead. Loyalty, if it is to exist at all, must stem from new sources.

There's a relationship between an employer and employee that can be constructive. Call it loyalty or mutual respect, the result of the relationship is clear: it makes the company seem like a good place to work and it makes his superior seem like a good man to work with. And it makes the employee enjoy his job more. Here's what's involved:

1. Imbue the employee with a feeling of loyalty to his group. When work problems are presented as cooperative ventures, a manager can build the feeling that the department is functioning as a unit, with each member's presence and best efforts essential to the success of the group. Accordingly, the man who feels himself a valued number of the group develops ties of loyalty to his fellow workers.

2. Foster loyalty to a profession or skill. Whether a man is an accountant, a production foreman, or a drill press operator, he is committed to a particular profession or skill. He is a member of a select group, and subject to the standards of that group. He *may* entertain the idea of working for another company, but isn't likely to *change his profession or job category.*

Managers who show employees that they can exercise their professional abilities most effectively and most rewardingly in their *present jobs* can build professional loyalty and derive the benefit from that personal commitment.

3. Create and encourage personal involvement in the work. When managers allow subordinates to share the responsibilities of planning and executing their own work, they provide a chance for self-fulfillment—and consequent emotional reward.

The manager who puts a subordinate on a challenging task, with clearly-defined and exciting objectives, is creating the conditions for job satisfaction.

A basic point should be clear: while the old loyalty was based on paternalism and the doling out of *material* benefits, the new loyalty is the result of acknowledging the integrity of the employee, and creating an atmosphere in which he can satisfy his *psychic* needs, the desire for accomplishment and work satisfaction.

➜ HOW TO BALANCE A TEAM

Recently, there has been a trend towards the task-force or project-team approach. This means the executive must devote some thought to the makeup of a task force he may create, so it may function effectively.

Small groups lack some elements that apply to larger ones. First, smaller units, of two or three members for example, cannot be "organized" in the same sense as a large group. And the question of leadership worsens. Consider the problem as it sometimes appears in the two-person relationship, marriage, and you get the picture—unclear division of authority, disagreement as to whose standards are to be accepted, and so on.

When you form a group of two or three people you are not simply adding their skills together. Dause L. Bibby of Remington-Rand put the relationship this way: "With the team approach there is a factor created, a new capability that goes above and beyond the mathematical addition of personalities." To line up an effective team, determine—

- what needs to be done
- the kind of skills required
- which people work best together
- what general guidelines to provide that will help them function together

Here are the considerations for each point above:

What needs to be done.   Different tasks impose different requirements. A team with an informational job must be able to gather data, to probe and analyze, and to come up with conclusions based on the findings. An organizational job would require the ability to plan, direct, instruct, motivate, and deal with unexpected developments. Once you have clarified the general nature of the job you are ready for the next step—

What kinds of skills are required.   Now you must pin down the personal skills of group members. For most purposes, your group is likely to be most effective if its members possess six key prototypes:

The Dynamo.   He's the pusher, the nudger, the one who's aware of deadbeats and deadlines.

The Hardhead.   He's the man who says, "I know it's never been done elsewhere before. Let's try it." He helps to keep the group's feet on the ground. He's apt to be called the realistic one, or a cynic—or even a stinker—but he may be the most important man in the goup.

The Analyst.   He's cerebral. While others may gloat over how well things are going, he's worrying about tomorrow. He digs below the surface, always wants to know *why.*

The Artist.   His specialty is creative thinking. He will produce ten suggestions, while others are laboring to come up with one.

The Detail Man.   He has a head for figures and the patience to stick with them. He will take pains, split hairs, double and triple check. For complicated tasks, he can be a lifesaver.

The Team Player.   His outstanding quality is loyalty to the cause. You can wake him at 2 in the morning and ask him to hop a plane to Tokyo and he will go without a grumble.

In putting together your team, remember two principles:

The rule of "likes."   Sociologists use the term *homogamy* to describe the fact that some husband-wife teams are formed on the basis of similar backgrounds, economic, educational, and so on. Generally, staffing your group with people who are similar in age and sense of values provides a good basis for mutual understanding and assures a minimum of friction.

The rule of "opposites."   Sociologists used the term *heterogamy* to cover husband-wife pairs who have selected one another on the basis of complementary traits. Teaming according to the principle of opposites works well when the individuals involved respect the differences and specialties of their teammates. While this approach may result in more friction, it often makes for a higher-powered team.

To the question how large should a group be, there are two guidelines:

Use the *smallest* number of people possible to eliminate communication lags and other human frictions that set in as a group grows.

Use the number that will give you the highest total of skill, and that will insure a capability to cover the scope of the job and the speed with which it is to be done.

Finally, it's usually advisable to give one of the individuals in even the smallest team, leadership responsibility. The leader not only sets the level of performance expected, but also decides on the means by which goals are to be achieved when there are differences of opinion. One way or another, the leader sets the tone and work pace.

⬧ HOW PEOPLE REALLY FEEL ABOUT CHANGE

People are supposed to resist change. And often they do. But the statement "people resist change" is a generalization that muddies the issue. You need clarification because group growth is based on change.

Allen B. Thomas, V.P. Personnel of the St. Paul Manufacturing Co. says, "I point out to people that change is an everyday norm. Often people want, like, and must have change. Those who resist it are usually insecure. They want to stay put while the rest of the world moves along." Thomas goes on to say that people resist certain actions which have been carelessly categorized as "change." For example:

■ *People resist surprise.* Few of us like to be caught off balance. A sudden announcement or development tends to throw individuals off balance and, understandably, they resist. On the other hand, knowledge in advance can give individuals the opportunity to digest the change and work it into their expectations for the future.

■ *People resist usurpation.* No one likes to have someone else come along and make changes in areas which they have thought of as "theirs." This is true in even the most innocent seeming situation. For example: a group of typists have been complaining about their chairs —they jiggle, they cannot be adjusted properly, and so on. A well-meaning executive decides to eliminate the irritation and orders new chairs. The chairs arrive and the girls are indignant. A dozen complaints are lodged against the new furniture: wrong size, shape, color, and so on. Needless to say, they would have been perfectly delighted with the very same chairs if they had picked them out themselves.

The solution, then, is to let people make the changes for themselves in their own areas of competence and responsibility.

⬧ PREPARING YOUR PEOPLE FOR CHANGE

Change has been in the cards ever since our ancestors came out of their caves. On the work scene, change has been a tangible and accelerating factor. And ever since World War II, change on the business scene has been developing with jet speed. Result? Employees— and sometimes even executives—view the shifts and alterations of the business environment with uneasiness, sometimes tinged by panic.

A recent study made by the Research Institute of America with a company going through the throes of computerization, turned up the basic fears—and questions—in the minds of employees facing the prospect of change. Understanding these questions can help you minimize the impact of change in your company or division.

Here are the kinds of questions employees ask, and some suggestions as to how to handle them:

Will I lose my job?   This is the big one, reflecting the greatest fear. And it may come from anyone—old-timers who long for permanent security, newcomers with plans and ambitions, even chronic gripers whose usual plaint is how much they *don't* like what they're doing!

Your answers will usually fall into one of three categories:

No.   Simple, direct, reassuring. The contemplated change will not affect the employee's job to any great extent, and he can function pretty much as he did before. This is the easiest answer to give—and the one most people want to hear.

No, but . . .   A company has issued a blanket promise: no one is to lose his job, *but* there will be some some shifting. Retraining will be necessary. Certain job categories will be eliminated, and people transferred to other departments. New procedures will be adopted, organizational changes made. There will be a place for the employee —*but* he will have to adapt.

Accordingly, you'll be talking to two groups: those whose jobs won't change, and those who face a somewhat uncertain future. Here again, you can reassure the people who will be unaffected. For the others, you'll have to walk a straight line between giving them as much information as you can, and not feeding their apprehension. For example: "No matter what happens, there'll be absolutely no changes until the first of the year. And the best brains in the company are making plans to minimize any possible difficulties. . . . "

Yes.   Unfortunately, some changes, particularly major ones, mean that certain people will be let go. A company may be cutting back, merging, automating, diversifying. Fewer workers may be required, or more highly skilled, or more experienced, or less. Just who will be kept on may depend on age, seniority (those with ten years or more will be retained, for example), job skills, even your opinion of an employee's growth potential.

It may be difficult to tell someone that he is no longer needed. The promise of liberal severance pay can soften the blow somewhat. But equally important may be an offer to help him in locating another job—finding out who's hiring, who needs what; working on job forms with him; adding a personal recommendation.

How will I find out about new methods, equipment, etc?   Employees look ahead to the immediate effects of job change—and wonder and worry.

There are many ways of imparting knowledge—it's only a matter of deciding on the best method, or methods, for your purpose. Your answer may include one or more of the following. . . .

Talks   by management, staff specialists, outside experts, yourself. These work well for "thoughtful" changes: company policies, the whys of reorganization, and the like. Care must be taken that they convey full, clear explanations, in the language of the listeners. Where possible, use visual material—charts, graphs, photos—to show the shape of things to come.

Group discussions   offer explanation plus a chance to comment, question, participate. There should be no pressuring of employees who speak up. Leaders must be ready to field all questions (even the most antagonistic), and communicate a spirit of optimism and positive thinking.

On-the-job training   by the best qualified person, be it you, your assistant, a technician, systems analyst, whoever. Such training should begin as early as possible, be comprehensive, allow for actual practice, raising of questions, test runs, and thorough review to make sure that all aspects are understood.

Off-the-job-study   may encompass anything from reading at home to in-plant classes and out-of-plant seminars. You may have little to do with the actual instruction—but you must follow it up. It's up to you to praise what a man has learned, how well he has learned it, and how soon he can use it.

How will the change affect day-to-day routines?   A change in the way of doing things is not a happy prospect for some people. It's unsettling, threatening, suggests inconvenience, even material loss. And employees fight it in a number of ways. They may become sullen or quarrelsome, produce less, ask for transfers, come up with a thousand-and-one pseudo-logical reasons why the change won't work. And when the change becomes fact, they may cheer over each little thing that goes wrong . . . and may even try to help the difficulties along a little.

The most constructive approach is *preventive*. In explaining, be very definite as to *what* is going to be done, *how* it is going to be done, *who* will be doing it, *where* it will be done, *when* it will go into effect. People often resist the new simply because they don't understand what is going on or what is expected of them.

And, while you stress the "good" of the project, admit that there may be some "bad." In anything new, errors and "bugs" are bound to crop up; how can they be avoided?

You want their ideas. Let them know that you can't foresee all the problems; that you respect their knowledge and experience; that you need their sugestions and help. And that you want it to be a continuing thing—the new way may have to be revised, little kinks ironed out. Can they come up with solutions?

Will new people be brought into the department? Many of today's changes herald the arrival of departmental newcomers. Sometimes they will be better educated, more highly skilled, younger than those already on the work scene. In other instances they may be lacking both knowledge and training. They may look different, talk different, act different. And on all counts, they may be regarded as outsiders, threats to the comfortable togetherness that had existed before.

To minimize the feeling of threat, clarify the kind of personnel that will appear, and the company's reason for hiring them. Don't hedge or equivocate—be factual:

"Two technicians start Monday. They're going to iron out the 'bugs' on Operation X. That means we can stop worrying about that headache and get our own work done."

Offer opportunities for advancement?   One step that will minimize the newcomer's threat is the knowledge that old-timers will be given the chance to better themselves. Where the opportunity exists, tell your people how they can learn advanced skills and procedure—and have a chance to bid for future job openings.

Equalize pay scales?   It's hard for a loyal, long-time worker to accept the fact that Joe Newcomer is making as much—or more—than he is. Yet this can be the case. Today, business hires at higher rates, pays more for education and training, and doesn't always put the same monetary value on loyalty and in-company experience. The hard reality of this situation should be tactfully explained to old-timers.

Will I have to move?   Even if an employee won't be going to a different building or department, major changes in the physical aspects of his work station may be upsetting.

When an employee is told that he has to move—be it across the street, down the hall, to a new machine, a strange department, an earlier shift—he may object strongly. As he sees it, he's being asked to leave the familiar and venture into unknown territory, where, in many respects, he will have to start anew. He worries. . . . "Why me? Can I handle a different setup? How will I fit in with the new gang?"

It's up to management to minimize the threat of the change. A three-step process may help:

Explain the reasons for the contemplated move.   Production bottlenecks, poor layout, constant equipment breakdowns, safety hazards, space and storage problems, employee retirements or dismissals. Whatever the reason(s), get him involved in the discussion.

Point out the advantages of the move.   More space, brand new lathes, air-conditioning, more efficient layout, chance to keep regular hours, earn more money, learn another skill. Whatever the advantage(s), emphasize the benefit to him as an individual—that's his chief concern. There's plenty of time later to talk about the good of the department, the value to the company, and so on.

Ask for his ideas.   Are there any improvements he'd like to see made in the new work station layout? Any suggestions on eliminating safety hazards? Ideas on what to do with old equipment? Suggestions on improving the comfort of the new operation?

Whatever the answer(s), listen to them attentively and when they're good, usable, tell him so. It he knows that some of his ideas are being incorporated in his new "home," he'll be happier about moving in.

How will the change affect my status? Chances for salary increase? Promotion?   We all have fundamental needs, and one of the most basic is security. On the work scene, this takes the form of money and the chance to make more, a job and the opportunity to better it.

Some changes do not affect either earnings or chances for advancement. For example, moving a man's work station from the right side of the aisle to the left, doesn't influence take-home pay. But switching the man to another department, or expecting him to learn another skill, *may.*

In such cases, put it on the line with employees. Make it clear that those who make good in new assignments will make gains. On the other hand, refusal to learn and grow could affect chances for promotion and raises adversely.

Faced with change, people respond in individual ways. One man will worry about the opinion of his peers. Another will be concerned chiefly with his status in the department. A third will fight zealously to guard any small prerogative, even something as simple as the desk nearest the window or the "chore" of collecting the time cards every week.

A person sees change from his particular viewpoint. Take an overworked machine operator who is assigned an assistant. Right away, he regards it as criticism of the way he is handling his job. Yet another employee in the same circumstance will see it as proof that he has "arrived"—now that he has an assistant, he feels that his status is that much higher.

Knowing your people and their individual needs can help sell them on change. Is Joe too gregarious for the silent confines of the supply room? Will Sol be more amenable to moving if his machine is placed first in line? Can Will be "turned on" by titling him "Squad Leader?"

Once you can see man-plus-need, you'll have a better chance of melding man-and-change.

Things were going along okay before. Why rock the boat? Some companies, particularly those that are technically oriented, move in an aura of change. Their employees learn to expect the unexpected, and thus have far fewer problems in adapting.

But in more static companies, it can be extremely difficult for employees to understand why "something different" is being considered for an operation that, at least on the surface, has been proceeding smoothly. Especially since the path of change, in the beginning, seldom does run smoothly.

The reasons will vary as much as the changes themselves. For example, the need to lower costs, increase output, improve quality, change a product, may spark major shifts. And the pressures favoring alterations may originate with the company, a department, or you. It will generally be up to you to explain them to your people. And in so doing it is important to relate the purposes and goals of the change to those of the individual. For example:

- The company is modernizing and expanding to meet today's competition.
- This means *your* department is going to have more work, and will be able to produce more.
- That can mean a bigger paycheck for *you*, Joe.

Don't gloss over the fact that any new system will have its delays and errors. And that it may take time to work them out. If people have been given a completely rose-colored view of change—and then things start going wrong—they are apt to react with an immediate "I told you so," and a subsequent loss of faith in your leadership and in management's sagacity.

In other words, don't oversell. And leave the group with two thoughts:

- Problems are likely to arise in the course of changeover. Expect them. Be ready to deal with them.
- The ability of the group will help solve or minimize almost any complications that come up.

Will it mean more work for me? Harder work? Less desirable work? People have different attitudes toward their job tasks. Some want the challenge of the difficult or demanding assignment. Others balk at any hint that they may have to work harder, longer, and so on.

Let's take typist Suzie Sloan, resisting the idea of acting as part-time receptionist—"You expect me to greet callers and type too!"

To employees in this situation, three points can be made:

- The fact that she didn't do the job before is no reason for it not to be added to her overall job.
- With the new task added, her workload is still not top-heavy. (You don't ask anyone to do nine hours work in eight hours.)
- The best way to see how a new assignment will work out is to give it a trial—a fair trial.

Right from the start, any shift in workloads should be spelled out in detail, with duties and responsibilities well-defined. The idea is to have everyone in the department know who is doing what, how much, and why. To make doubly sure of perfect understanding you might have each employee make out a chart of what he thinks his new duties and responsibilities are. When his version doesn't jibe with yours, you can work together to bring the two versions into line.

What if I can't handle the new job? In our highly competitive world, the idea that what a man knows isn't enough, or that what he does is no longer in demand, can be frightening and confidence-destroying. So it's only natural that employees will voice doubts about their abilities to learn new skills and methods. In some cases, *they may be right.*

One way to manage this aspect of change is to set up a probationary period. This may be thirty days, sixty days, or longer, based on the intricacies of the new job and an estimate of how long it should take the average worker to master it. And the time span should be made clear to the employee. While there may be difficulties, basically he should absorb the new ways and be able to utilize them in that period.

What if, despite all the breaks you can give him, he still fails to make the grade? Perhaps he can be returned to his old post. But realistically, such moves are not always possible: the position may no longer exist, or it may be filled by someone else. Then a transfer to another department may have to be arranged. Or, the employee may even have to be let go, if he's fairly new in the company.

But remember, the problem of retraining is largely psychological. Most doubts arise from fear of the unknown, the untried—or a lack of self-confidence. You can do much to dispel them if you show a man that *you* have faith in his ability to handle the new job. Encouragement can truly work wonders.

➡ EIGHT WAYS TO START A COST-IMPROVEMENT PROGRAM

For some executives, the problem of controlling costs is one of motivation:

"How can I get my staff to develop their cost-consciousness?" is the way some executives see the problem. Perhaps your people are not suffering from disinterest in costs. You may never have that problem. But a brief catalog of "starts" may be useful to help cost-cutting efforts. The items below are specific. They aim to win the interest and cooperation of your people. Finally, they tend to lessen the aura of gloom and the frequently damaging consequences of the "cut-10%-across-the-board" approach:

1. The "consultation" start. One executive describes this use of the idea: "It's almost like a ritual. I find my key man or men and we begin to talk about the need to tighten up on the cost line. What often happens is that this key group comes up with an idea, a point of departure, an approach that puts cost control in proper perspective."

2. The "performance review" start. Some executives get their bearings in the cost area by appraising the performance of departmental operations for a given period: annually, semiannually, quarterly.

Analysis of operating records is an effective starting point: production records, recheck records, sales volume, customer complaints, service records, down time—almost every aspect of departmental operations helps clarify the cost picture.

Out of this review and analysis of past performance can come new resolves and new goals. Says one executive: "Maintenance costs are dragging down our overall performance. We have got to zero in on that area. . . . "

3. The employee meeting. In certain situations, executives find that a full-dress meeting of the entire employee roster is an effective cost-improvement starter. Most successful examples of this approach involve getting employee participation and involvement. Here are a set of notes used by an executive for the agenda of a cost-control meeting:

    a. Introduction. Tell the group why our costs must be cut: competition, need to maintain profitability of selling price, and so on.
    b. Relationship of the division to the company. Describe the impor-

tance of our unit to overall company performance: the lower our costs, the better the department's and company's performance record.

c. Individual employees. Tell of the importance of each employee's activity to departmental performance.

d. Rewards. Describe what increased profitability will do for the company ("We will be able to grow," etc.) and for the individual employee (perhaps higher salaries, greater career opportunity, and so on).

e. Improving procedures. Ask: What can we do; what are your ideas for getting us moving?

The important thing, says the executive who uses the above approach, is to listen to the solutions and ideas suggested, and put them to work as far as is possible.

4. The "dramatic device" start.   Flamboyant executives can profit from the example of an Oklahoma City plant manager. He got a large photostatic blowup of a stage money bill and used it to spark a "save-the-buck" campaign.

There are numerous ways to dramatize a cost-saving effort:

- Mount scoreboards in each department or area showing recent sales or production figures, or possibly for expenses such as the cost of materials, or maintenance.
- Another executive staged an "idea day." After several weeks of prepublicity, employees were asked to turn in their cost-cutting ideas. Since employees were not limited to "one to a person," it was found that the average was 3.6 ideas per employee. Out of this vast number of suggestions, the company was able to adopt 76 that paid off.

5. The key operation start.   Some managers prefer to select the element of their unit's operations that is critical, where improvement will have the broadest effects. They then get the best brains among their staffs working on the key areas.

6. The "grain-of-sand" start.   Instead of seeking a single large area, some executives prefer a comprehensive tightening up of all areas of operation. One executive had his supervisors work out with their respective groups the many small ways that lead to operating losses. For example, a supervisor in charge of a polishing room spotted these "loss leaders": machines left running when not in use; breakage due to careless handling of stock; sandpaper being "borrowed" for personal use; pumice wasted; polishing wheels discarded before full use had been obtained.

This pinpointed approach may sound like paperclip saving, but for the executive who can get participation down at the grassroots level, the small savings add up to an important percentage of operating costs.

7. The red tape start. Companies often become entangled in forms and formalities. When communication channels become clogged, when procedures get slowed down, when people who need attention or material or equipment cannot get it because of "procedures," your red tape is going to turn into red ink.

The effective supervisor looks for procedural bottlenecks or red tape and improves efficiency and profitability by eliminating them.

8. The interdepartment team. Many companies find a major source of wasted effort and delay exists between departments. Each department may work well on its own but the department's activities are not well-meshed.

For example, Department A produces work and stacks it in the corridor for Department B to pick up and process, but "B," for various reasons, does not move the work right away, or sometimes the lots are mixed, and so time—and money—is lost.

In a Texas electronics firm, an executive sat down with a colleague also in charge of a major operational area. They proceeded to list a series of questions:

- At what points do our operations touch or overlap?
- What inefficiencies occur in these areas?
- How can we minimize these?
- How can we get better cooperation between the staffs of the two departments?

A list of revealing questions of this kind can help turn up answers to close an operational gap through which wasted dollars have been flowing.

➲ FILLING PERSONNEL GAPS DURING VACATIONS

The vacation period frequently leaves a work roster looking like Swiss cheese. The checklist below can help you cope with this situation:

- If regular employees will take on duties of those who are away, will they require some breaking in, such as brushup training?
- In the case of the assignments of vacationers, can you hold off on some crucial aspects till they return?
- Can you use the vacation period as a trial period for some of your people—that is, give them the opportunity for new assignments?
- If you are going to need replacements or temporaries, have you decided how many, and what their qualifications must be?
- Should you take up the question of replacements with Personnel at an early date?
- Do you know of any skilled ex-employees who might be willing to serve as fill-ins on a temporary basis?
- Can you use the "buddy system" to help temporaries break in— that is, have veteran employees act as guides and sources of information for the newcomers?
- Can you modify work methods to meet personnel shortages—for example, have two subordinates share a secretary when their regular assistants are away? (Be sure the secretary knows it's temporary, and ask your subordinates to eliminate low-priority typing.)

➲ WORKLOAD ADJUSTMENTS DURING SUMMER VACATIONS

When the vacation period strikes, you may have to do more than hire temporaries or ask your experienced people to take over someone else's assignment. Adjusting the workload may be essential. Moves such as those below can help:

- Can you move critical jobs up on the schedule, or defer them till the return of vacationers?
- Can special arrangements with other executives ease some of the standard problems?
- Can consultations with your superior lighten workloads or flatten out work peaks and valleys?
- Can you "trade" work with other departments?
- Can you make mutually helpful transfer of employees with other executives?
- If you plan to hire temporaries, can you have them come in for training beforehand, so that they'll know the ropes when they report for active duty?

➜ **MEETING A CRISIS**

Avoid undue hesitation; speed up decision-making. Then—Move! Talk and act fast.

Get your people into the act—ask for help.

Tell everybody what's going on—especially your superior.

When you give orders, use the autocratic method. At this stage, you only want your decisions implemented.

Borrow people, material, machines from other departments.

Develop backup solutions.

Ride herd on solutions and be ready to modify them in action.

Don't leave crisis procedures in force when the crisis is over.

➜ **CHANGE OF PACE**

Monotony can put a damper on employee job interest; increase the number of errors employees make; increase the possibility of accidents; depress their output.

What makes a job monotonous depends largely on the individual. But if you sense a harmful degree of monotony in work situations, consider some of these relief measures:

■ **Rotate assignments.** Many executives consider this one of the best ways to build job interest. Filing duties might be rotated among a number of employees, for example; so could posting. Note too that this does more than introduce variety into the job. It enlarges each employee's understanding of departmental operations. It gives you greater flexibility in the face of unexpected absences or periods of pressure.

■ **Reduce endlessness.** Psychologists have repeatedly demonstrated that "signposts" are necessary to the feeling of progress. Managers put the principle to work when they break the day-long job into a series of steps. Processing invoices in sets of twenty-five, for example, would be one way of doing it.

■ **Off-the-job missions.** An executive points out that these can be rotated among those employees who seem to show the greatest restlessness. Frequently, trips off the premises are all undertaken by one employee. This may be the more efficient way of handling it. But placing such assignments on something like a roster basis gives more people a chance to "get away."

■ **Emphasize challenge.** "This isn't just a routine assignment,"

Executive A tells his assistant. "If you can come up with a promising plan for promoting this new product, it will be the first time it's been done in this division. . . . "

READING THEIR MINDS

The Clue	Common Inference	Alternatives
No complaints, gripes, or grievances	Smooth sailing ahead	Explosion brewing, or apathy building up
Eagerness to confer with superior	They like you, respect your knowledge	Sagging initiative, overdependency
No questions being asked	Everybody in agreement	Afraid to show ignorance, or doubt boss
Arguments among themselves	Friction and internal strife	Healthy exchange of ideas

Executives pride themselves on their ability to take a "reading" of their group. "The mood is up," one executive says. Another one's report is, "There's a feeling of tension and dissatisfaction."

It's important to be aware of group mood. However, there is a tendency to misinterpret. The chart above gives you an opportunity of checking some common evaluations of group feeling.

But when it comes to readng the mind of your group, here's how to avoid mistakes:

1. Check alternative theories. Don't latch on to the first explanation that comes to mind. No matter how well it seems to tie the clues together, keep trying new possibilities.

2. Look for additional evidence. Don't let one clue—or even two —establish your theory. A single observation can be very revealing, but at best it requires verification. Getting further proof should not be difficult. If the situation suggested by the clue has any significance at all, it's bound to create additional evidence. Look for it. Sometimes it pays to go after more evidence on your own—instead of waiting for things to turn up.

If you're relying primarily on detective work for information about what's happening, you have a strong clue that regular communications are sagging. Spend more time talking to your people. Probe beneath the surface behavior to get real feelings. It will pay off in terms of understanding and your ability to improve the well-being and performance of your people.

➍ WHEN THEY ALLOW TOO BIG A MARGIN OF SAFETY

> *Every sub-system and structure (of the Apollo spacecraft) was designed with what North American engineers call the "50 percent fudge factor." That is, it was half again as strong and durable as it supposedly had to be.*
>
> —New York Times

Like North American engineers, every business tries to build a margin of safety into its operations. Budgets, inventory controls, production and quality controls, all contain such a cushion. But many people try to build in a little extra protection of their own, if they get the chance.

An employee wants his production quota set low, so that he won't have too much trouble looking good. A well-meaning employee may "hide" some scarce material, so he won't get caught short at his machine. The consequences can be immobilizing and expensive.

When you find subordinates building in their own fudge factors, playing *too* safe, consider:

1. Are they revealing over-anxiety?   The man who lives in terror of being caught short clearly is afraid of the snapback—a severe reprimand, loss of status, and so on. If this seems to be the case, the fault may lie with his supervisor. Everyone—from top to bottom of an organization—should have a certain amount of freedom to err. Without this freedom, little initiative can be expected.

2. Are they making a power play against a colleague?   "Ted would rather have a man stand around idle than let him share his backlog of work," asserts a colleague bitterly. The subordinate who hoards, whether it's manpower, equipment, or materials, while a colleague suffers from shortages, obviously hasn't gotten the idea of team play and cooperation.

3. Are they aware of the cost facts of life?   "Why shouldn't I keep these hundred drums in reserve?" a mixing-room leadman in a paint factory asks his boss. "You wouldn't want us to run out of solvent, would you?" The cost of storage, the cash tied up in the materials, apparently is not appreciated by this well-intentioned employee. His boss owes him a man-to-man session on hidden costs.

4. Does use of the fudge factor suggest unsatisfactory controls? These may be at the level at which the fudging is taking place, or at the next higher level up the line. A supervisor whose worksheets reflect excessive hours of employee idle time *may* be providing himself with too much standby manpower. Or, he may have a legitimate complaint: "I never know from one day to the next what kind of orders the Front Office is going to load on me."

Admittedly, there never can be a perfect balance between ability to perform and performance requirements. However, using a fudge factor beyond accepted limits often reflects either anxiety or uncertainty. The conditions that cause these problems must be spotted and dealt with to control the fudging.

➲ WORKING WITH TEMPORARIES

Your secretary comes down with a sudden illness and she's out, several days or weeks. Or one or another of your staff is out for reasons of health, vacations, and so on. These days, the use of temporary help has become a pervasive practice on the work scene. And the range of job categories made available by the temporary agencies has been increasing. Stenos, typists, clerks, engineers, salesmen, the list continues to grow.

Temporary help can be an excellent solution to a roster gap, but temporary workers also represent a tough problem—that of getting them into the act quickly. Here's how to make temporary help more productive sooner, a method that you may want to pass along to your subordinates, if and when they have to hire temporaries:

1. Specify the kind of help you need. According to one agency, success of a temporary depends 90 percent on the quality of the job description. Requesting a "typist" gives you a slim chance of getting what you *really* need. Copy typist? Manuscript? Statistical? Each requires different skills; you won't get what you need unless you specify

2. Keep your department in the know. An unexpected face invites speculation. Has the regular man been fired? Is the new person really there to see which jobs could be automated? Don't let rumors start. Tell your department a temporary is coming to *help them.* Keep them informed, and they'll be eager to cooperate.

3. Plan work and prepare supplies. You waste time and money trying to organize assignments and equipment after the temporary arrives. Decide in advance which work will be his responsibility. A checklist can help you be sure you have all supplies ready. Where possible, have the regular employee help in the preparations.

4. Give complete instructions. A temporary comes into your department cold, and you hope he'll perform like an experienced hand. It's not "the impossible dream"—if you give complete instructions. A job instruction sheet, prepared by you or the regular employee, helps you cover all points, and lets the temporary review them. Or, if you give instructions orally, encourage him to make notes of key points. Work samples help him get it right first try.

5. Explain company procedures. The temporary will feel like a member of the group, not an outsider, if you explain rules regarding lunch hours, rest periods, smoking, etc. This prevents mistakes which would annoy you and embarrass him. If possible, use a "buddy" approach: assign a seasoned employee to help with routines.

If you've chosen a reputable agency, the temporary has been tested, trained, and placed according to skills and personality. He is a professional and should be treated as one. Expect good work, and you'll get it.

7. Leadership and Motivation

Leadership has been defined by the late President Eisenhower as "the ability to get people to do what you want because they want to do it."

This statement also includes the concept of motivation: the ways and means of getting people to *want* to do whatever is to be done.

Some management observers feel that the idea of leadership is outdated. The traditional image of the business leader who stands at the head of his "troops" and guides them along, doesn't suit the image of the modern executive. Motivation has come to be the preferred concept and to some extent it encompasses the ends of leadership. However, the burial of the leadership concept is premature. The average executive has good reason to want to keep up-to-date on the subject of leadership, as well as motivation. Accordingly, you will find both areas covered in this section.

➲ WHY LEADERSHIP WORKS

Everyday experience plus the assurance of industrial psychologists tell us that leadership on the business scene is an important element in effectiveness. And yet, as important as this fact is, very seldom is the question asked, Just why is it that leadership works?

Analyzing the response of the *individual* and of the *group* to good leadership yields considerable insight into managerial effectiveness:

1. Leadership and the Individual. Individuals working in constructive relationships with their superior can accomplish tasks that surprise even themselves. Personal productivity and creativity take an upward bounce. Often, individuals can make constructive innovations in their jobs and on the entire work scene. Here's why:

▪ *Goal alertness.* The president of a New Mexico public service company puts it this way: "I get my people lined up on the target, make them aware of what contributes to our goals and what does not." Leadership that is expertly exercised makes individuals aware of desired goals, steers them away from dead ends.

▪ *Talent latency.* A New Jersey electronics manufacturer reports that one of his managers without prior factory experience became one of their most capable men. Explains the executive, "His boss was able to arouse an enormous amount of talent that the employee didn't even know he had." There is latent energy and untapped talent in every individual—no matter what his position, no matter at what level he is performing. The good leader is able to bring out the wealth of these hidden gold mines.

And a key point is this: the improvement in performance *doesn't* come about by the employee working himself into a lather. The man doesn't work harder, he works smarter—to use an old axiom.

▪ *Self-doubt eradication.* Most people are affected with varying degrees of self-doubt: "I can't do that assignment, I've never done it before." Or an employee will accept an assignment—and spend hours worrying whether he can fulfill it. His performance is bound to be adversely affected.

A good leader gets a subordinate to improve performance by breaking the chains forged by self-doubt. Superior performance results from this upsurge in self-confidence.

2. Leadership and Groups. There are times when the manager wants his work force to tackle an assignment as a team. Good leadership turns individuals into team members. Here's what happens:

■ *Common goals.* "The leader creates a concept of common goal," says a Pennsylvania manager. "I can take machinists who are out for themselves and help them see that it's more important for the unit to win the ball game, so to speak, than for each one to try to hit home runs."

■ *Mutual help.* A South Carolina cotton mill manager recently presided over the installation of semiautomatic equipment in his department. "I realized," he said, "that if the men would help one another learn the new ropes, we'd have fewer mistakes. The faster learners could teach the slower ones, not leave them to fend for themselves." By talking to the men, he was able to get them to help one another. Soon the entire department had mastered the new equipment. The reason? Good leadership, which created, in this instance, a department-wide atmosphere of good will and mutual helpfulness.

■ *Team effort.* The leader takes an aggregation of people and molds them into a team. You see it done by good sports coaches, on the diamond and gridiron. You see it on the work scene, when masterful managers are at the helm.

The leader who knows his business can put the work of individuals in phase with the work of colleagues. "I can modify a man's assignment," said a California aircraft manager, "or put him on a different task entirely, until his work is ready for him. If I do my job right, individuals work smoothly, in step with one another. There is less time wasted, fewer starts and stops."

The result of this "phasing" of the work, and the result, too, of providing common goals and a spirit of mutual helpfulness, has been expressed as: the whole is greater than the sum of its parts. It is the sign of the effective leader.

⮡ A BRIEF REVIEW OF APPROACHES TO LEADERSHIP

Historically, leadership concepts have been of three types:

The trait approach. This explains leadership in terms of the personal traits of the leader. Ever since the dawn of the human race, people have been aware that leaders possess qualities that set them apart. Personal courage, for example, was one of the traits generally ascribed to early tribal leaders.

The trait approach has advocates in our own day. There are some management authorities who say, to be effective, a leader must—

be enthusiastic
know himself
be mentally alert

be self-confident
have a sense of responsibility
develop a sense of humor

The list is far from complete. Dozens of items could be added.

No one can really quarrel with the value of many of these traits. However, the trouble with the trait approach is that it's about as useful as a handbook on traffic rules would be to the motorist who needs a road map. No one would deny that an enthusiastic leader can be a highly inspiring one. But, if the would-be leader is not *naturally* enthusiastic, he could work himself into a nervous break-down trying to develop an enthusiasm he did not feel. And the insincerity of phony enthusiasm can be disastrous.

The same handicap pertains to other leadership traits—they're fine in theory, but not very practical when it comes to developing leader-ship, or applying it.

The situationist approach. Some experts feel that the situations in which the leader operates hold the key to effectiveness. Accordingly, this concept stresses the characteristics of leadership situations. Norman F. Washburne, in *Nation's Business,* lists a number of actions performed by a good leader that reflect the situationist approach:

A good leader initiates action.
He gives orders that will be obeyed.
He uses established channels within his group.
He knows and obeys the rules and customs of his group.
He maintains discipline.
He listens to subordinates.
He responds to their needs.
He helps them.

Although Washburne's ideas go a step further than the trait ap-proach, we need something more. The trouble with the situationist approach, in general, is that, it's *descriptive* rather than *prescriptive*.

For example, we have all verified the fact that a good leader initiates action. However, the statement "a good leader initiates action" raises more questions than it answers. *What* kind of action does the leader initiate? *When* does he initiate it? And, exactly *how* does he do so?

The social activist approach. Some authorities view the role of the leader as one of putting together the elements, human and material, required for successful performance. This method includes the assignment of individuals or groups to specific tasks, and stresses the nature of the relationship between the leader and his followers.

The method of Selective Leadership, the next item in this section, is an example of this approach.

⮕ SELECTIVE LEADERSHIP: A SYSTEMATIC APPROACH

Should a manager approach an experienced subordinate in the same way as a novice? Should one manage a group of laborers the same way as one might a group of scientists? What difference—if any— does the personality of a subordinate make in his boss's approach to him?

In the early 1950's Auren Uris developed a systematic approach to leadership. The concepts and practices that make up Selective Leadership derive from key experiments by psychologist Kurt Lewin at the University of Iowa. To explore the nature of leadership, Lewin set up experimental groups of two sorts:

One type was dominated by an "autocratic" leader, who determined policy, decided what was to be done and how, assigned tasks, and chose work companions for each member. He was personal in his praise, criticism, and general comments.

The second type was led by a "democratic" leader, who brought up matters of policy for group discussion, encouraged group members to choose their own work companions, and was "objective" in his comments.

Then came an unexpected development: observers noticed that one individual playing the role of "democratic" leader created an atmosphere different from that of other "democratic" leaders. He exercised virtually no control over the group; he permitted group members to shift for themselves; he let them tackle problems unaided, as best they could. The group's response to this technique was so different from the reactions of other democratic groups that Lewin set up a third kind of group under a type of leadership which he termed "laissez-faire."

Significant differences emerged in atmosphere, behavior, feelings, and accomplishments:

Autocratic. Group members were quarrelsome and aggressive. Some individuals became completely dependent upon the leader. When the leader was absent, activity tended to stop altogether. Work progressed at only a fair rate.

Democratic. The individuals got along with one another on a friendly basis. Relations with the leader were freer, more spontaneous.

The work progressed smoothly, and continued even when the leader was absent.

Laissez-faire. Work progressed haphazardly, and at a slow rate. Although there was considerable activity, much of it was unproductive. Considerable time was lost in arguments and discussions between group members on a purely personal basis.

Actually, each method has built-in strengths and weaknesses; each method has its value. The three methods developed in the University of Iowa investigations provide the framework of the Selective Leadership approach, welding the Lewin concepts into a unified and systematic method.

Using the Selective Leadership approach, the manager selects whichever one of the three tools is most appropriate:

Autocratic leadership. The leader mainly seeks obedience from his group. He determines policy and considers decision-making a one-man operation—he, of course, being the one man.

Democratic leadership. The leader draws ideas and suggestions from the group by discussion and consultation. Group members are encouraged to take part in the setting of policy. The leader's job is largely that of moderator.

Free-rein leadership. (Lewin's "laissez-faire" method) The leader functions more or less as an information booth. He plays down his role in the group's activity. He exercises a minimum of control.

These definitions provide the basis for a systematic approach to leading people. Autocratic, democratic, or free-rein methods may be considered as three tools of the management leader. Contrary to common belief, the three approaches are not mutually exclusive. No one has to choose among using autocratic, democratic, or free-rein methods. That would be like telling a golf player he must choose between using a driver or a putter; in the course of a game he will use both.

Note Manager X in action:

He *directs* (autocratic method) his secretary to make a report.

He *consults* (democratic method) with his employees on the best way to push a special order through the shop.

He *suggests* (free-rein method) to his assistant that it would be a good idea to figure out ways in which special orders may be handled more smoothly in the future.

This type of leadership suggests that mastery lies in knowing when to use which method. In short, Selective Leadership is a logical adaptation of autocratic, democratic, and free-rein techniques to appropriate situations.

Once the three basic approaches are understood, it remains only for the manager to learn to suit the appropriate approach to a given situation. For example, the personality factor is taken into account in this fashion:

The hostile subordinate. With an individual of this type, the autocratic method is likely to be most effective. While he resents authority, he respects it at the same time. Accordingly, his hostility must be met by a show of authority. The autocratic approach has the effect of channeling his aggressions, confining his energies to constructive ends.

The group-minded individual. The subordinate who is team-minded, who enjoys "team play," will probably function best if led by democratic techniques. He needs less direction, regards work as a group job, and is willing to accept group goals as personal ones.

The individualist, the solo player. He usually thrives best under the free-rein type of leadership. He likes to develop his own methods and ideas; the more he is given his head, the greater freedom he has to mobilize his creativity.

In addition to adapting to the personality factors of a situation, selective leadership also takes into account the nature of the response the manager seeks in any given context. For example:

Compliance. If the subordinate or group is working along routine lines, with well-established goals, the autocratic method is appropriate.

Cooperation. A rush order may put a group under pressure to perform above standard. Calling the group together, describing the nature of the crisis, asking for help and suggestions, are democratic techniques that will best help meet objectives.

Creativity. Productivity can be stimulated slightly by autocratic, means, considerably by democratic approaches. But creativity poses different problems. When novel ideas are sought and imagination is needed, the free-rein approach is usually most effective.

(A brief description of Selective Leadership is also included in Section III, Key Management Concepts.)

➔ THE CHARISMA COMPONENT

The experienced executive knows that above and beyond the procedural and rational aspects of leadership, there's something else. Intangible though it may be, it can make major differences in results:

- Some executives "do things all wrong" and still run effective departments.
- Some executives "do all the right things" and still get only the most meager payoffs.

What is this X factor? One explanation is *charisma*. "Charisma," says the dictionary, is "that special personal quality in some men that makes others want to follow their lead." King Arthur had it. So did Joan of Arc. And, in our own time, John F. Kennedy had it—in outstanding fashion.

Can a leader "develop" a charisma, improve this highly personal aspect of his leadership? Unexpectedly the answer is *yes*. Keen observers of outstanding managers in action report that the charismatic leader is usually one whose dedication, involvement, and sincerity regarding his work and goals are self-evident, *sufficiently so to rub off on his subordinates.*

The executive inspires his people, spurs them on, motivates them, gets improved performance, in ways ranging from increased output to more wholehearted participation. In ultimate development, the well-led employee views the company's problems as his.

YOUR PERSONAL LEADERSHIP STYLE

"In a society overrun by people trying to be carbon copies of one another, anyone with the nerve and verve to be different can lead an exciting life filled with a sense of personal satisfaction."

These words are from the recent book, "They Dare To Be Different," by Elmer G. Leterman and Thomas W. Carlin.

There's no doubt that for many individuals, the path of individualism and nonconformity can lead to high achievement. The names and accomplishments of some of Leterman's fellow biographees make the point: Commander Edward Whitehead, bearded Englishman who sells Schweppes' tonic to American markets by publicizing his own distinctive appearance; Helen Gurley Brown, the Californian whose best seller ripped the veil from the subject of sex and the single girl; Dr. Wendell Phillips, whose unique approach to exploration and development of oil lands made him one of the wealthiest men in the world.

What does "daring to be different" mean for executives? Answer: unconformity represents a style, a *working style,* a way of thinking about and doing things. And as such, it deserves your objective consideration.

There's no doubt that the executive who moves out in new and untraditional directions may well come up with novel ideas and solutions to problems. For example:

Department head Bill Woods has a production problem. Ordinarily, he would set about solving it either by consulting with Engineering, or by getting his most experienced employees together for probing discussions. But, Bill Woods decides to try a different tack: he arranges to have a working lunch with three or four of his fellow managers, and along with the food, he puts his problem on the table.

The example is not only illustrative, but suggestive, because the executive reading the Bill Woods tactic, will make the logical observation: "Woods's fresh approach *may* work if his fellow managers have some knowledge of the circumstances surrounding the problem."

In other words, unconformity, "daring to be different," has a good chance of working *if* certain conditions prevail:

- If "daring to be different" isn't simply being different for its own sake. In short, the differentness must give you an edge on the field.

- If the new tack, or approach, takes you in a direction where there's a possibility of finding pay dirt. (As pointed out, discussing problems with colleagues may yield results *if* the colleagues have know-how in the problem area.)

Tough-minded executives know that a concept is only as good as its payoff. And they need only look about on the work scene to know there must be more than one road to the top. No one concept can claim to be "the way" to success.

Accordingly, executives evaluating the worthwhileness of "being different" may say, "Sure, taking the unorthodox, unprecedented approach to things is one way of accomplishing objectives, if it happens to be your thing. But it's not the *only* way."

Doubtless there are benefits to "being different." However, studying the work patterns of successful executives, we see that there are other keys to success. For example, some outstanding managers owe their achievement to persistence, sticking with a problem till a solution is developed. Others accomplish objectives by making the best possible use of resources on hand. Here are a number of keys to leadership success, philosophies of work, tactics for achievement—call them what you will:

- "being different"
- persistence
- mobilizing available resources
- attention to detail
- follow through
- analyzing a problem accurately
- knowing how to get and use expert help
- other

In scanning the list, ask yourself, "Which of the items have I used, or do I use, separately or in combination?" Remember, each has the virtue of potential success. To a large extent, the question, "Which is best?" is answered by three other questions:

- Which suits the particular problem best?
- Which can I implement best?
- Which suits my natural propensities or "personality" best?

Perhaps you'll decide that being different is your thing. Or, you may see the advantages of another alternative, or combination of alternatives.

In any event, the increased awareness gained by thinking about the approach to work and work problems can improve one's leadership performance. The executive who knows what "his thing" is, has a much better chance of doing it well.

WHAT TO TELL A MANAGER WHO'S JUST STARTING

Occasionally, executives face the task of putting a new man in a supervisory job. His qualifications naturally have been found adequate. But a personal "message" from you can help him approach his responsibility with more understanding—both of his job and your expectations.

The following suggestions probably won't be made in one sitting, but over a period of time. These "principles of supervision" have helped many a starting manager make the grade:

Be firm, but fair.   You can lead, direct, coach. You can—and should —speak and act with strength and conviction. But it's also important to realize that circumstances change people; people change situations. What works in one instance, won't in another. What's fair for one person may be all wrong for someone else. A good supervisor knows how to be flexible, in order to be fair.

Take advantage of the experience and abilities of other people.   No one is so much of a genius that he knows everything. Be receptive to the ideas and advice of others: your subordinates, your boss, staff people, other department heads. Being interested in what they have to say can provide a twofold benefit: they'll be stimulated by your interest; their ideas may save you many a headache.

Don't show off authority.   Make suggestions, but issue few orders —you get a lot more out of people by direction than by command. Assume that others are working *with* you, not *for* you, for the mutual benefit of the group—and the organization.

Admit your mistakes. Even the greatest executive can't always be right. When you goof, don't alibi, don't try to shift the blame to someone else. Just admit that you were wrong and offer a brief explanation, if you think it's pertinent. This applies whether the mistake covers one person or all the people in your group.

Be truthful. Even when it hurts. Don't be afraid to tell someone he's doing a poor job—it's for his own good—but at the same time point out how he can improve. That way, you make him feel that even though he's low now, there's no reason why he can't move up. Remember the reverse side of the coin, as well—give credit where and when it is due. Everyone welcomes a word of praise and appreciation for a job well done.

Be consistent. People won't willingly follow a leader who goes from mood to mood, who flatters one day and frightens the next, who talks a blue streak in the morning and won't open his mouth in the afternoon. They simply end up confused and unsure.

Maintaining an even disposition isn't always easy. Sometimes you have to bite down hard on your tongue so you won't say something you'll regret. Or it may take a colleague's blunt, "What's the matter with you?" to alert you to your attitude. Accept such comments in good faith—and snap back to normal.

Don't be afraid to train assistants. Recruit the kind that can serve as good right hands, take over when you're not there, move into your spot when you go higher. The executive who "runs scared," who holds onto each bit of his job and authority lest someone else prove smarter than he is, is missing the boat. A good assistant can make a good manager look even better.

Be a self-starter. Don't wait for someone else to set the rules and the pace. Be open to inspiration, learn to translate thought into action, dramatize action with salesmanship. To sell an idea, stress its good points, tell people what it can do for them, and for you as well.

And . . . when you start something, see it through to the finish. Don't be disheartened when something doesn't run smoothly. Give it time, patience, and some enthusiastic follow-through. It may work.

Keep people informed. Don't try to put things over on your group, to keep them in the dark. If you expect them to work as a team, you have to treat them like a team, one that is in the know about what's going on and why. This builds their confidence in you as a leader—and keeps morale high.

Keep reading and learning.   Moving from supervisor to executive demands new knowledge, new techniques, almost a new way of thinking. You progress with experience, from reading and listening. A course in labor relations can prove invaluable. The same holds true for books and magazines dealing with various phases of management. One part of management is common sense, but another is knowledge and know-how. Both are available—if you know where to look for them.

➲ WHEN YOU NEED VOLUNTEERS

No executive has ever complained that he had too many volunteers. Complaints, if any, are usually: you need help, but no one comes forward. To make sure you can count on helping hands when you need them—

1. Clarify what you want done.   That includes how long the job will take. "I need someone to stick around with me for an hour or so Wednesday night," says the head of the Computer Room. You can cross Johnny's name off the list for all future volunteering, if he gets stuck till midnight.

2. Stand ready to pitch in.   Where a job's being carried through on a voluntary basis, the manager should be prepared to lend a hand himself. "You inventory the first aisle, I'll take the second," is the attitude that gets lasting cooperation.

3. Highlight your appreciation.   That's a time-honored rule, but it's too often disregarded in the rush to get home. Whether you're dealing with one volunteer or twenty, it's always good practice to make a curtain speech: "Thanks a lot for the way you've all pitched in to clean up this job."

4. Reward their efforts.   They'll like that best of all. And they'll give you the most in return. Be sure to include their record of cooperation in merit rating and progress reviews. "I'm putting in a pitch for you," is sweet music to any man's ears.

Follow these rules, and you'll be much surer of seeing the hands go up, rather than the thumbs down when there's a call for volunteers.

➲ WHEN YOUR LEADERSHIP IS CHALLENGED

Occasionally, and for a variety of reasons, an executive may find his leadership rejected or evaded by his group. Even the most seasoned executive may run into trouble. The important thing is to recognize the development in its early stages, and eliminate causative factors before the virus spreads. Here are some of the symptoms:

■ **Excessive need for discipline.** You find increasing instances of people bypassing regulations, becoming negligent, even acts of insubordination.

■ **Grievances galore.** Complaints of all kinds begin to pile up. The trivial matter that's passed unnoticed for months suddenly becomes a major issue. A grievance you considered settled flares up again.

■ **Cooperation down, goldbricking up.** Tom, Dick, and Harry, the faithful three you could always count on to stick out a job till it's finished, beg off on staying overtime. You find you've got to do more arguing and explaining, to keep your group on their toes.

■ **Performance records skidding.** "Look at the errors made last month!" That may be the soundtrack on your first picture of leadership trouble. Or maybe the mail is accumulating in the correspondence department, and the typists are falling behind, with no increase in the workload.

■ **Leadership ignored.** They stop asking questions. They no longer look to you for advice. They make their own decisions on matters that normally require your okay.

Any one of those situations calls for a two-dose treatment:

Keep your head. Start out by dealing with the individual cases. Don't use any single case as a test of strength, to show you can crack down. Resist the temptation to "make an example" of the latest offender. That may be the spark that sets off the explosion. Instead, look for the underlying cause of the trouble. Check up on the answers to the questions in this self-examination:

1. Have you been failing to make decisions when they were called for?
2. Have you been getting all the facts before making a decision?
3. Have you been selling your decisions by explaining the "why"— or have you been relying on your authority?
4. In running your "shop," have you been influenced by personal feelings—friendships, animosities?
5. Have you been getting your staff in on the solution of group problems?

6. Have you been taking positive steps to underline the group nature of the work—group goals, group achievements?

THREE TYPES OF MOTIVATION

Why do people do things? For example, what makes an employee get out of a comfortable bed to brave the problems and ordeals of a job? What makes an executive apply himself to a task, work overtime to complete a particularly challenging project?

In general, people are moved to act by three types of motives:

1. External motivation. Many people do what they do because they're *told* to do it. A parent tells a child he must get high marks in school. A teenager mows a lawn because his father orders him to do so. Or, a young man goes to college because his parents believe it's essential for his future. On the job, an employee "obeys the boss."

2. Social pressure. Many people are motivated by social or group pressures. For example, 90 out of 100 people work because our society expects them to. Similarly, many people get married when they do because society expects them to. Or, on the job, individuals seek advancement because it's expected by their employers or colleagues.

3. Self-motivation. Occasionally, we find people who take action on their own. They do something because *they* want to do it.

The self-motivated individual in many cases lives where he wants to, in the manner he prefers, and works toward objectives that he has decided are desirable for him. For the executive, it's important to understand these three basic types of motivation. The executive who is most effective in motivating his subordinates is the one most able to get them to act *not* because they are commanded to by a superior, *not* because they are pressured by the expectations of those around them, but because they are aware of the desirability of attaining the objectives of their efforts defined by their superiors.

What self-motivation comes down to, finally, is the individual's conviction that he desires the fruits of success, that he wants them so badly that he's willing to strive for them with all his heart and mind.

TELLING THEM WHAT'S IN IT FOR THEM

You're explaining a new policy to your group, and you want to get their full support. Or you give an individual an assignment, and he very properly seems to hesitate, because he's not clear on his stake in the success of the effort. In cases like these, the key to effective motivation may be in explaining to the individual, or group, the benefits they stand to gain. Perhaps the most crucial specific application of this approach lies in the cost-cutting area. You, as a representative of management, know the importance of holding the cost line. Some of your people may be reluctant to "knock themselves out" to save the company "a few bucks."

A considerable amount of insight into this problem is gained when you hear the answers given to a probing question: "If your company announced a cost-cutting drive, what would it take to get you to cooperate?" The answers given here provide the key to effective motivation, not only in cost cutting, but in any other job project where the employee may be unclear as to what he stands to gain:

- **Personal payoff.** "I'd want to feel," said a New York City insurance office clerk, "that my boss would notice me if I did a good job. And I'd expect him to remember my cooperation when it came time for a promotion or a raise."

- **Dollars and cents.** A Connecticut bakery employee said he'd want to know the dollars and cents of the matter. "Let my boss show me figures. If I saw figures showing, say, that $1,200 went down the drain every month on unnecessary electricity, wow! I'd sure turn off lights. But if my boss just talks about 'waste' or 'high costs,' that's too abstract for me."

- **Necessity.** Says a California aircraft worker: "I'd want the company to tell me they're in financial trouble. Or if they told me my job depended on it, yes sir, I'd try to cut costs. And I'd want to be kept informed of the progress made: how we improve each week after the drive goes into effect."

- **We're all in the same boat.** Said a Chattanooga factory worker: "Why me? That's what I'd ask my boss. I've got a sense of responsibility like everyone else, but I'd want it appealed to honestly. If I thought that somebody higher up was just passing the buck down to me, I wouldn't do anything. But if I felt that everyone above me was getting into the act, sure I'd help out."

Should this hardheaded attitude be discouraging? *Not at all.* Notice that each employee indicated that *he would be perfectly willing to participate* in cost-cutting efforts *if*—the reasons behind the activity were made clear, his position were given some consideration and justification, and so on.

If your company and your department plan to do any belt-tightening, try to think what each man in your department would react to—then spur that interest. For some employees it will be involvement—just asking for help, getting them into the act. For others it will be the carrot—or the stick. Chances are, you'll have to use all of the techniques at your disposal. Your flexibility with these techniques—the aptness with which you satisfy each employee's "What's in it for me?"—will determine *how* your staff cooperates.

➜ WHY PEOPLE WORK

Chances are, each one of your subordinates wants:

- recognition as a person—treatment as an individual, not as a "cog in the machine"
- fair treatment—a square deal
- job security
- suitable working conditions—reasonable schedule, comfortable facilities, protection against hazards
- a chance to be heard
- pride in his work—the feeling that he is useful
- knowledge—the meaning of the job, clear instructions
- the help of leadership—guidance where he needs it
- challenge—a chance to prove himself
- the sense of belonging—acceptance by the people around him

➜ EIGHT DEMOTIVATORS

Obviously, not every case of lack of motivation among your subordinates is your fault. But, without being aware of it, the executive can contribute to a subordinate's apathy. Watch these areas:

- *Freezing them out*—Employees who don't have sufficient contact with you will begin to feel that nobody cares about them.
- *Chewing them out*—Make sure criticism is reasonable and accompanied by constructive suggestions for improvement.
- *Letting them flounder*—Let employees know what you expect of them. When you don't communicate clear standards, they may decide "anything goes."
- *Ruling by whim*—When you don't enforce rules consistently, you are depriving workers of the strong leadership they need.
- *Aiming too high*—When goals are set too high, people give up, say, "Why should I knock myself out?"
- *Aiming too low*—If employees are not challenged, do not have a chance to use their full potential, they become bored.

■ *Skimping on equipment*—Inferior tools or materials will "turn off" the employee who is trying to do a good job.

■ *Insufficient recognition*—Failure of a boss or leader to register awareness of an individual, either on a day-to-day basis or in appreciation for notable performance, may lead to demoralization. The ritual "Good morning," and "Good night," may have litle value in today's working relationships, but they're better than no recognition at all. And the subordinate who feels that his accomplishments go unnoticed, regardless even of a high natural level of inner incentive, tends to lose steam.

These demotivating factors suggest a key principle: high levels of performance from subordinates are forthcoming not only as a result of positive motivation, but also in the absence of actions that demotivate.

➲ HOW TO CRITICIZE

You want the improvements resulting from criticism without demotivating side effects. Accordingly—

Focus on the act, not the person.   Don't tell the man he's unworthy. Get the facts, concentrate on them. Tell the worker that:

■ An error has been committed.
■ Good people have made the same mistake in the past.
■ They corrected their errors and he can too.
■ The way to correct the error is thus-and-so.

Be specific about the error.   Avoid generalities, exaggeration.

Be specific about the remedy.   Spell out just what the employee can do to improve.

Watch his reactions—go slow enough so that you are sure he gets it. As soon as he understands—stop.

Choose the right time and place.   Make it private. Avoid criticism just before lunch or closing time. If possibly, allow for a second, constructive talk the same day.

Use only friendly humor.   If you can't keep it friendly, avoid it.

Follow up on criticism.   Don't repeat your criticisms or instructions. Follow up to:

■ Reassure him that you're in his corner.
■ Give him a chance to ask questions.

➲ HELP FOR THE GOAL-MINDED SUBORDINATE

Not everybody wants to be president—either of the U.S.A. or Acme Universal Manufacturing Co. On the other hand, for many of your subordinates a feeling of career movement is necessary to maintain morale and performance.

• In considering the attitudes of your people to their work, you'll find that they tend to fall into three groups:

- Those who are happy in their routine. These are the small minority.
- Those who are happy just knowing there is some place to go— even if they do nothing about it.
- Those who want to go places. The better your staff, the more such people you have.

Yet everybody isn't qualified to move ahead. Or the nature of the work may be such that there is no opportunity for advancement. If your people get the feeling of being dead-end kids, you're going to have disciplinary problems, absenteeism, high turnover, frequent gripes and grievances.

How can you prevent the dead-ender from getting the "I'm-in-a-rut" feeling? Keeping in mind the special condition in each case, see which of these recommendations apply.

1. Are there chances for promotion or transfer? Give this point a pretty thorough going-over before throwing up your hands. And don't let a man's present performance, by itself, guide your thinking. We all have undeveloped potentialities.

Search his work record. His present job may have thrown him off an old course. He may have past work experience that can be reapplied.

Talk to him about his interests. They may reveal additional possibilities.

2. Can you expand his job? You may be able, without any loss of efficiency, to incorporate other operations into the job. They may be steps that either immediately precede or follow the employee's regular task. Or they may be entirely unrelated, but still make use of his special abilities.

3. Can you improve his job methods? Without changing the old-timer's job, you may still be able to increase its efficiency, raise quality standards, or both. That gives him a sense of progress in the job without involving progress to a new job.

4. Can you put him on his own without losing control over his various activities? The old-timer may tend to set himself up as a "separate department." This may be a good solution. A feeling of independence usually carries with it a sense of responsibility.

But you don't want to create a problem situation. If you give him the feeling that he can run things his own way, you'll have trouble if that way doesn't agree with yours. In other words, you want to give him independence of action that makes it possible for him to get results, without removing him from the group and your leadership.

You can accomplish this by subjecting him to a lesser degree of direction. "Just put through that report. With your experience, I don't have to look it over."

In addition, this attitude on your part gives him the feeling of superior status.

5. Make him realize that he's doing a useful job. The employee who's in a rut will be more content if he has to stay there, when he knows that he's accomplishing something worthwhile. He, more than any other type of worker, needs a constant reminder that his work is necessary. Give him:

. . . an understanding of his relation to the company, how his job fits in.

. . . an understanding of how the company serves the community, our national interest, and so on.

8. Dealing with Problem People

One of the most exasperating and demanding parts of the executive's job involves his dealing with individuals who represent difficulties in his working relationships—a recalcitrant employee, a careless one, an apparently well-intentioned, but destructive individual—may wreak havoc with an otherwise high potential for achievement.

Dealing with problem people is best viewed as a separate and special kind of human relations area. This is particularly true because the individuals who must be dealt with are usually unique problems, and because the whole matter of dealing with problem individuals requires policies and practices that are specific to this area. Accordingly, you will find two elements in the section that follows:

- A discussion of what makes an employee a "problem;" one of the difficulties is often a failure to understand *when* an employee is a problem employee—and when he *isn't*.
- Specific suggestions on dealing with typical "problem people."

➲ WHEN IS A "PROBLEM EMPLOYEE" A PROBLEM?

The phrase, "problem employee" is traditional in management literature. Early in the development of human relations awareness in business, executives became aware of the "different," or "nonconforming" individual. He usually seemed to represent a work difficulty, and often did. But fully as many destructive beliefs began to flourish around the "problem employee" as did helpful practices for dealing with him. Some typical myths:

- An individual who doesn't conform to group standards—in behavior, attitude, dress—is a problem, and must be dealt with summarily.
- A nonconforming individual automatically threatens group unity and teamwork.

Both of these ideas are usually false. The fact is, an individual who is "different" from his fellows, no matter how much he may deviate from group norms, is not a problem *unless*—

- He actually interferes with the progress of the work.
- He interferes with fellow employees in their work activities.
- He damages the image, reputation, or services of the company.

If none of these damaging consequences apply, the individual is *not* a problem employee, regardless of what he looks like, or what his values or behavior may be.

And a final point: as far as the nonconformer threatening group unity, most groups are surprisingly accepting of nonconforming individuals. Workers have a live-and-let-live tradition on the work scene. They know they're there to earn a living, and are willing to give others the same privilege.

Actually, the executive is a key to the "problem child's" reception by the group. The group will generally follow the leader's mode. If he treats the nonconformist more or less the same way he does other contributing members, the others will do likewise.

But dealing with an actual problem employee *is* a problem—and a tough one. The pages ahead offer a number of suggestions.

➍ **MAJOR PITFALL TO AVOID**

Don't play psychiatrist. It's a tendency that occasionally trips up an executive—and the consequences can be catastrophic. There are several excellent reasons to avoid donning the psychotherapist's mantle:

- You haven't got the time.
- You almost surely lack the skill—unless you've been trained.
- You can get trapped by your own emotional entanglements in the problem. This can make you the most regretful person standing in line at the psychiatrist's door.

And finally—

- You don't have to play the psychiatrist to provide sound effective help to your people, and solve the company's part of the problem at the same time. Other approaches, detailed in the pages ahead, show you how.

➍ **SHOULD YOU PLAY BIG DADDY?**

It's natural that your subordinates should see you as a person of power, possibly a father image. As a result you may find that some of your people, particularly those who are more dependent, may look to you for assistance with their personal problems. Obviously, some requests will be unjustified and embarrassing. On the other hand, you often can help employees, to their own personal improvement and the betterment of their work attitudes.

In part the answer seems to lie in *how* the help is given. These pointers can give you the benefits, avoid snap-backs:

1. Don't see yourself as Big Daddy. Before you give help, think through your relations to your employee. If you see yourself as Big Daddy, the benign, "I'll-take-care-of-everything" parent, you are harming him before your help has even begun. The role of Big Daddy suggests an overprotection that does violence to his dignity. He is not a child, no matter what kind of trouble he's in. He's an adult in need of adult advice.

Seeing yourself as Big Daddy is wrong, too, because it exaggerates the nature of what you are planning to do. You're going to offer help because of your unique position. You're not involved in the situation, and can see things about it that your employee may not be able to see. Being on the outside you can be objective, bring your experience to bear.

2. Don't take on his burden. Once you decide to help your employee, act in such a way that the problem remains his. Unlike a doctor or a lawyer, you will not be giving the kind of help that requires the employee to put himself in your hands. On the contrary, the advice you give will be strictly limited, requiring that the employee continue to *think through his problem.*

3. Don't recommend only one expert. In some cases, you may suggest that the employee get professional help—it may be as simple as saying, "Go to an eye doctor." The employee asks, "Whom do you recommend?" It is important that you recommend a *number of sources.* Or that you refer the man to your company doctor for a list of names. Or you may want to put him in touch with an organization—such as a local chapter of the American Medical Association—that can give him such a list.

The point here is that you want the *employee* to make the choice of whom to consult. If you give him only one name, in effect you have chosen the consultant, and your prestige, rightly or wrongly, is linked to the professional's success or failure. It's a chance that you don't have to take—and you shouldn't.

4. Describe alternatives. Maybe you've pointed out that if a man moves, he will be able to solve a commuting problem.

Being objective, having a clearer view of the situation, you can suggest alternatives that he overlooked. He makes the decision, although you may help him with the process.

Shown the alternatives, the employee recognizes that the way to resolve the question of which course to take is to start ruling out alternatives until left with the best one. You broaden his horizons when you suggest options, help him reach a solution possibly based on combining the best features of several alternatives.

5. Don't let him escalate you. You suggest a bank as a possible solution to a man's financial troubles. He takes your advice and discusses with a bank officer how to get a loan to consolidate his debts. It works. Then he comes to you one day and says. "You were so helpful on that loan problem, could I ask you another question?"

You say, "What?"

He says, "Well, my brother has a problem. . . ."

He is reflecting a tendency that people have, which is to become more and more in need of the executive's helpfulness. And you, without knowing it, may experience an equal pull in the direction of giving him this extra help. Don't. Impose reasonable limitations on the help you offer.

5. Don't judge moral issues. Sometimes the personal problems dumped into your lap involve the shady side of human conduct. The problem may revolve around gambling, drink, immorality, even infractions of the law. But you're not going to help by being horrified.

Accept such information as matter of factly as possible. Above all, make sure you are sympathetic and friendly—so that the individual does not feel his personal position is even more difficult because you know. Then steer him on to professional help—a lawyer, psychologist, minister.

6. Don't betray a confidence. Only the most unusual circumstances could ever justify repeating the information the employee has imparted.

The employee has come to you in good faith, seeking you out as a friend and as a leader capable of helping out in a pinch. It would be a breach of faith for you to reveal to a third party anything that you've learned. And the loss of prestige you would suffer from such an error could be immediate and devastating.

➲ WHEN YOU HATE HIS GUTS

Occasionally, an executive faces a difficult situation; his subordinate is quite capable, but for one reason or another he dislikes him. The hazards of the situation, both in terms of the individual's performance and even in staff morale, are obvious.

However, once the problem is identified, a certain amount of resolve and candor makes several steps possible.

1. Spot the bug. For several reasons, you should try to understand what it is about the employee that's bugging you. This analysis may turn up the conclusion that you've judged a person unfairly. One manager, for example, discovered, "One of the girls in my group wore a constant smirk. I always felt as though there was some sly or sneaky feeling she had against me. Thinking about her, it suddenly became clear that what I had construed as a sly expression was really a grimace that simply revealed nervousness and tension."

In some cases, executives have discovered that they tended to transfer hostility or dislike to an innocent victim simply because he reminded them, unknowingly, of someone else. Understanding can quickly relieve this type of misdirected feeling.

2. Do not broadcast your attitudes.   Do the best you can to cover up your negative feelings towards a subordinate. While getting a load off your chest may bring relief, it may also cause your people to wonder what you say about *them.* In addition, you will be punishing the man you dislike, since an employee becomes a marked man, and may lose standing with his group, if his boss's low opinion of him is known.

3. Lean over backwards to be fair.   The manager may have to make a special effort to see he's administering equal treatment. He should establish standards, either publicly or in his own mind, that apply to discipline, assignments, raises, and so on.

Once these standards are established, you have double protection. You can be more certain that everybody's getting a fair shake. And, if your judgments are questioned, you can spell out the thinking behind a decision.

4. Agree to disagree.   Is the source of the trouble a conflict of viewpoints? Men with widely differing ideas about life—very liberal and very conservative, say, or very gregarious and very quiet—can get along with one another by "agreeing to disagree."

In essence, they decide not to challenge each other in their areas of difference, to concentrate, instead, on cooperating in those areas where they agree. This is more likely to work when feelings between you and your subordinate are known to each of you, and accepted as a matter of course.

5. When you can't make peace, make distance.   What about a transfer for your subordinate? This is frequently a good solution, if it is in the interest of the company, and the men involved. A special project or job where you and he do not naturally come into contact may ease the situation. And in some cases, time may improve the situation.

⦁ **THE PESSIMIST**

Male or female, young or old, the individual who is excessively pessimistic is licked before he starts. Give him an assignment that is a little different, set up a goal for him to shoot for—and he is sure he'll miss the mark. Of course, his pessimism is a problem because it tends to minimize his performance. Sometimes, he even succeeds in wet-blanketing others on your staff because of his gloom.

Dealing with him is a matter of probing with questions like these:

1. Is this condition curable?   Experience with overly-tough assignments may be weighing him down. Lack of your personal interest or encouragement can leave a gap in his enthusiasm. Where factors like these add up to a pessimist, you can do a lot to ease the mental load.

But you may find an employee who hangs on to his pessimism regardless of what you do. In such cases, these points are worth considering.

2.   Can you keep it from spreading?   If you're introducing important changes, don't assign him to lead off. *Pessimism is infectious,* and he could use his to wet-blanket the entire proceedings.

3. Can he learn to live with it?   Some changes in his assignments may be inescapable. One executive suggests this shot-in-the-arm: "I know you're doubtful about how this is going to work out, Tom—but then don't you always do about twice as well as you expect to?"

Fortunately, optimism is infectious, too.

⮑   **THE OVER-OPTIMISTIC SUBORDINATE**

Optimism is usually a virtue—except when it is so excessive it blinds the individual to the facts or reality of a situation. For some people, optimism is an escape hatch from failure. Errors are shrugged off, not mended. "Things could be worse," he points out.

Behind over-optimism may be a considerable degree of irresponsibility and immaturity. In attempting to modify his viewpoint, plan a continuing campaign:

1. Start by putting solid ground underfoot. Stress the importance of each of his assignments at the outset—plus the necessity for success.
2. Tighten up on the reins in the course of his work. Have him report back to you on progress. And introduce intermediate deadlines.
3. Bring other members of your group into the act. When his slap-happiness interferes with their work, stand back; let them tell him the score.
4. Take your final leaf out of his book. Show him that you, too, can be optimistic: "O.K., let's look at the bright side—by making

sure there is a bright side, next time." And then go on to suggestions that will assure success.

⮕ DEALING WITH THE ALSO-RANS

For every promotion you make, there may be one or two people who have been left standing by the roadside. For every person who merits praise for outstanding performance, there are those who may have tried and failed. These people who never quite make it, these failures in the competitive race that marks the typical work scene, deserve attention because they can be helped to succeed.

Of course, some people may lack the innate ability or skill to perform at outstanding levels. But before you conclude that personal deficiencies explain their failure, look into these factors:

1. Did you motivate the employee sufficiently? Almost everybody would like to be promoted—but not everybody is willing to work for it.

Many people don't know what possibilities of self-betterment exist in the company. If your people are to improve, they have to see what specific goals are within their reach. Don't assume that the average employee knows the line of promotion. Tell him.

2. Did you define clearly the standards you use in deciding on promotion? In addition to knowing what the next higher job is, the employee must understand what qualifications he needs.

This factor is important, both in preparing people for possible promotion, and in explaining to the also-ran why he didn't get the job. If you've never told him the standards, his disappointment at not making the grade can turn into anger at you, for not giving him guidance.

3. Have you suggested to your employees study possibilities that would qualify them for advancement? A highly-skilled subordinate may put himself in line for promotion simply by spending a few evenings a week at a vocational school. Your people may look to you as the one with the experience and judgment to make such recommendations.

4. Have you taken steps to give your people additional training on the job? A Grade B mechanic might need just a half-hour's instruction a week from an old-timer, over a period of several months, to put himself in line for promotion to Grade A mechanic.

⟡ HANDLING THE "JOHN ALDEN SYNDROME"

You may have an employee like the historical John Alden, who hesitates to speak for himself or on his own behalf.

Instead he'll tell you, "Bill Jones thinks thus and so, . . . or Tom Blakely says we ought to. . . . " His failure to advance his own views or interests can cost you information, ideas, and a valuable point of view. In addition, it creates a communications barrier between him and others.

To get him to speak for himself:

1. Tell him why you want his opinions. "It's important for me to get everyone's views, John. That's the only way I can get a complete picture."

2. Coax him along. Frequently, he holds back because he's not sure of himself. Good antidote is to start by asking him questions to which he's likely to know the answer. Note his relative strengths and weaknesses in these areas:

- Facts. Giving information about his work usually finds him on firmest ground.
- Opinions. Making comments about other people's ideas for work situations is next easiest for him.
- Ideas. Here's where he needs most encouragement. Show him you like people who voice their views—gripes or otherwise; that you applaud suggestions, even if they don't pan out.

⟡ THE LONE WOLF

The loner may be a productive employee. Or he could be one you are just about ready to fire.

Either way, remedial steps might save a potentially good employee, or improve present performance. Many different factors can turn a man into a lone wolf. To start the de-isolating process answer these questions:

1. Is his loner tendency creating a problem? The answer may be *no.* If so, no action is called for. Or it may be *yes:* he's not cooperating with people he must work with, or he is not communicating sufficiently with you. If this latter is the case, you must probe further.

2. Was he always a lone wolf? Just check your memory; perhaps a comparatively recent development, such as difficulties at home, problems in his personal life, cause his craving for solitude. In some instances, a special competence may mean that his boss left him alone because he could go it alone. However, instead of building self-reliance, this move may have further built up his need for a protective shell.

At any rate, further your understanding of the situation by trying to pin down the reason for his behavior.

3. Can he be given assignments that minimize the effects of his tendency? If in your opinion, the lone wolf, because of his personality makeup, really prefers isolation, your most effective move may be to give him assignments where he will be operating independently. For example, it can be an advantage to you if a subordinate with this preference took on assignments at remote places, after hours, and so on.

4. Can a low-pressure program of interpersonal contacts improve the situation? You may decide that your problem child is a shy sheep in lone wolf's clothing. Accordingly, he would like to mix with the others, but finds this difficult to do. You can help by establishing a bridge to others on your staff; or in arranging at first, minimum contacts with some of your friendly nonaggressive people, then building the contacts when you see he's beginning to respond.

5. Should you consider a transfer? It's seldom that even the worst, the most extreme representative of this type is fired. But where the loner's tendencies are a definite handicap to job achievement and all your efforts are in vain, you may be able to do both yourself and another executive a good turn by arranging a transfer to another department, where his behavior will not represent a handicap.

➲ **THE SNOOPER**

This individual is a problem because he goes to ridiculous lengths to get into the act. Anytime something is going on, he feels he must thrust himself into it—whether advisable or not. He may have a neurotic need for recognition, and may be more sinned against than sinning.

Consider:

1. What makes him run? *Ambition?* Does he barge in to get the chance to show how much he knows? Here your problem is to learn why he takes this particular tack. Has he been denied opportunities otherwise open to the rest of the group? Been brought into group decision-making as much as the rest?

- *Exclusion?* His workplace may be the answer. Or it may be the nature of his work. He may, for example, perform a task that's finished later than the rest. Does this put him out in the cold? Relocating him may be the answer.

If his ostracism is a "personal" matter, you have a tougher nut to crack. But whatever the cause, you'll want to make certain that the group isn't withholding information or work that prevents the problem child from doing his job properly.

2. Does he crave recognition?   In many cases this person needs the feeling that he is important—at least as important as other people around. The more you can do to build his self-image, the more you make him feel that he's a respected member of the work group, the more you can ease his compulsion to barge in. Accordingly, recognize his performance; show him that you approve of his accomplishments. Praise his outstanding achievements.

➜ THE IRRESPONSIBLE EMPLOYEE

Often he's a youngster, new to the world of work. But he also may be an older, but immature person. Because of his attitude, a situation that seems obvious to you may be obscure to him. He may become involved in important matters, without realizing the consequences.

The typical job, with requirements for promptness, conformity with working rules and policies, obedience to instructions, may seem unnecessarily confining and "an establishment approach" that demands to be flouted. If the problem of his irresponsibility is not too extreme—

1. Give him the big picture.   As clearly as possible, preferably in the early days of induction, acquaint him with the history, traditions, objectives of the company, the department, his job.

The older, mature worker understands the general pattern of his job life. But the youngster often has no experience on which to draw. Perhaps curiosity may bridge the gap. At any rate, encourage questions about company operation, product, marketing, and so on.

2. Go out of your way to give the reason why.   That goes for whatever comes up: work, instructions, pay rates, inspection procedures, schedules, and so on. Keep your explanations clear and nontechnical. Don't hesitate to repeat them at a later date, if you are not sure he has grasped the point. Assign an experienced dependable worker as an official or unofficial "buddy." A friendly relationship with a fellow employee can help eliminate a certain amount of the immature employee's recalcitrance, and a well-informed sidekick can answer the many small questions that may arise. The individual can pick up a good deal from such a buddy in terms of facts and attitude.

Use care in selecting the partner. He should have understanding and tolerance.

3. Treat him as an adult. Particularly in the presence of others, don't talk down, show any impatience you may feel. They may take their cue from you and begin making life unbearable for the individual. Even when you deal with him in private, don't let your interest in his life appear patronizing.

4. Give him responsibilities and hold him to them. Do this gradually. Don't overburden him with responsibility. He may seem to be eager to take on big assignments; but in part the explanation may be his intention not to take them too seriously.

Test him out step by step. Check up regularly on the assignments that you give him. See that he follows instructions closely.

5. Keep his achievements and goals constantly before him. This individual is likely to be easily discouraged by failures. Emphasize what he has accomplished, and show him how he can turn his abilities to further self-improvement or advancement.

6. Utilize his energy. Suiting the challenge to his capacities is an important aspect of developing this individual. It can be particularly effective to use his energy capabilities for the benefit of the group as a whole. Success here can make him both a hero and a permanent member of the group. Keep him occupied. Help him to continue to learn. Use his curiosity and maintain his interest by a variety of assignments. This will also help him develop a broader understanding of his job responsibilities as a whole.

THE SUBORDINATE WHO IS NEVER WRONG

He says it, often: "Of course I admit when I'm wrong—but I'm never wrong."

Even if he doesn't say it, that's his feeling. Generally his braggadocio is a cover-up because he has a hard time holding on to his self-confidence. He may have been over-criticized or over-praised in childhood.

Consider these steps in your general dealings with him:

1. Let him know it's no crime to make mistakes.
2. Avoid unnecessary criticism.
3. When criticism is in order, don't criticize *him* but the *method* he used.
4. Build his self-respect by appropriate praise when he does an outstanding job; then he will have less need for a phony defensive shield.

THE OVERLY DEPENDENT INDIVIDUAL

He or she is thought of as a clinging vine. The strange fact is that often he is a capable individual, and he clings not because he needs help, but because he needs reassurance.

It takes time to get the unsure or overly cautious employee to stand on his own feet. But if you want him off yours—

1. Go light on the criticism.   It isn't so much that you have to pull your punches. It's just that a small amount will have a strong impact. Usually he overreacts, magnifies a correction into a major dressing down.

2. Watch him for signs of trouble.   If he does get into a tight spot that he can't handle, be ready to assist as soon as possible. This doesn't necessarily mean that you take over. When he gets into deep water, the best help you may give him is to help him figure his own way out.

3. Keep feeding the ball back to him.   When he comes to you for help prematurely, without trying to cope on his own, help him see that he does have the answer: "How do you think we should handle it?"

4. Can you consult him?   To reinforce his own self-confidence, let him participate, where appropriate, in discussions of problems and so on, and from time to time consult *him* on decisions *you* have to make when you can use his help.

WHEN HE'S TOO POPULAR

Social lions are great in the living room, but hell on the work scene. Occasionally, the executive is confronted by the problem of dealing with an overly popular subordinate. What with phone calls, visits by friends from other departments, there's a constant social merry-go-round. Usual result: performance goes down as his disturbance rating goes up. To exercise some reasonable control:

1. Check your own performance first.   If you are extending special privileges—such as long or excessive number of personal calls, you may have to change the signals and make him live up to the same rules as others do.

2. Avoid a frontal attack.   Direct criticism of his misplaced social activity might leave you open to the charge that you are "butting into my personal affairs."

3. Focus on his job performance.   It is appropriate for you to call the turn if his activities affect the work. These points apply:

- Disturbance with the work of others. Even if they don't complain, your observation is enough to bring action—and warning.
- Slapdash work, to make up for lost time. This gives you an opening to discuss the quality of his work and the need to perform up to standard.
- Low-quantity level. Be specific in discussing his below-standard performance. Refer to a recent job in which he ran short of expected goals.

⮕ THE ALCOHOLIC

Of all the problem employees you may be called on to deal with, an alcoholic will be most difficult. According to Dr. J. J. Walsh, Medical Director of Union Carbide, "Some of our best employees are alcoholics." And it's heartbreaking for the executive to see an individual of outstanding ability victimized by an addiction that destroys him both as a functioning employee and as a human being.

One of the reasons that makes alcoholism so difficult to deal with is that two things tend to hide the problem:

- Alcoholics tend to become extremely ingenious in covering up.
- Social drinking is an accepted aspect of our society, and it isn't easy to make a clear separation between the social drinker and the one who is a victim of the bottle.

When you are faced by a suspected case of alcoholism, it is the height of wisdom to think through your actions, if any. To clarify some of the aspects of the problem, consider the following information and insights developed by medical and psychological experts.

A booklet, *The Alcoholic Employee*, put out by Alcoholics Anonymous, states that there is general agreement on these basic facts—

1. There is a distinction between the heavy drinker and the alcoholic. While the former may overindulge on occasion, he does not let alcohol disturb the pattern of his living or obscure his objectives.

2. Once a person crosses the invisible border line between social drinking and compulsive drinking, he is never going to be able to drink normally again. A single drink may be enough to start the alcoholic on his merry-go-round. Alcoholism may be arrested, but it can never be cured.

3. The only way for an alcoholic to cope successfully with his unique problem is to abstain completely from even the smallest quantity of alcohol in any form.

Alcoholism, a pamphlet issued by the U. S. Department of Health, Education, and Welfare, suggests indications of alcoholism:

"One of the more obvious early signs of a pre-disposition to alcoholism is that the individual drinks more than is customary among his associates and makes excuses to drink more often. This is an indication that he is developing an insistent need—or a psychological dependence—on alcohol to help him escape from unpleasant worries or tensions.

"As the condition progresses, he begins to experience 'blackouts.' He does not 'pass out' or become unconscious, but the morning after a drinking bout he cannot remember what happened after a certain point. If this happens repeatedly or after taking only a moderate amount of alcohol, it is a strong indication of developing alcoholism.

"As his desire for alcohol becomes stronger, the alcoholic gulps, rather than drinks, his beverage. He senses that his drinking is getting out of hand and he starts drinking surreptitiously so that others will not know how much he is consuming.

"Finally, he loses control of his drinking. After one drink, he feels a physical demand so strong that he cannot stop short of intoxication. Suffering from remorse, but not wanting to show it, he strikes out unreasonably at others. As he realizes that he is losing the respect of his associates and hurting his loved ones, he tries to stop or drink moderately, but he can't. He becomes filled with discouragement and self-pity and tries to 'drown his troubles' in more liquor. But his drinking has passed beyond the point where he can use it as a way of coping with his problems, and he is faced with the disease of alcoholism."

To act constructively when dealing with an alcoholic employee consider these guidelines:

1. Don't act until there is work interference. While this point applies to problem employees in general, it has particular cogency in relation to a heavy drinker.

2. Develop a realistic view if he has an off-the-job drinking problem. Occasionally, an executive is contacted by a wife or other member of an employee's family with the information that his drinking is a problem at home. As much as you might like to help, it is unwise to do so in your professional capacity. Any moves you make could justifiably bring the accusation from the employee that you are meddling in his personal affairs. This point must be made clear to the relative, even while you are conveying your interest and sympathy.

3. Avoid moral judgments. The least effective and most damaging action a superior may take is to criticize an employee's drinking. The perfectly commonsense statement, "You have just got to stop drinking. You're ruining your health and your career," will be completely useless. This point is clarified when you—

4. Understand the psychology of the alcoholic. There's no point in telling an alcoholic that he is ruining himself for one of two reasons. One is that he won't believe you, no matter what the circumstances are. The other, deeper reason, is that often he is drinking for precisely that reason. It's *because* drinking is in some cases a form of slow suicide that the individual is an alcoholic. He seeks self-obliteration in a limited way, just as the suicide seeks the ultimate permanent form.

Some authorities feel that alcoholism is physiological, that is in its later stages the body develops a need for alcohol that must be satisfied in the same way a starving man must have food. This concept explains why the strongest arguments become meaningless to the alcoholic. He almost never has sufficient will-power to stop simply by wanting to.

5. Make your approach nonthreatening. The most effective thing you can do when you approach the subject with the individual is to do so on a nonaccusatory basis. You may not be able to get him to stop drinking. You *may* be able to persuade him to take some action that may help. If you can, make a specific suggestion. You may want to suggest that he see the compay doctor or psychiatrist, or other agency that you know about.

The Alcoholics Anonymous groups have a good record of rehabilitation. But perhaps the employee will refuse to accept your recommendation that he seek help from any source that is so easily identi-fied, since he may not be willing to see himself as an alcoholic. For this reason, the visit to a doctor or psychologist may be a more prac-tical suggestion from you.

Nevertheless, it's helpful to know that most large communities have alcoholism information centers operated by volunteers affiliated with the National Council on Alcoholism. These centers provide informa-tion about the problem, have resources for limited support or coun-seling, and can make referrals to doctors, psychologists, clergymen, family agencies, and hospitals in the community.

Most large companies have sufficient experience with the problem of alcoholism to have both a policy and a tested procedure for dealing with the problem. It would be wise for you to check with your superior or appropriate person in Personnel to get their recom-mendations in dealing with this type of problem individual.

⊃ EMOTIONAL FIRST AID

It can be an upsetting experience: one of your subordinates displays emotional disturbance. It may either be a fit of crying, a prolonged or intense display of anger, a low mood verging on depression.

The following approach is based on suggestions made by the pro-fessional staff of BFS Psychologist Associates of New York City.

Of course, you don't want to play amateur psychologist. If the behavior displayed is extreme, what's called for is immediate medical assistance. However, if the emotional storm is within normal limits—such as reasonably justifiable anger or tears, there are steps that you can take to help matters. What you do will vary, depending on the nature of the problem.

1. In case of crying or other similar behavior:

   a. Show your serious concern to the individual. Make clear your desire to help.

   b. Take her to a private place, your office for example, as unob-trusively as possible.

   c. Give the employee a moment or two to compose herself. Avoid exerting pressure, to make it clear that you're not an-noyed by the situation.

   d. Ask, "What's wrong?" If the employee doesn't wish to re-spond, however, don't press the point.

   e. Ask, "How can I help?"

f. When the tears have subsided, give the employee the choice of returning to work or leaving early, if it's in the afternoon.

g. If the employee explains what's wrong, listen; offer sympathy. If it's a complicated or highly personal matter, don't prescribe. You may want to suggest that she seek professional guidance.

2. For an outburst of anger:

a. Face the individual firmly and assert your authority.

b. Show a strong mien. Be firm without showing anger. Make clear your intention to have things cool down before any action is taken.

c. Isolate him by taking him off to a corner or separate room.

d. If you don't know, ask the reason for his upset.

e. Listen to his complaint. Generally this will help calm him down.

f. Be prepared to deal with his shame or sheepishness. Usually, there's a revulsion of feeling in which the individual is sorry for his display of temper. Alleviate this feeling by assuring him that it's "just one of those things."

g. If he needs counseling or guidance, suggest that he see a professional person. Preferably, don't use the phrase, "See a psychiatrist," or anything similar. This suggests that you've made a diagnosis of abnormal behavior, which probably will be resented.

3. In case of despondency:

a. Approach the individual and show your concern.

b. Isolate the individual.

c. Ask for the reason for his feelings. If this confidence is refused, don't press the point.

d. Show your friendliness and desire to help.

e. If the individual begins to cry, don't interfere. Weeping in this case might be a desirable alleviant.

f. If the upset suggest serious causes, recommend that the individual seek professional help or guidance. If your company has a medical department, leave it up to the nurse or doctor to refer the employee to proper channels.

In all cases where there may be some kind of reaction from other people, talk to them to make sure that they keep their curiosity under wraps. As far as others are concerned, try to smooth over the situation as quickly as possible to help bring things back to normal.

⮕ THE CARELESS EMPLOYEE

"The employee was careless."

The statement is often used to explain an error or accident on the work scene. But seasoned executives know the "carelessness" designation is a coverup, rather than a diagnosis.

The trouble with attributing mistakes or mishaps to carelessness is that it automatically puts the problem out of bounds.

It is practically impossible to cope with carelessness—as such.

Experts of the Institute of Scrap Iron & Steel have analyzed "carelessness." They found it to be a catchall term, covering many forms of failures. Through their analysis, they revealed that many of the specific faults that hide behind the carelessness designation *can be* dealt with. Here is the list of possible employee faults disguised by the term "carelessness":

( )   He didn't follow instructions.
( )   He didn't follow rules and regulations.
( )   He didn't use safe work methods.
( )   He didn't follow standard procedures.
( )   He didn't pay attention to what he was doing.
( )   He didn't foresee an action or movement.
( )   He didn't wear personal protection equipment.
( )   He didn't think ahead and plan his actions.
( )   He didn't consider the consequences of his own actions or the action of a machine or equipment.
( )   He didn't know his own physical capabilities or limitations.
( )   He didn't have the physical fitness necessary for the work.
( )   He didn't have the skills necessary for the work.
( )   He didn't know the limits of strength of materials.
( )   He didn't know the properties or actions of chemicals.
( )   He didn't use tools or equipment properly.
( )   He didn't anticipate safety or health requirements.
( )   He didn't use good sense.
( )   He didn't look.
( )   He didn't think.
( )   He didn't have a good safety attitude.
( )   He didn't care about the consequences.
( )   Other.

The value of the list is that, unlike "carelessness," most of the items suggest remedies. For example, the man who "doesn't follow instructions" can be asked *why* he didn't. Weren't they clear? Any development interfere with following the original orders? Could he have prevented the failure by informing you of unexpected changes? And so on.

9. Dealing with Interpersonal Problems

"Among the touchiest, most explosive problems an executive must face," says Lee J. Smith, president of Tri-Tex Advertising, of Dallas, "are those dealing with attitudes, values, or habits of subordinates."

What's referred to here are situations that arise on the work scene that cannot be dealt with on a simple matter-of-fact basis. For example:

A valued employee tells you he's leaving for another job.

You must fire a subordinate.

An employee complains to you about the offensive body odor of a neighboring worker.

Problems of this type can tax an executive's understanding of people, and his resourcefulness in developing satisfactory solutions. In the pages ahead, you'll find some of the most challenging interpersonal situations that turn up on the work scene, and suggestions for dealing with them.

➜ WHEN AN EMPLOYEE SAYS, "I QUIT!"

When a valued employee unexpectedly tells you he plans to resign, there may be a good deal at stake in your reaction. Consider these points:

1. Decide what the employee really wants. Harold Ickes, Secretary of the Interior under President Roosevelt, used to "quit"—again and again. "Mr. President," he'd say, "I've got to leave." To which the President would reply: "Now Harold, what is the matter?" Roosevelt sensed that Ickes didn't really want to leave. What he wanted was a sympathetic ear.

The good executive follows Roosevelt's example. He listens to the words the employee says, and looks for the meaning behind him.

Of course, there are some employees who talk about quitting, when they really want a raise. Here are some of the other gambits that are used:

"I have another job and I'm giving you notice."

"I'm thinking about leaving."

"I'm just not happy. Perhaps I ought to leave."

Each of these speeches means something different. The first is final. The last is so tentative, it's obvious this employee can be made to stay—if you want him.

2. Decide if you want to keep the employee.   There's a natural response you must make when someone says, "I want to walk out." The executive tends to object—and perhaps he shouldn't.

If you believe the employee is serious about leaving, mentally review the record, decide on the spot if this is a valuable employee. If he's not, clearly you shouldn't try to keep him. A certain amount of turnover is healthy, brings in new blood. A quit in some cases can be a desirable development.

3. Get the employee's story.   When an employee walks in and says he's through, ask yourself, "Is there something causing a problem in this man's work situation?" Maybe it's going to affect other men under your supervision. Maybe it already has.

How do you find out? By encouraging the employee to talk freely. You want him to tell his story. That story may suggest what's gone wrong. It certainly will suggest lines of questioning.

Needless to say, the executive has to be careful that nothing the employee says elicits argument or criticism. You must be a fact finder in this situation, not a judge.

4. Get the "picture."   Let's say the employee has told you his story. But your mind's been racing: thinking of what another employee let slip last week, what one of your fellow managers said, and so on. What you're doing is seeking the real reason for this employee's desire to leave. A quit may be a complicated thing. Experienced executives find that employees who say they're quitting for one reason may have different, more basic reasons.

You can find the deeper reasons by tactful questioning after the employee tells his story. And, perhaps, the employee's statement suggests questions to be asked of the employee's co-workers, one's own colleagues, Personnel, if need be.

5. Decide how far to go.   Based on what you learn, you decide whether the employee is serious about leaving or just wants some handholding—or a raise.

You may want to offer inducements. *But watch out.* Don't make unrealistic promises that only kick back. Regardless of how good a man is, it's wiser to let him go than to make efforts to keep him that you'll regret later on.

In general, your moves are likely to take you in three directions.

■ *Eliminate or alleviate a source of dissatisfaction.* "I just can't start at nine," a typist may say. You may want to permit her to make a change—start at nine thirty—keeping in mind that your reasons must be good enough to explain to others why you did so in one case, and are not bound to do so in another.

■ *Offer reassurance.* In some cases, an employee may actually have better prospects in his present job—chance for a better position, higher wage bracket—than he's aware of. Make sure, then, that if an employee is dissatisfied because he sees no chance to improve his situation, that he's set straight—if it's in the cards.

■ *Offer tangible improvement.* It may be anything from special privileges to a raise (if deserved). But, again, there must be justice and logic in the move, to protect you from a parade of "quits," aimed at winning some advantage.

Finally, if you think a man is too good to lose, you may want to pass the question upstairs, let your superior in on the problem. There may be steps that he knows about, that he will feel are worth taking for a key employee.

➲ HOW TO FIRE

Of all the situations that confront the executive, the one that seems to put him through the wringer, that represents the greatest personal ordeal, is that of firing a subordinate.

And, strangely, this fact may be true even when the dismissal is fully justified or when the prospects for the reemployment of the individual are excellent.

When you must fire an individual, these steps insure that you are being fair, and minimize the possible adverse effects:

1. Use existing procedures. Your company probably has a specified method for dismissal. While the details of such procedure may differ from one company to another, generally the steps follow a pattern. For example, unacceptable conduct calls for—

■ A verbal warning informing the subordinate of what he is doing wrong and possible consequences.
■ A written warning informing the employee that the offense is continuing and that his job is hanging in the balance.
■ A final warning to the employee informing him that if by a

specified time the infraction has not stopped, he is liable to dismissal.

2. Back-up for your decision.   If you are on the point of firing an employee, it's desirable that—

- You have some kind of written record in which the history of the employee has been kept.
- If the employee is supervised by a manager on your staff, remind him that a dossier should be kept in case the decision is in question. The record should contain dates and descriptions of the infractions and corroborating evidence or statements, if available.

3. Try to make the dismissal interview constructive.   Occasionally, an executive fires a subordinate under the spur of anger or frustration. Generally, such off-the-cuff dismissals are undesirable. As a matter of fact, if the executive finds himself in a highly emotional state, it is wise for him to postpone action until a later time, when he can have his final conversation with the employee in a quiet and relaxed atmosphere.

To make the final discussion as helpful as possible, it is wise to avoid recriminations, accusations, or derogatory descriptions of the employee's performance. Any such opinion should have been communicated to the employee at a much earlier time in the "warning" phase of the dismissal. The actual firing should give the employee a chance to have his say. But for the executive's part, it must be a firm but friendly parting of the ways. If the situation permits, the executive may insure the constructive aspects of the action by—

- Commenting on the favorable or worthwhile aspects of the employee's tenure.
- Making suggestions as to possible future employment.

If the employee raises the question of references for a future employer, you may tell him at this time just what you feel you can say honestly, that will either help him get a job or at least not interfere with his job finding efforts.

➔ HOW TO FIRE AN EXECUTIVE

To begin with, very few executives are ever fired. (When they are, it may become front-page news. Remember the furor caused by the firing of the president of the Ford Motor Company in 1969?) One reason the top echelons are usually fire-safe is that while lower-level employees are still, in a sense, "hired hands," executives are "family." Other reasons: it's bad public relations; it hardly speaks well of the management that hired him.

However, executives obviously *are* separated from time to time. Here are some of the methods used to bring about a parting of the ways:

- *The Siberia assignment.* An executive is given an undesirable task, a come-down from what he's been doing. He usually takes the hint.
- *New assignment: "Find yourself another job."* Usually on full pay, and even without a time limit, the manager is told to seek another affiliation.
- *"We'll help you find something else."* Some companies retain guidance counselors, employment agencies or executive recruiters to help their undesirables get new situations.
- *The bypass technique.* This harsh method is sometimes employed when no top executive is willing to face the man and tell him he's through. Instead, his name starts being omitted from important memoranda; he's excluded from conferences; etc. Eventually, he catches on and starts job-hunting.

No matter what technique is used to break the news, even when the man is told directly that he's through, the art of face-saving has been highly refined. Devices like these are considered almost mandatory:

- *"He has chosen to resign."* For example: "Our vice-president is leaving us because he's always wanted to go into consulting."
- *"It's a matter of health."* For example: "J.D.s wife needs a change of climate, and so, reluctantly, we must accept his decision to leave. . . ."
- *"He's gotten an attractive offer."* For example: "Tom was offered an opportunity he couldn't afford to refuse. . . ."

One of the reasons for management squeamishness in this area is the identification, often subconscious, of the executive who has decided to fire, with the firee. "There but for the grace . . . etc., etc." However, much of the sensitivity about firing relates to an obsolete tradition. These days, executives tend to be professionally much more mobile, and with the aid of career counselors and executive recruiters, the executive job market is a fairly lively place.

WHEN BEAUTY BECOMES AN UGLY PROBLEM

The executive, told that a beautiful girl may represent a work problem, is likely to say, "It's a problem I'd like to have."

He probably is underestimating the magnitude of the complications that may arise.

It's said that beauty is skin deep. But that's deep enough to cause trouble. Executives face these difficulties:

- *Favoritism.* Justly or otherwise, they are accused of treating the Keen Kates better than the Plain Janes. And, sometimes, attempting to lean over backwards to avoid the digs, executives have been blamed by the superbeauties of unfair treatment.

- *Social whirlpool.* The beautiful employee becomes the center of a situation that may involve one or more ardent admirers, or one or more envious females. And it's even been known to happen that the presence of a latter-day Helen has caused upset even in the executive echelons, when a higher-placed official may be drawn into the emotional maelstrom.

At any rate, if you decide in favor of beauty on the job to the point of recruiting and hiring one or more, it is helpful to know what to do and what not to do to prevent the beauty queen from turning the executive suite into an overheated trouble spot:

1. Avoid the ridiculous. Don't try to keep admiring colleagues in line by adopting arbitrary rules of the "boys can't talk to girls" variety.

2. Build an invisible barrier. The executive who knows how to play it cool builds a sense of propriety into the working atmosphere. For example, horseplay or teasing on a boy-girl basis is kept within reasonable bounds. Or, if a girl must work overtime or come in on Saturday, she shares the work with another girl. (A press dispatch from Manila sometime ago described how a local executive, in an effort to keep excessive romance under control set up a rule prohibiting "overtime for attractive female employees." The press dispatch did not say how he was ever able to get any female volunteers for overtime thereafter.)

3. Apply the rule of reason. Appeal to the common sense of the girl who is too popular for her own good. Make it clear that the office is a public place. Conduct that might be perfectly proper at a summer resort or the beach is not necessarily acceptable at a desk.

- *Try to prevent explosions.* Of course, any relationships after hours and off the premises are outside your province. But when a situation is causing difficulties on the job, discreet action is called for.

- *Keep the conversation businesslike.* Make it clear that your concern is for the smooth progress of the work and the state of mind of others who may be affected. To emphasize the friendliness in your approach, you may want to use the "people are beginning to notice" line.

4. Final step—transfer or dismissal?   If your low-pressure, friendly efforts fail, if the consequences are becoming increasingly serious, you may want to warn the man in the case that if he cannot cope with the situation, someone may have to be transferred, even discharged.

Remember, under no circumstances, can the executive in such a delicate situation, see himself either as a censor or a wet blanket. A cardinal rule should be to make no move unless there is actual interference in the work of the department.

⮑ HANDLING EMPLOYEE FEUDS

When two of your employees are in conflict, the consequences can involve your entire staff. The case may even resound in the highest echelons of your company.

On the other hand, it's easy to distort differences between two individuals. A mild disagreement, even a quarrel, may represent a temporary state of affairs. People, being human, don't always like or respect one another.

However, when you become aware of friction between employees there are steps to take to avoid a widespread conflagration:

1. Should you act?   Even a violent quarrel may not signal a call to action on your part. It's not unusual for people under tension to let fly at one another with angry words. When the tension relaxes, the hard feelings go with it and often the feuding pair will repair the situation themselves and be thankful that no one has interfered, formalizing the trouble and making it more difficult to smooth over.

2. Think your way through.   Once you decide to take the initiative, give some thought to what you are going to do:
 ▪ It's important that you understand the reason for the disagreement, even though you will probably *not* want to judge the merits of the case, and exonerate one individual and find another "guilty as charged." (Of course, the assumption is that this is not a situation where one individual is bullying or victimizing another. In this situation, your intervention may be desirable at an early date, with the full weight of your authority thrown into the approach, if necessary.)

■ Keep in mind that your objective is to terminate the conflict, making it as easy as possible for the individuals to get back to normal without any scars.

3. The procedure you use.   With the preliminary steps taken care of, you want to talk to the feuders either individually or together. Which one of these two approaches you use depends on the nature of the quarrel and the character of the individuals involved. Then consider—

■ *Timing.* Delay may incubate the trouble, but overeagerness may be as bad. Again, the nature of the disagreement and the characters of the principals tell you whether they will be easier to handle the day after a flare-up or on the spot.

■ *Breaking the ice.* This may be the toughest part of the procedure. You may want to take up the problem head on. "Men, we have got a situation here that we'd better deal with before it gets completely out of hand. . . ." Or else, directly, "You both must realize how important it is for us to have a friendly atmosphere in the office. . . ."

■ *Third party?* In some cases, the presence of another employee not directly involved in the feud may help. This is especially true when he may have some information that will help clear the air.

■ *Place for the discussion.* Your choice of a meeting place may make things easier. An invitation to go out for lunch or a cup of coffee may smooth the way.

4. The agenda.   Once your discussion is under way, there are three points to be covered, preferably in this order:

■ *Areas of agreement.* If the quarrel hinges on differences of opinion, you may be able to point out that there are points on which the arguers agree.

■ *Areas of difference.* In many cases, if you clarify the nature of the differences, a basic misunderstanding may be found at the bottom of the hard feelings. In any event, spotlighting the differences will put the situation in better perspective.

■ *Means of ending the disagreement.* If possible, leave it up to the principals themselves to resolve the situation. If the argument is about some action or decision that must be made, a flip of the coin, a compromise by one of the individuals admitting he was wrong, or that the issue was petty, may do it.

5. Strengthening the bonds.   A well-set break in a bone often turns out to be the strongest section. In the same way, a rift between two people, after healing, may find them on better terms than ever before.

Frequently, such improved relationships happen as a natural result of the best efforts you have made. But there may be additional ways you can help. Any moves that show your goodwill toward both individuals to assure both that bygones are bygones, and that you have not taken sides or placed blame, will help mend the situation.

➔ HANDLING A COMPLAINT BY ONE EMPLOYEE AGAINST ANOTHER

A subordinate comes to you saying that a fellow employee borrowed a fairly large sum of money several pay days ago and now refuses to pay it back within the agreed time. Would you—

a. Tell him it's not your affair and refer him to a lawyer.
b. Call in the second worker and try to work out an agreement.
c. Hunt up the second worker privately and bawl him out.
d. Try a fourth alternative.

This apperently simple complaint raises several questions you would have to answer to make any move:

Are the circumstances described by the employee correct—that is, did he *really* lend the money?

Was there an understanding about the time within which the debt was to be repaid?

Why does the second employee refuse to return the money?

Once the facts raised by these questions have been verified, it's possible to act. What is essential here is a gradualistic approach. It is not unreasonable for the employee to look to you for help, but it is unreasonable for you to move in with the full weight of your authority. Accordingly, alternative (b) originally suggested is a wise opening gambit.

And since your authority really doesn't cover collecting debts for your employees, the ultimate move would be the suggestion to the lender that he may have to take legal recourse.

➔ WHEN A KEY EMPLOYEE STARTS THROWING HIS WEIGHT AROUND

One of your subordinates is a highly skilled man, who knows he can get another job for the asking and would be hard to replace. He has been taking advantage of the situation—coming in late, giving you arguments instead of cooperation, and even, you suspect, talking slightingly of you to other employees. Should you:

a. Recommend his discharge.
b. Close your eyes and hope for the best.
c. Appeal to his team spirit.

d. Warn him to get on the ball or he will have to go.

e. Try to find out what's bothering him.

f. Try another alternative.

Two of the alternatives above should be used in sequence. Start with (e); try to find out whether he's being annoyed, frustrated, or troubled by something in the job situation.

Eventually you might have to apply (d) if your efforts to win his cooperation fail. Not only is his recalcitrance lessening his value to you as an employee, but such undisciplined behavior is likely to affect the morale of your entire work group.

It goes without saying that early in the game it would be advisable for you to make plans for getting a replacement should this become suddenly necessary.

➡ HANDLING OFFICE PILFERAGE

Sums of petty cash and small stores of postage stamps begin disappearing from your desk drawer. Should you:

a. Change the locks and let it go at that.

b. Call your group together and issue a mild warning.

c. Keep a weather-eye open, snoop around, and try to catch the thief.

d. Try to figure out who the prime suspects are and give them individual, clear warning.

e. Try a fifth alternative.

Definitely avoid (d). Problems of petty pilferage are difficult to handle because in one respect, they're acceptable. There probably isn't an executive who hasn't taken a handful of clips or a few sheets of graph paper home to his kids. But once you get out of this relatively small and unimportant pilferage area, it's important to act because the problem may mushroom. In this case, start with alternative (b) above. Let your people know that there is a problem. Try to get their cooperation to stop it.

Certainly go in for new locks and any other move that will eliminate temptation. Finally, if a thief is caught, it's probably wise to turn him and his fate over to Personnel, since pilferage tends to be a company-wide problem and undoubtedly your Personnel Department has a policy on how to handle it. Needless to say, you must have a foolproof case before pointing an accusing finger.

➡ WHEN YOU GET A COMPLAINT ABOUT A NOISY EMPLOYEE

It may be a youngster who whistles—gratingly. Or it may be a would-be drummer who practices on a file cabinet. A variety of noisy habits may draw protests from other employees who feel put-upon. It's a thorny problem because you have to tell the nuisance he *is* one, without hurting his feelings over something that is essentially trivial. These steps can bring both quiet and peace with honor:

1. Don't be trigger-happy. Be sure that the noisemaker is a nuisance before you act. If the whistling or other habit does not upset anybody, there's no reason to clamp down. You've got a problem only if the habit upsets others.

But if the complaints begin coming in—

2. Blow the whistle. You can break it to the noisemaker gently: "Tom, would you mind killing the canary? Not that there's anything wrong with your whistling, but it is out of place here. . . ."

The light approach is best because the situation is not serious; but make it clear that you mean business.

3. Try to head off a feud. It's natural enough for the nuisance to resent the complaint. Usually there is no point in telling him who complained, unless you are sure there will be no ill-feeling. Best bet: make it seem like your own idea.

4. Make it stick. Once you've served notice on the noisemaker, your job is usually finished. But sometimes it takes repeated warning, even the promise of disciplinary action. This, of course, should be in proportion to the misdemeanor—usually mild.

5. "Gag up" the penalties. One executive solved this problem by levying a nickel fine at each infraction after the warning. You may adopt this approach or devise some other kind of penality that puts the situation in proper perspective.

➲ THE B.O. COMPLAINT CAN BE TNT

"Mr. Jones, I hate to bring up this matter, but . . . that new girl works right next to me, and she has such a bad case of body odor I can hardly stand it. . . ."

From time to time, executives get a complaint about the appearance, behavior, or other aspect of an employee from a co-worker. The culprit may be accused of smoking a smelly pipe, or using too much perfume. Whatever lies at the heart of the complaint, you're faced by a delicate problem.

Consider the "bad breath" problem. Contrary to the message of a TV commercial for a well-known mouthwash, the problem can't be handled by leaving the anti-bad-breath product on the offender's desk. Even less realistic is the expectation that the offender will welcome the attempted assist. You're in a highly booby-trapped situation. One wrong move and the whole works will blow up in your face.

The problem is usually intensified by the urgency of the complaint. As in the case mentioned above, Susie says, "I just can't stand it any more." And the fact is, the complaining employee may come to you under the pressure of strong upset—further complicating your situation. Don't minimize the difficulties of handling this type of situation. Then, consider these suggestions to help you think through the difficulties:

1. Check the charges. There's always the chance that the complaining employee is distorting the facts. This may come about either because of hostility towards the other employee, or an exaggerated reaction. For example, an employee may come to you and say, "I just can't stand the outrageous dress the new girl is wearing. It's okay for hippie-land but it's out of place in an office like ours— and it bugs me terribly."

On checking, you may find that while the new girl is wearing an unorthodox costume, it's within acceptable limits. Then the problem is to calm down the complainant and gently persuade her that her feelings are somewhat exaggerated. For example, you may point out that she's the only one registering the adverse reaction.

2. Figure out the course of least trauma. Once you verify the situation and feel action must be taken, your immediate objective is to act in a way that will stir up minimum fuss.

Don't underestimate the sensibilities of the individual involved. Even the best-natured person will resent being told of his personal deficiencies. It's not easy for anyone to accept the fact that he or she is guilty of unknowingly offending others.

Consider then that you may not be the best person to broach the subject. As a matter of fact you may seriously want to—

3. Let someone speak for you. Executives in the past have discovered that their most effective approach is through a mature individual from the group. For example, in handling the body odor problem, an executive went to one of the motherly and discreet people in the department and explained the problem to her. She agreed to talk to the offender in an informal heart-to-heart chat.

Another possibility: a good friend of the offender may also be an effective intermediary. In any case, the person who conveys the message must do it without any suspicion that *you* have initiated the action.

4. Avoid going through channels.   One executive *thought* he was taking the easy way out. He got the head of the Personnel Department to agree to talk to an engineer who was the source of trouble, in this case an overly free use of obscene language. The interview seemed to go fine. The technician listened while the Personnel manager delivered a well-reasoned lecture on the undesirability of obscene language in the hearing of the people who couldn't take it.

The executive complimented himself on his perspicacity. But the employee failed to show up the next day, or any other day thereafter. Once Personnel had gotten into the act, he felt a "big thing" had been made of it—and his resentment registered in the form of a quit.

5. When the problem can't be eliminated.   All that has been said up to this point suggests that your subordinate *can* eliminate the complained-of problem. For example, if it's something like body odor, bad breath, and so on—it's been assumed that intelligent use of soap, deodorants, mouthwashes, and so on, will successfully erase the fault.

But some difficulties of this category aren't easily dealt with. Where the difficulty can't be eliminated, you may have to think of making changes. One manager, for example, gave an employee of excessively sloppy personal habits a workstation next to an employee with whom he spent a lot of time outside. Or, a person whose appearance upset one employee was given an assignment in which she worked next to an individual with much less sensitivity to this particular attribute.

One aspect of the problem may mean it will be coming your way more often. We live in changing times with values and attitudes undergoing revolution. For example, language that might only be whispered in privacy is now trumpeted to mixed audiences from stage and screen. Accordingly, you may be getting complaints from traditional-minded older employees who find some aspects of the "new behavior" difficult to take. In a sense, what you'll be asked to do then is to help bridge the generation gap. You may have to work on both the "accused" and the "accuser" to get them to compromise a little.

10. Improving Your Own Effectiveness

The performance of the executive is a crucial factor on the work scene. The effect of the efficient, result-getting man is multiplied many times through the consequent activities of his subordinates. Another way of conveying the same fact: a 10% improvement in the efficiency of an executive can boost the performance of his department, division, or company, 20%, 30%, or 40%.

Improvement depends not only on doing things "better." Also involved is the long-range development of personal and professional skills and management capabilities.

For the career-minded executive, especially, self-improvement is the order of the day. The ideas in this section can make you more effective in your job, and can speed up career progress and development.

(The specific matter of optimum time usage by the executive as a means of improving effectiveness is covered in the first part of this section, starting on page 2.)

➜ HOW TO DICTATE

Most executives can do dictate letters, for instance. But considerable time can be saved by dictating other material—reports, long memos, articles for business journals, and so on.

Anyone who can speak can dictate. Practically everyone can develop a reasonable dictating skill sufficient to cut writing time by 50 percent or even more.

There's no mystery in how to go about mastering the dictating skill. These points can help you:

1. What to Dictate While almost anything that is to be written can be dictated, there are some types of writing that effect greater time savings by dictation than others. Reports, for example, are particularly worthwhile for dictation, since they tend to be lengthy; undictated they represent large investments of time.

Unsuitable for dictation are long lists of names or other proper nouns, numerical tabulations, and highly mathematical copy (i.e., where more than half of the copy is comprised of equations).

2. Girl or Machine The dictator may have a choice between a stenographer and dictating machine. Recent years have seen dictating equipment refined. Machines are lighter, operate more easily. Some companies have dictation systems where one dictates into a mouthpiece or telephone: a recording tape or other medium, in a centralized location, records the dictation, which is subsequently handled by a typing pool.

Regardless of the particular mechanism, machine dictation and dictation to stenographer have advantages and disadvantges. A comparison of the two is on page 152.

3. Getting Started Gather your information, background material, and so on, in advance. Don't start your dictation and be forced to interrupt yourself because you are missing a piece of reference material. Have available all the backup material you will need—if possible, in the order in which you will use it.

Make a rough outline. An outline has the virtue of giving a track to run on, a framework on which to build your final product. And, except for lengthy or complex projects, you needn't get involved in the kind of elaborate outlining that is sometimes taught in school. At a minimum, a number of words or phrases that give you a logical sequence of ideas will do the trick. For example, here is the outline that was used in dictating this article:

Introduction: Benefits
Everyone can do it to some degree—
a. What to dictate
b. Girl or machine
c. Getting started (after the preparation steps)
d. Common hang-ups and how to overcome them
e. Improving your copy
f. Reviewing your weak and strong points and improving your technique
Conclusion: By-product benefits.

4. Common Hang-ups and How to Overcome Them Discussions with individuals who have attempted to dictate material other than letters or memos reveal some common problems:

"Writer's block." Some people say that when faced by the need to start dictating, they freeze. This is similar to the paralysis that occasionally stops even the professional writer in his tracks. To counter this problem, check back and make sure that all your preparations have been made. In some cases, the feeling of not being ready to dictate may be the obstacle. Then, start! Throw hesitation to the winds. Don't worry about finding the "right" word, phrase or sentence. Plunge in!

"I can't get down to brass tacks. I ramble and digress." The solution here lies both in having and *following* an outline. If you find you're straying from it, go over it to make sure it covers your subject adequately. Then stick to it, forcing yourself to stop when you seem to be digressing.

"It's disconcerting to have a stenographer waiting for me to grope for an idea." Try using a machine; or, change stenographers; or make some disarming or humorous comment, letting your stenographer know that you don't expect to talk smoothly and incessantly. If you have not been doing much dictating, it is no disgrace to admit it, and to imply that your stenographer will have plenty of time to catch her breath while you gather your thoughts or grope for the phrase you want.

"I never liked gadgets, and talking to a lifeless machine is disconcerting." Try a stenographer. Or, the particular make or model of your dictating machine may be a poor choice for you. In today's market, one can find a wide variety of dictating equipment, involving everything from tape to plastic sleeves. If you are having trouble with a machine that you have tried, a trip to an office supply company will make it possible to test various types of equipment.

"I lose too much time searching for a word or phrase or even an idea." This is a common and major hang-up for many people. To overcome it, bull it through—put down any word or phrase that will get you over the hurdle, knowing that you will be able to improve the word or phrase or idea later on.

The important thing is to work for a *rough draft*, because once you have your copy in black and white, you have something to work with. The professional writer will often push on to complete his draft, regardless of how many word gaps or idea gaps there may be in his copy.

5. Improving Your Copy The greatest misconception about dictation is that you say it once and that finishes the job. *Neither* the dictated nor written copy is "right" the first time. Every potential writer will tell you that the *rewriting* is an essential part of the operation.

So consider the typed pages you get either from your stenographer or from the typist who has worked from your machine-recorded material as merely a draft, a preliminary version. What you should strive for is to turn your first rewrite into what professional writers call "final copy." In some cases, you may have to do two rewrites; that is, revise your copy twice before you have a final draft. It's in the editing or rewriting that you can eliminate any oral habits that are objectionable.

6. Improving Your Technique After you have tried dictating once or twice, review your technique. Use the above discussion of hangups as a kind of checklist to spot your weak points. Then try to improve your technique via practice. Even someone very much used to dictating letters cannot expect to undertake longer communications without some preliminary difficulties.

If first attempts are discouraging, try again, dictating material on

which you have a good grasp. Don't give up too quickly, because the rewards of success can be substantial. Repeated attempts can help you
score a breakthrough. Then, not only do you save time, but you're more
likely to undertake a long but important report with goodwill, even
zest. The quality of your writing will benefit from your new attitude.

● STENOGRAPHER VS DICTATING MACHINES: HOW THEY STACK UP

Stenographer

Advantages:

Useful rapport can exist between steno and dictator.

Can make corrections and insertions on the spot, and supply
quick readbacks.

Can be helpful in giving instant feedback to dictator (in terms of
reaction to wording, ideas, etc.) Can ask questions immediately if
something is not clear.

Disadvantages:

Usually works eight-hour day or less, and may resist overtime.

May tire after an hour or so.

If steno is absent from work and has not completed transcription
of her notes, chances are no substitutes can read her shorthand.
This means a delay until steno returns to work.

Dictating Machine

Advantages:

Doesn't complain, has no personal habits or traits that can irritate
you. For example, doesn't chew gum, manhunt or get long calls from
boyfriends.

Available twenty-four hours a day, and is tireless.

Some people are less self-conscious when they dictate to a machine.
There is no need to apologize for pauses or interruptions.

Conserves secretarial time, and can be taken along on a business
trip without precipitating office gossip.

Disadvantages:

Can lend themselves to corrections, but some people find machines
difficult in this respect.

Cannot supply a missing word or phrase.

If transcriber has difficulty in discerning some words or phrases
dictated, the dictator may not always be available to be asked.

Transcriber might feel it's a waste of time to listen to the entire
recording before typing it, preferring to take it down in shorthand
to facilitate transcription of corrections, changes, and punctuation.

➲ **ON BECOMING A BETTER LISTENER**

The average manager spends up to 70 percent of his time listening. But psychologists know that the average listener forgets about ¾'s of what he hears in a few hours.

What can be done? How can you listen more effectively at conferences, discussions, seminars, interviews? Dr. Ralph Nichols of the University of Minnesota has these suggestions to improve retention of what you hear:

1. Know what makes a poor listener. Mainly, it's the difference in time that it takes to say words and to think them. Even the most rapid speaker can think words several times faster than he can talk. So listeners tend to race ahead of the speaker, anticipating his words, and then "tuning out." Frequently, the listener's mind wanders until continuity is broken completely and key points lost.

Dr. Nichols advises listeners to use constructively the time difference between thinking and hearing. Evaluate what is being said. Is it supported with facts? Can you find a weakness in the presentation? Or use the extra thinking time to go back and review what has already been said.

2. Avoid distractions. Another common listener's fault is allowing oneself to be distracted. However, concentration is no easy trick. In addition to tight discipline, it takes *involvement*. You have to find a reason to want to listen—and stay with it. But look out for this common trap: you can work so hard at trying to listen and appearing to listen that you don't hear a word.

3. Don't "argue." You'll need to analyze your own emotional reactions, especially the "red flag" variety. This can be a major barrier to effective listening. Certain statements—those with which you violently disagree—can arouse you to the point where you feel you *must* interrupt to make an opposing point. And if for some reason you cant interrupt (you don't want to offend, or it's a formal speech), you likely will do so mentally and miss the words and thoughts that follow.

4. Listen selectively. The really good listener doesn't listen indiscriminately. He selects. He searches for what he can use— professionally or in private life. Whenever possible, decide in advance what you will listen to and eliminate topics that, for you, are of little or no interest or value.

5. Make notes. Few of us listen for listening's sake. The purpose of listening is to retain the important aspects of what's being said. In "formal" listening situations, such as a lecture, or seminar, listening acuity can be improved by note-taking, in two ways. First, the notes you make help put the ideas and information you're hearing into permanent form. And second, the process of note-taking itself, forces you to analyze what's being said, so that you zero in on the significant points and ideas.

Finally, it's been said often enough to require only passing mention here: we hear what we want to hear. The statement has pertinence because it pinpoints the motivational factor. If we are eager to get the opinions and views of a speaker, we tend to adopt all the proper listening methods automatically.

➲ FRIENDSHIP WITHOUT TEARS

The problem of friendships on the work scene have troubled many an executive. You can avoid the hazards and maximize the rewards of friendship by a better understanding of exactly what is involved:

First, realize the difference between two different ideas:

Friendliness implies a warm and sympathetic attitude.

Friendship involves intimacy and special consideration.

If you develop friendships on the job, you must—

- compensate for it by even greater efforts at friendliness with others;
- make it clear to your friend that he, like yourself, must be prepared to pay a price for the friendship. You have no choice but to lean over backward, since you cannot allow your friendship to interfere with your judgment on the job.

Then, to protect your friendships, show real friendliness to all your people. These guides can help.

- Show no favoritism for one employee over another.
- Don't accept friendly overtures from cliques. While it may be pleasant to be "in" with one group, it's likely to lead to your being "out" with everybody else. Try to avoid showing recognition, and hence, approval of cliques. A barrier between you and the nonclique people would become unavoidable.
- Show friendliness to newcomers and to those who have less standing in the group. This move boosts their morale and emphasizes that you play no favorites on the job.

Finally, to maintain friendships with colleagues or others on the business scene—

1. Don't be overly selective. It's not simply a matter of avoiding the accusation of snobbishness. More important: the need to make your friendships across the board for the fullest rewards and enrichments.

2. Act with a sense of the appropriate. This isn't a matter of a stuffed shirt concern with "what people think." For your own sake, good judgment must temper the contacts you foster.

3. Be aboveboard with the other person. Your motives, your real feelings toward a superior, a customer, or a subordinate, may be neither simple nor clear. If you have doubts about the motives of your friendly interest or feeling toward an individual, think twice before undertaking any social gambit. Nothing is as cold as a chilled friendship.

➔ FOUR KEYS TO PERSONAL EFFECTIVENESS

An analysis of individual case histories of successful executives suggests that four areas are keys to effectiveness.

1. Mental fitness. The capable executive, regardless of age, keeps his mental outlook, attitudes, and emotional tone at a constructive and useful level.

2. Personal efficiency. An ability to organize the details of his job and to use his energies economically is a conspicuous quality of the high executive achiever.

3. Physical fitness. Good physical health is a characteristic of almost all productive people. The health area is one in which an individual can help himself considerably. Advances in medical knowledge and technology have increased our understanding of the role of diet, exercise, sleep, and so on, in their relationship to physical well-being. Regular checkups and proper medical guidance will deliver considerable benefits.

4. Mastery of one's profession. Accelerating technologies, new types of business operation, mean obsolescence for the individual who fails to keep up with change. Stay on top of developments that affect your profession. Develop a knowledge hunger that will lead you to appropriate courses, books, seminars, industrial and professional meetings. Anticipate and capitalize on changes. Don't wait for them to threaten.

➜ ADJUSTING YOUR SIGHTS TO CHANGE

The executive, in addition to helping his people meet the challenge of change more frequently these days, faces the same challenge himself. To help yourself ride on top of the crest of the future—

1. Prepare yourself emotionally. For some people this may be easier said than done. But the man who regards the future with apathy, is likely to be steamrolled by it. The one who makes the effect to adjust will have the best chance of riding the future to new triumphs. Accordingly—

- Don't kid yourself and hang on to the idea that, "It can't happen here." Eventually, it *will* happen. The only question is exactly *how soon* and to *what degree*.
- Reject defeatist thinking and anxiety about age or capability. Attitude—not the calendar—determines "youthfulness' in this situation. And there is a pleasant surprise in store for many: some will find they're *even better suited to the future* than they were to the past.
- Concentrate on your professional assets—experience, skills, general know-how. These are the tools that can help you assure a place for yourself in a changing situation.

2. Learn how your company might change. Watching current events will suggest the broad outlines. However, some alterations will be unique to your company. There are two good sources for clues as to the nature of the changes that are on the way:

- *Other industries.* In some cases, what will happen to your industry has been foreshadowed in others. This is true because technological innovation moves through different industries according to individual patterns. For example, in some respects food processing production and selling will parallel changes that took place in chemical and oil refining years ago.

Ask questions like these: How will my company's products be produced in ten years? What basic changes will they reflect? What implications will these changes have for management?

- *Your own industry.* Stay up-to-date on developments in the companies that lead the parade in your industry. The things being discussed by the pacesetters may well give you clues as to what your own company will be doing tomorrow. And, of course, if your company has a Research and Development arm, perhaps some of these staff people can provide clues.

3. Prepare yourself practically. You have professional and family obligations, as well as a personal one, to prepare for the changes ahead.

Go back to school? Why not? Education centers in the 1980's will be designed to make learning a continuing process. The manager of sixty may very well find himself in a closed-TV center (classroom), sitting next to twenty-year-olds in need of the same information. Of course, companies will do a considerable amount of the updating in the education area.

Along with company training, the most direct solution may be as simple as taking refresher courses at a local university, or working out a systematic reading program. Areas to cover include both the technology of the products or services you deal in, as well as such skill-increasing subjects as report-writing.

Don't overlook conferences, conventions—and conversations. Discussions with fellow managers and executives, as well as experts in your industry, broaden your horizons and may provide you with specific clues as to what's ahead.

4. Management specialization. The day of the "generalist" will never be over. Companies will always need men with a broad understanding that cuts across departmental and functional lines. However, paradoxically we'll be entering an age of super-specialization. Sign of the future: some years ago, a single executive could take care of all his company's financial problems. Today the financial function is often broken up into a number of specialties, such as taxes, investments, fund raising, and so on.

The increasing technical content of management will see the innovation of new staff functions. Managers in production and departmental operations will be served by specialists in operations analysis, statistics, and so on. Purposes: to bring new knowledge from many disciplines to bear on operating problems, and for strategic planning.

5. Watch for opportunities of change. Examine each development that comes your way from the point of view of the new chances it gives you. Remember, almost every problem can be turned to advantage when examined constructively.

Finally, to ride the wave of the future will require a positive and active participation. You will have to respond to challenge and do your homework. No matter what the tomorrow will bring, the qualities of flexibility, energy, and creativity are never out of date.

➲ THREE KEYS TO JOB ENJOYMENT

The more you enjoy your job the better you do it—the better you do it, the more you'll enjoy it. It's a benign cycle you'll want to operate in your favor. Accordingly, consider these suggestions for increased joy in your job:

1. Use your job for personal growth. "My job is one of the strongest maturing experiences I've ever had," says one West Coast executive. "It enlarged my vision of people, of relationships, and of myself."

A biologist, head of a pharmaceutical laboratory, says, "The executive job with its many contacts with people, its complex situations, is like a growth medium in which the executive is steeped. If he doesn't grow, there's something wrong."

2. Increase the challenge of your job. Challenge. The word has gone through the cycle from "in" word to cliché, but challenge adds excitement and stimulation to a job. How do you add challenge? Three ways:

- Be frontier-minded; seek the new, the leading edge of innovation in your business.
- Seek to perform the standard part of your job at higher levels of excellence.
- Set yourself a special project, something *not* required of you.

3. Make your job or career your personal monument. Develop what Bennett Cerf, well-known publisher and TV personality calls an "edifice complex." The desire to build something of value and permanence in your work can represent an ongoing and exciting target.

➲ PUTTING THE MOST INTO YOUR WASTEBASKET

Many how-to subjects have titles such as "how to get the most *out of.* . . ." The wastebasket is a major administrative tool and to a large extent, the more you *put into* it, the greater the benefits you reap. Here are some golden rules of wastebasketry:

1. Take care of the physical details. Size, shape, and location of your wastebasket should reflect not only functional requirements but also personal performances. Obviously, the basket you use should be big enough for all you can feed it. And it should be convenient to your hand, rather than occupy a spot determined by the whim of your maintenance people or even your secretary. Some executives with limited capacity requirements find that a small, flat-sided basket works out well, particularly where it can be fastened to a wall bracket or a panel of the desk inside the knee-hole area.

2. Pinpoint the extreme cases. In your use of the wastebasket, two types of material pose no problem:

■ *Natural wastebasketables.* A mail order ad for a product of no conceivable use to you, written announcements of developments with which you are already familiar, fall in this category.

■ *Obvious retainables.* Weekly production figures that you keep on file, information you will need at a later date, require processing other than by wastebasket. The chart below can further help you decide on the wastebasketability of materials that lie between these two extremes.

For the Wastebasket	**To be Retained**
1. *Use and discard.* A memo announcing a conference, for example, can be tossed out after you've noted the conference date on your desk calendar.	1. *Reports.* Key periodic reports that fit into a series you use for comparison, etc.
2. *Extra copies.* You may be sent several copies of printed material. Where you need only one for the record, the others may be discarded.	2 *Items with a future.* You'll hold correspondence that contains: a. queries that require reply b. information you need for an as yet unmade decision c. ideas on which you'll want to follow up
3. *Unnecessary bulk.* Voluminous material of which you need only a summary or portion can be abstracted.	3. *"Evidence."* Letters sent you "for the record"—terms of an agreement, for example—are file material.
4. *Irrelevant material.* Circulars, form letters of no interest to you should seldom survive at desktop level.	4. *Reference material.* Manuals, instruction booklets, etc., for equipment or procedures in your area.
5. *Recorded elsewhere.* Sales figures that are posted on a centralized permanent record may be noted and disposed of.	5. *Carbons of your own memos, letters, etc.* These help clarify the record in case of misunderstanding, or qualify you for "credit," if due.
6, 7, 8, etc. Add your own!	6, 7, 8, etc. Add your own!

A common executive practice requires your examination. It's summed up in the question, "Should you use the other fellow's wastebasket?" From time to time, you receive material of no importance to you. Routing such matter to a colleague who may be interested can be of real help. However, occasionally this procedure becomes the means by which an executive evades a wastebasketing decision. Before sending along a letter, brochure, or memo to a fellow executive, clear it with your conscience.

➲ PREPARING FOR YOUR OWN VACATION

Your absence need not shut down your operation cold or handicap the staff you leave behind. To keep things moving when you're away, consider questions like these:

☐ Have you scheduled your own time off so that it will handicap operations least?

☐ Have your immediate staff, your assistant, and so on, been informed well enough in advance of the time you are going to be away?

☐ Have you arranged to tie up loose ends of important pending responsibilities?

☐ Have you arranged to notify those outside the company, suppliers, customers, etc., who should be informed of the time you are going to be away?

☐ Does your boss know when you are to be away?

☐ Will you be able to make satisfactory arrangements for a fill-in or an assistant to take over routine operations while you're away?

☐ Has your assistant or replacement been fully briefed for the take-over—

☐ (a) key jobs described?

☐ (b) critical equipment pinpointed?

☐ (c) manpower problems discussed?

☐ Do you want to leave instructions as to where you can be reached in case of emergencies (for your own peace of mind, as well as your assistant's)?

☐ Do you know when *your boss* plans to be away, so that you can settle crucial matters before *he* leaves?

➲ HOW TO SAY NO

An abrupt no is usually painful to the person to whom it is addressed. What is worse, it can sever a relationship, sever communications.

As a rule, a no is necessary in three types of situations:

- an offer of service from a subordinate
- a question asked for the purpose of getting information
- a request intended to produce a favor or benefit

If a no is followed by thank you, the offer of service shows the individual your appreciation and will usually conclude the exchange satisfactorily.

A no to the second query is usually a simple matter of fact.

But it's in the third instance, when you have to turn down a request, that trouble appears. For example, an employee asks, "May I have the afternoon off?"

You may have this thrown at you, followed by any one of a number of reasons—a visit to the doctor, special shopping, "personal business," an early weekend start.

Analyze the request and note the three possibilities:

1. The request may show a poor work attitude. You're going to say no, but remember that you're saying no to the basic attitude as well as the request.

Lay your cards on the table. Tell the worker you feel the request isn't justified, and show that the job rates more attention than it's getting. And since an attitude of this kind is usually built on a fundamental dissatisfaction, try to find the real cause and discuss it.

2. The request is justified, but because of the work situation, must be refused. Assume that the worker has a good reason for wanting time off, but his absence will mess up your schedule. Or the effect on the rest of your staff will be bad—what you grant to one, you can't very well refuse to others.

You're going to say no, but you want the worker to see it your way. "No, we can't spare you this afternoon," isn't very satisfactory. Try this:

"No, Mary, much as I'd like to, I can't let you go this afternoon, because. . . ." and from there on be frank.

Unlike your worker who has a poor work attitude, Mary is basically conscientious. When you tell her why you're saying no, she may even go back to her work with a renewed sense of importance—if your explanation plays up her part on the team.

3. The importance of the reason for the request isn't clear. Before saying no, be sure you understand the real reason behind the request.

Here's the same request that calls for two different answers.

a. Frances wants time off to go to the dentist because she has a severe toothache.

b. She wants to go to the dentist to have her teeth cleaned.

In the first instance, of course, you say yes. In the second, you probably say no, and after explaining why, suggest that she make an appointment outside work hours. But this is clearly a case where you have to get the facts first.

In general, the simple no, has the sting of a crack across the knuckles. *In all cases, no by itself is no answer.*

➲ HOW TO BE A "COMER"

"How am I doing?" It's a question that executives are asked by their subordinates. And for the progress-minded executive, it's a question he asks himself.

A series of questions about you and your job activities constitute a realistic self-audit that can give you an idea of how solidly you are progressing, and help you locate any soft spots in the road:

▪ Have you recently sat down to assess your knowledge of company policy and the reasons behind it?

▪ Can you cite specific instances where policy has changed in the last year?

▪ When is the last time you had to grapple with an ethical question in carrying out your responsibilities?

▪ Can you describe the traditions of your business?

▪ Your company has added new equipment, methods, etc. Have you stopped to think what basic implications these changes have for your job?

▪ The last time you made a comprehensive report, how well were others able to grasp what you were driving at? If they did poorly, was it because of lack of facts? Assumptions and impressions not identified as such? Incomplete examination of alternatives in light of overall effect?

▪ Have you broken any new ground in the past year, taken on new tasks? If not, why not?

▪ Did your company make more money last year than the present one? How much of the gain or loss were you responsible for?

▪ When was the last time you defended the organization against attack from within or without?

▪ How many proposals did you come up with in the last year for new products, procedures, materials, handling personnel?

▪ How many of your basic responsibilities do you still handle in the same way you did two or three years ago?

■ How often in the past six months have you asked why something is done one way rather than another?

■ When is the last time you were in the minority, defending an unpopular proposal in which you believed?

■ Can you recall occasions within the last year when you got upset about your work? If so, was it because something went wrong in an area you deemed important? Was it because somebody else couldn't see the value of what you were doing?

Naturally, this isn't the kind of self-test on which you can give yourself a score. For one thing, some of the qualities the questions imply are more important to your job than others. But wherever you had trouble answering, or your answer troubled you, you have uncovered an opportunity to sharpen your management skills and strengthen your potential.

➲ HOW TO HANDLE YOUR BOSS

You can ask the question, "What are good boss relations?" and come up with as many opinions as there are people to answer. To get insight into the ingredients of a satisfactory relationship, it's helpful to analyze some of the deterrents.

To begin with, relations can be *too* smooth between you and your boss. No matter how excellent a performer you are, a boss can make you muscle-soft by too easy acceptance of your ideas, incessant approval of your accomplishments.

Think back to your school days. Don't you feel most respect and gratitude toward the teacher who put you over the jumps, but in so doing developed your interest and capabilities in his subject?

An examination of many case histories in which both the manager and his boss agreed they got on well together showed these elements:

1. mutual respect
2. mutual approval
3. mutual stimulation
4. a more or less tension-free personal relationship

Why Strains Exist   Certainly, the logic of the subordinate-superior relationship itself cannot explain the frictions that frequently arise. Both parties have every reason to want a good relationship. What forces explain the contradiction? Several possibilities suggest themselves:

Difference in standards.   One company vice-president stated recently, "The president and I are at loggerheads. His opinion on a major policy matter was so unethical, it ruined my opinion of him irretrievably."

Unacceptable authority.   "It's extremely difficult for me," said the division manager of a plastics plant, "to take orders from a man I don't respect."

Feeling of threat.   "My boss thinks I'm trying to take over his job," reports the manager of a bank department. "Accordingly, the better I do my job, the tougher he becomes."

It's silly to suggest that the man who has poor relations with his boss is always "doing something wrong." Obviously, it's just as possible that the boss is at fault. Yet, you cannot change *him.* Fortunately, poor relationships can be improved, and good ones can be made even better, by the efforts of the subordinate executive. The aim is to probe the relationship itself.

What Can Be Done
1. Search for the roots.   The first step when relationships are unsatisfactory is to track down some causes. Many symptoms have standard origins:

"My boss is afraid I'm going to take his job." Whether the difficulty stems from an overly aggressive subordinate who actually has been thinking too big or from a supersensitive boss, the remedy is the same. It's up to the subordinate to ease off sufficiently to remove the element of threat. Get time on your side.

"My boss doesn't think much of my abilities." Regardless of the abilities in question, the subordinate has failed to impress.

To reverse the situation, action in two directions is necessary:
a. a review of past incidents that may have led to such an evaluation
b. development of ways to eliminate negative impressions and to build a more favorable evaluation

"I have hostile feelings I can't altogether cover up." It's common enough, and the last thing called for is a feeling of guilt. But analytical thinking can pinpoint and ameliorate causes. A grievance, real or fancied, may explain the hostility. "Once I got to thinking about it," reports one "cured" executive, "I realized that I had always resented my boss's snobbishness. He came from the right side of the tracks, and I didn't. Once I dragged that realization out into the daylight, I could properly ask, So what? I even realized it was my attitude rather than his that made the difference seem important. . . ."

In addition to healing specific ailing relations, you have other ways to deal with a tough-boss problem that can help make a poor situation good and an impossible one, bearable and constructive.

2. *Ask for the tools.* In some cases, the core of an executive's problem with his boss is simply that the superior expects a particular set of results, without being willing to provide the means for his subordinate to achieve the expected performance.

In other words, the superior says, "Here's what you'll do," without completing the plan by adding, "And here's what I'll do."

Specifically, the difficulties may show up in terms like these:

"I'm supposed to keep my people informed. But nobody tells me!"

"The boss needles me on output, but refuses to discuss maintenance schedules or machine replacement schedules."

The more strongly a superior presses for a given result, the more justification there is for a realistic discussion with him of the ways and means by which the result is to be achieved.

3. *Selective contact.* "My boss is unreceptive to new ideas," one executive says. Another complains, "My boss is too demanding." The explanations for poor relationships, as we've already seen, may range all over the lot. But they are based on the unsound assumption that the superior, unlike other people, is a monolithic, one-faceted individual.

Often an outstanding quality is singled out as the cause of the friction. But, like any other oversimplification, it hides certain facts. Every person, viewed objectively, has weak and strong points, attractive and unattractive features.

"My boss," an engineering executive reveals in confidence, "is unimaginative. Half the ideas he turns down are wasted, simply because he lacks the imagination to understand what I'm talking about."

But if the engineering executive is correct in his assessment, he ought to know the answer to his problem. Perhaps his boss is eye-minded rather than ear-minded. Accordingly, he ought to frame his ideas in the boss's own language. For example, rather than presenting his idea with a thumbnail sketch and minutes of enraptured prose, he might get further with detailed drawings, and step-by-step visual illustrations of what he has in mind.

Some people resist the idea of dealing with the boss in his strong areas because it seems to be "playing up to him." The issue is one of intent. Talking to a superior—or any person—in the language he best understands, is the way to facilitate the business at hand. It is not like seeking a special privilege or self-ingratiation for personal advantage.

The principle of selective contact applies in other areas. Suppose the boss is obviously annoyed by a subordinate's preoccupation with projects to improve work methods. A wise individual would reduce his efforts in that direction and back up his boss's efforts, for example, to work out a better cost-reporting system. By scoring successes in the latter area, he may eventually achieve better understanding and working relationships.

4. *Show "the real you."*   Naturally you want your boss to know of your virtues or successful performances, etc. How about your weaknesses? Should you hide them?

There are good reasons for *not* hiding them.

Knowing your weaknesses, your superior is in a better position to help you—to back you up in the areas of critical performance.

If you outgrow your handicaps with his aid, he cannot help being favorably inclined toward an improvement in which he has played a part.

The boss who has a real feeling for people (and most of them have, you know) wants to know the whole man, strengths and weaknesses both, rather than feel he's getting only part of the picture.

More specifically, if you can avoid rigidity and formalism in your communications, the boss at once gets a clearer idea of what he must do at his end to click with you.

In general, the strongest move is to use one's talents and resources to lighten the boss's load. Work with him, not against him, and he'll be *your* man as much as you're *his*. Out of this mutuality will surely come the productive, stimulating, tension-free relationship that takes an enormous part of the executive burden off your shoulders.

➲ PLANNING A SUPERIOR EXECUTIVE-SECRETARY TEAM

General rules can offer only rough guidelines. Every executive's relationship with his secretary is unique, because it involves two unique people. Nevertheless, some rules are basic and meaningful:

1. Hire for compatibility.   When you go about hiring or selecting your own secretary, you face the problem of evaluation. You judge the candidates on a number of key points: job skills, appearance, intelligence, experience, education, knowledge of your particular job activity, and so on.

Not likely to appear on any personnel rating sheet is the factor of *compatibility*—how well you and the candidate hit it off. But the fact is, it's crucial for good teamwork. The average executive will do much better to hire a less skillful girl, but one with whom he'll get along well.

Does this suggest that you favor your biases? Absolutely!

Don't misunderstand. This approach is not recommended for hiring in general. If you're the president of a company looking for a marketing executive, obviously a biased personal preference has no part in your choice.

A secretary is something special. Normally, the executive spends more time with his secretary than with his wife—and we're talking about the normal working relationship.

In the Loesser-Burrows musical, "How to Succeed in Business Without Really Trying," the audience is assured at one point that, "a secretary isn't a toy." Indeed, she's not. But she *is* a crucial status symbol. *You* are judged by *her* efficiency, appearance, and manner. An overly slick chick outside an executives door imparts an air of frivolity and pleasure-before-business. On the other hand, an attractive, dignified, efficient secretary signals a person of laudable stature.

In a literal sense, you must live with your secretary, in close quarters. "If you want to know a man, work with him" goes the old saw. For the secretary that goes double. No man is a hero to his barber. If he is one to his secretary, it's probably because she knows all about him and likes him anyway.

2. Try to understand her. The story is so old, it's got whiskers. But amazingly enough, it continues to happen, and happen, and happen:

The young executive, confident and dynamic, zooms into his office. "Good morning, Miss Train," he says, and sits down to his day's work. As the morning wears on, he vaguely becomes aware that there's something wrong with his secretary. He rings for her to give some last-minute instructions before going out to lunch. No answer. With some annoyance, he steps to the office door, and there at her desk is Miss Train sobbing convulsively.

He rushes to her side. "Miss Train," he says desperately, "what's wrong?"

Through her tears she stutters. "Everybody else sent me a card—or wished me Happy Birthday—and not a *word* from you. . . ."

There's no avoiding it: you must give some thought to the girl who works for you. You must find out what kind of person she is; what her interests are; what kind of life she leads on the outside; who her friends are within the company.

And you have to do this simply and tactfully, without seeming to pry, without getting too personal. If necessary, keep a record of her birthday (Personnel has this information); her hiring date (in some companies, this "anniversary" date is celebrated rather than birthdays); names of her family—husband, brothers, sisters. Make notes at the beginning of the year when you get your new desk calendar, so that you won't have the sad experience of Miss Train's boss. To what end? A birthday card, a birthday (or anniversary) lunch, here, certainly, it's the gesture itself, not the expense, that's important.

3. Give her "voting stock." In some areas, you must be autocratic in your dealings with Miss Friday. You give direct orders; you brook no questions about what you want done or how you want it done. But these areas should be relatively limited. For the most part, get your secretary into the act. Encourage her to make suggestions about procedures and arrangements that are within her area of operation and competence. For example, let her design the filing system for your correspondence, or the record of departmental expenses—if the business office has no uniform method. After all, she's the one who uses the material.

But further: in matters that are squarely within your province, but on which you'd like another opinion, try her.

Henry Jones is head of the collection department of a large Midwest department store. From time to time, he must write to customers who have rolled up large debts. Their letters in response to his requests for payment occasionally are difficult to interpret. He calls in his secretary:

"Anne, read this letter and tell me whether you think Mrs. X really means she'll pay within the next couple of months, or whether it's just a stall."

How far should you go in soliciting your secretary's opinions depends on two factors—you and her. If you can consult without abdicating, if she can advise without getting a distorted idea of her own importance, then the more the better, within reason.

The things to watch for are two:

Overdependency. Don't weaken your own effectiveness by using her as a crutch. One executive describes his plight:

"My ex-secretary was a bright, capable woman with a need for power. She started making suggestions, then recommendations, and pretty soon, she was preempting me in most routine decisions. Finally, I realized I had gotten myself in the situation where I scarcely made a move without calling Miss Lincoln. It was all my fault, of course, but eventually it became so nerve-wracking, that I simply had to have her transferred."

Inconsistency. It's generally inadvisable to set up rigid boundaries on job activities or job roles. On the other hand, even worse than rigidity, for rattling a secretary, is inconsistent behavior.

"A girl was in here just a few moments ago," a personnel manager explains, "practically in hysterics. Her boss kept changing the signals on her. One week he'd give her almost a free hand, the next week he'd play things close to his vest. He just wouldn't let her know what was going on."

You may not want to put it in writing, but at least get it straight in your own mind—the procedures you put in her hands, those you retain for yourself, and those in between, where you consult her before taking action.

4. Rule emotions out of bounds.   We're not talking about romance or love or an affair. But any stickiness, a tendency to become overly friendly, to make the relationship a social one, will undercut the secretary's usefulness to you.

Chester Burger, in his book, *Survival in the Executive Jungle*, points out: "By nothing more than the tone of your voice or the look in your eye, you can draw a line between you and your secretary which must not be crossed. . . . Your secretary must always realize that she is your employee, not your social acquaintance, however friendly you may be."

5. Use her as a bridge, not a barrier.   Marilyn French, in *American Business*, points out that a secretary may either aid or impede her boss's communications with outsiders, as well as those within the company.

Certainly a key part of a secretary's job is to screen calls and callers. Being closer to the work group than you are, she often can keep you in touch with developments through the grapevine that otherwise might never reach you.

But in order to maintain her as a constructive communications aid, you must instruct her, that is, give her directions as to who you will see and who you won't, for example; and make sure you don't put her in the role of informer.

There's a thin line between listening to the things she brings you from the underground and pumping her for more than she's willing to tell.

6. Feed her ego a reasonable diet.   You want to praise and encourage her, without overinflating her sense of self-importance.

In situations when she acts for you, you will want to back her up. This means, among other things, not to pass the buck. Don't blame your failings on her. A letter you've neglected to dictate shouldn't be explained by, "I guess my girl forgot to send it out. . . ." Even further, when she has made a mistake or slipped up, try not to string her up by the thumbs. When you do criticize, make sure to follow the traditional human relations injunction, "Criticize the behavior not the person." And as mildly as the situation allows.

➔ REMOVING OBSTACLES TO A GOOD RELATIONSHIP WITH YOUR SECRETARY

The behavior that rankles most painfully with the secretary is *neglect:* her boss's failure to say good morning or good night, his failure to observe the small amenities. These oversights can create her greatest job dissatisfaction. Three explanations account for the bulk of such instances of executive misjudgment:

1. Thoughtlessness.   Under the multiple pressures of executive life, amenities are easily forgotten. When the executive is preoccupied with thoughts of the new ad campaign, he literally may think of his secretary as a working machine, expected to deliver service, not to receive it.

2. Callousness.   Embittered or cynical, some men consciously take the stand that, "These girls are paid to do a job. Let 'em do it, and if they don't like it, let 'em quit. They'll get no head-patting or soft soap from me."

It must be admitted, however, that few girls of the Marilyn Monroe type suffer this particular indignity. It's usually the secretary who has already been hurt by lack of attention and insufficient regard, to whom coldness seems a particular affront.

3. Lack of communication.   "I'm not afraid of hard work," the secretary to a bank official says. "But the thing I can't stand is this feeling of being completely out of touch with my boss."

Some secretaries say they resent lack of contact with their superiors more than they would be disturbed by rudeness or sternness. Contactlessness grows out of the inability or the lack of desire on the part of the executive to communicate. It represents both a procedural and psychological hazard:

"My boss just refuses to keep me informed of his plans," averred one overwrought assistant to an East Coast real estate executive. "It gets to be so bad that I don't even know from one day to the next whether he's going to be in the office at two o'clock. He may be a thousand miles away seeing a customer. What am I supposed to do? No wonder I'm a wreck at the end of the day."

The positive aspect of "removing obstacles" involves all the elements of a good working relationship: a feeling of friendliness, mutual respect, open communications, and the kind of pleasant attention to her individual likes—from Christmas cards to birthday lunches—that make clear your appreciation.

➲ HOW YOUR SECRETARY CAN HELP YOU

"Happy is the man with a wife to tell him what to do, and a secretary to do it," says the English nobleman-humorist, Lord Mancroft.

You may or may not let yourself be guided in your career or your day-to-day job by the suggestions of a helpful spouse. But there's no doubt at all that your secretary is a major factor in helping you get things done on the job. And how you train and guide her in her job performance, can make a major difference in easing the strains and pressures of your responsibility.

Here are some guides to maximize the contribution a secretary can make to her boss's *joie de vivre* on the job:

1. Let her in on your worries—and your hopes.   When your secretary is privy to your worries, she can help offset some of your anxiety. It's not at all a matter of misery loving company. Rather, she knows the problem, the factors that enter into the situation. You gain a certain amount of reassurance in feeling that you have an informed person with whom you can discuss the problem and bounce ideas or solutions around. But balance this off by sharing pleasant anticipations about the department's work, growth, prospects.

2. Let her take over tasks you don't like—and that she can do. This does *not* mean buck-passing, or handing over the hot potato. For example, if you have to fire a girl in the department, it's your assignment, not one you can delegate. But there are many nasty little problems that come up in offices that secretaries can often handle more tactfully than the boss. For example:

A female employee in your group is going to be married. What should you give her as a wedding gift? Your secretary not only can discreetly discuss the subject with the employee, or one of her close friends, but can also do the shopping for it.

Or, you're miffed at the lack of cooperation you're getting from a supervisor who reports to a fellow-executive. You don't want to lodge a formal complaint. But your secretary, if she's on friendly terms with the offending supervisor, can act as a good-will ambassador to repair relations.

3. Let her screen nuisances and timewasters. In the life of every executive, some rain must fall. Good-hearted, but verbose people drop in to pass the time of day—and take an hour to do it. Over-dependent subordinates, seeking a shoulder to cry on, adopt the boss as an emotional parent. He is then expected to listen to and discuss highly personal matters—everything from marital relations to what to do about a hostile mother-in-law.

Then, there are salesmen, fund-raisers, community organization people—all deserving different degrees of time and attention. Screening her boss's callers is a vital function of a secretary. *But* you must take care that she performs this delicate function both efficiently and with finesse.

Your own public relations, as well as efficiency, is at stake. Never to be forgotten—and certainly to be learned by your secretary—is the need to respect the dignity and worth of every individual at your doorstep.

In almost all cases, it's the executive who supplies the cue. A secretary who is disdainful and arrogant, who gives the red carpet treatment to the people "who matter," and the back of her hand to the unimportant ones, almost invariably takes her lead from her boss.

Your attitude, even more than your instructions, will set her style of screening. If you show by your manner that you consider a salesman a worthy professional—even when he's making a cold call—she, too, will be courteous when she tells him that you're not available.

WHAT YOU SHOULD—AND SHOULD NOT—EXPECT OF A SECRETARY

"It was a revolting sight," an executive says. "I walked into this executive's office, and his secretary was massaging his neck and back muscles, presumably to 'relax him'. . . ."

The executive as Oriental potentate doesn't look too good to his peers. Yet, there are a number of small personal services that a secretary *can* perform—short of becoming a personal masseuse—that are acceptable and gratifying to the executive ego. For example:

Morning coffee, always permissible. When a visitor is included— "Would you like some coffee too, Mr. Smith?"—the atmosphere of pleasant relaxed work pace can be most enjoyable. Deskside lunch and dinner also fit in here.

Personal shopping—gifts for a wife, children, a business friend— can bring to bear both better taste and judgment than the executive may have, and also gets him out from under a chore.

Additional small personal services depend on the exact nature of the relationship, the kind of individuals involved. In general, it's a good rule to request no services that the secretary resents giving. For example, one executive almost caused a crisis by asking his girl to return a purchase made by his wife. The girl hated "returning things," and while she didn't mind doing a favor for her boss, she resented his thinking that this personal service was transferable to the distaff side.

➡ FIVE STEPS TO PERSONAL CREATIVITY

Everyone capable of thinking at all can produce ideas. Sometimes, all that's lacking is a systematic approach. Here's one that has stimulated many executives to creative thinking:

1. Problem directedness.   Don't start by looking for ideas. Instead, start by thinking over a problem or difficulty.

The problems should be written down, in detail, so that the mind has something concrete—words on paper—to work on. Any problems can be listed, for any obstacles or bottleneck can benefit from an apt idea or solution. But the number of problems that the supervisor thinks about should be restricted to three or four; otherwise, energies may be scattered.

2. Mind loosening.   Some executives limber up their thinking about the problems under investigation. Says a Toronto executive, "When I'm looking for a workable new idea, I tell myself, anything goes. I'll let my mind think about any thought I get, even if it seems unorthodox, contrary to all my experience, or just plain dumb."

3. Fact ingestion.   "It's true you've got to examine a problem to come up with an idea," says an executive. "But it's rare for a man to look at a problem and—presto—solve it. I have to go outside the problem first; research it.

"I had a materials handling problem," he adds, "and I went to a friend of mine, an engineer, for some advice. He told me about similar problems that managers in other companies were having. When I got home, I wrote down what he said, then put it in a folder which I marked SIMILAR PROBLEM—OTHER PEOPLE. By the time I wound up talking to friends, reading articles, I had six different folders. One was marked HISTORY OF MY PROBLEM, another: SOLUTIONS RECOMMENDED TO ME. And so on. The fact I was classifying everything kept me from getting lost in the data I was collecting."

4. Mental rambunctiousness.   When all the preliminaries are done, it is time for your creative thinking to start. This doesn't mean your thinking must proceed in a straight line. On the contrary. In many instances, the creative process finds you shuttling back and forth between the problem and various ideas.

But at some point, you take the problem in front of you and start thinking of solutions, ameliorating ideas, and so on. Questions like these can start you off:

What are the different parts of the problem?

Is any one of them the key to another part?

What can I borrow from another situation that will apply to this one?

What if I carry this to extremes? Could exaggeration help?

What's the opposite of the "normal" way?

5. Triggering the unconscious.   It sometimes happens that ideas come—and then have to be discarded. They're not the "right" idea; or, you're after a better one. Perhaps your unconscious can help.

You contribute little to this step—directly. You simply rest from any form of conscious thought about the problem by seeking recreation or sleep (if you've been working on the problem at home), or by thinking about other problems (if you've been working on it at the job).

If you have concentrated on the problem, and stored up considerable data, the unconscious is most likely to spring into action. That's the way we get "inspiration," the sudden idea that bursts into the mind.

One manager reports his success at stimulating his unconscious. He is so successful, in fact, he carries around a small notebook when he's idea hunting:

"I'd been having a tough problem meeting a specification. I'd tried everything: defined my problem, researched it, asked myself hard questions about it, even let my mind just roam. I got nowhere.

"I went to bed that night and was about to fall asleep—when the ideas began popping like firecrackers. I got up, went to my bureau, wrote them down on a laundry slip, and went back to bed. Five minutes later, I had to get up and write down another idea: on the back of a check. Within minutes I was up again: two more. I spent half the night looking for scraps of paper to write down ideas."

Many people find that the greatest discovery they make is their own potential creativity. The human mind is a tremendous idea machine—possibly the most underused resource in the world. With a minimum of stimulation and direction, we can all become that much-admired, sought-after individual—the idea man.

⮕ MAKE YOUR READING TIME MORE PRODUCTIVE

Most executives, busy as they are, need to read to learn about new developments in their fields. The main problem is: how can they read with greater speed, comprehension, and enjoyment? According to Norman L. Cahners, chairman of a Boston publishing firm, *the good reader isn't primarily a reader at all.* He's a detective, explorer, scientist, critic, and editor—all active, seeking roles. Writing in IBM's *THINK* magazine, Cahners points out that the effective reader wants information—*he uses reading as a searching technique to get what he wants.*

As Cahners sees it, reading is a kind of treasure hunt. The trick is to find one's way to the gold nuggets in the most direct fashion, and in the shortest possible time. Unfortunately, reading habits, as usually taught, aren't too helpful in this approach.

Cahners claims there is no point in telling a time-hungry executive to seek a relaxed posture in reading, or to insist on quiet or freedom from interruption. Most of a manager's reading has to be done under pressure and with constant interruptions. He has to read whenever he can snatch a few minutes.

Here are the author's ideas on how you can get the most out of your scarce reading hours:

▪ *Make a habit of casing a book or article before actually reading it.* Who wrote it? When? What are his qualifications? What is he trying to get at? How has he organized his material? Take a few minutes to answer these questions in advance, and you may find it's not worthwhile reading the book or article. Or, you may identify what it is you want to look for, what it is you want to learn.

▪ *Be impatient.* Don't wait for the meaning in writing to "come to you" through long meaningless paragraphs. Reading requires your active participation. *Go in and get the meaning.* Make a habit of opening the sandwich and getting at the meat. If you pick a dozen business letters at random, you will find that most of them are constructed like a daycoach sandwich—a thin slice of meat between two slices of spongy and conventional prose.

▪ *Organize what you have read. The reason for reading is to recall a useful idea later, when you need it.* The secret of retrieving an idea, according to Cahners, lies in spotting the dominant theme. The main theme serves as a magnetic field around which facts cluster in patterns like iron filings. Any method that helps you organize the meaning, will make it easy for you to rebuild the details when you need them later. For example, when you finish a session of reading, ask yourself, "What have I read?" Close your eyes for a minute and try to recall it.

■ *Find time to read.* Merely by trying harder, most of us can double our customary reading speeds without loss of comprehension. Paradoxically, the swifter your reading, the more effective it becomes. Another source of more reading time is to learn to read in snatches—such as on a commuter train. Cahners mentions that the great Methodist leader John Wesley, read history, poetry, and philosophy, mostly on horseback. If you can't read in snatches, try to set aside a specific part of each day for concentrated reading—ten minutes, an hour—however long you decide. The definite spot on the agenda is a way of saying, "There's a time and a place for everything. This time belongs to reading."

WHICH JOB COMES FIRST?

When you have two or more jobs to be done, which comes first? Essentially, what's involved is the establishment of a priority.

Of course, when the urgency of one project is obvious, there is no problem. But frequently the sequence in which to tackle a series of projects isn't self-evident. In such a situation, consider these four principles:

Principle No. 1: Do the easier job first
With the easy job out of the way, the executive can concentrate on the tougher one without worrying about the other hanging over his head.

Principle No. 2: Start the longest of equally easy jobs first when they must finish together.
This is the old lamb-chop-and-baked-potato principle used by the kitchen-wise housewife. She starts with the potatoes baking first, puts on the chops later.

When your requirements are such that all items must finish at the same time—as when you must make a shipping deadline—this principle is decisive.

Principle No. 3: When the products of both jobs are equal in value, do the short one first.
The virtues of this course include the following—

- With the brief assignment out of the way, the decks are cleared for you to go all out for the remaining item on the agenda.
- In the process of getting the shorter task completed, you may have partially mobilized resources which can then be swung on to the bigger job.

Principle No. 4: Question off-the-cuff judgments and check the accuracy of estimates. Assigning priorities to a job often means you've got to guess at some pieces in the puzzle. In one case, it's the time it will take to repair a machine. In another, it's the completion time of an unfamiliar job. It's wise to ask questions about estimates, get other opinions. Now you're better able to set job sequence.

You're the one who has to make the decisions. But that doesn't mean you can't use the experience of others to guide you on the preliminaries.

⮕ QUALITIES OF A "GREAT" EXECUTIVE

What's the difference between a good executive and a great one? Dr. Mortimer Feinberg, a consultant psychologist to American big business for many years, gives this definition:

"The best corporate officers, the men who are recognized as tops, have a lot of energy and drive. They do many different things simultaneously—not all of them well, necessarily—but they are *driven* people. Napoleon could do seven things at once. Look for such traits in your subordinates.

"I have never seen a top executive who was passive, contemplative. Hamlet would never have become a good executive, in my view. There may be some Hamlets around, but they aren't holding the top jobs. Fred Friendly, a former president of CBS News, was known in the industry as 'Frenzied Fred,' because he expected others to tackle projects with his own clock-defying zeal. He was described as always looking as if he had just got off a foam-flecked horse.

"There are some other, more subtle characteristics that distinguish the potential presidents from the also-rans on the executive staff:

"*Dedication.* Just plain, sheer devotion. You call in the man and you say, 'Listen Jack, you've got to fly to Chicago and get that order. Get out there tonight.' Occasionally, he may have a good excuse— his wife is sick or his child is in hospital. But if he goes 99 percent of the time, he is committed to the game of making your company successful.

"*Competitiveness.* First-class executives can't bear to lose. They are only interested in winning. They are constantly evaluating themselves against the competition and striving to do better at each opportunity. They change their frames of reference. One executive, a self-made man, told me when he was on the way up: 'Here I am, sitting at the feet of the elephants, and I'm just a mouse. They might kill me. Just by accident. Because I'm a mouse and they are elephants.' I asked him, 'What are you going to do?' He said, 'I'm going to become an elephant, too.'

"*Honesty.* How honest is he with himself? Does he wear expensive suits and dirty underwear? Is he aware of some of his own limitations? How honest is he with you? How consistently does he produce what he said he would produce? Are his aspirations out of touch with reality? Or, are they close to what he can actually achieve? If he says, 'OK, I didn't do too well that time, but I learned a lesson and I'll do better next time,' then he's honest with himself.

"*Realism.* He has his feet on the ground. He doesn't just dream about how great he's going to be someday. If he's always seeing the big picture and never the details, he's in trouble. The outstanding executive is looking at how he's going to get where he wants to be; he is almost compulsive about the little things, the short cuts.

"*Maturity.* He knows that his own future rests on what happens to other people. He can fire a man who does not contribute to the good of the organization. He respects differences of opinion. He doesn't meddle in office politics and he refuses to manipulate people. He is patient. He doesn't accept the first solution when it presents itself. He bounces back when he's hurt.

"Finally, a potential president is able to handle multiple pressures. A New York boss puts it this way: 'Anyone can do a good job if you give him one problem at a time and all the time he needs to solve it. But when I see a man unwilling to pay attention to anything else until he gets his own little problem solved, I worry. That kind of man never knows there's a fire next door until the whole company burns down.' "

⟳ ETIQUETTE FOR THE EXECUTIVE

The subject of etiquette for the executive is as much a joke as it is an area of concern. Look at some of the books that have been written on the subject, and it's all too clear that good manners on the business scene are a simple extension of etiquette in everyday life.

Then, what are business etiquette books about? The well-intentioned authors, after stressing how important it is to businessmen to cultivate good manners and good appearance, then go on to such vital matters as how to dress, how introductions are to be made, and so on. But once these areas are exhausted, the writers tend to take one of two paths:

- They go into the lore of etiquette *in general*—visiting cards, orders of precedence, and forms of address (one English book on business etiquette goes into great detail on how to address mail to the royal family, and dukes and duchesses of royal blood.)
- The other direction in which the subject-matter-starved writer tends to turn: that of business situations. And these don't involve etiquette as much as they do management procedures. For example, one authority discusses meetings and committees, offering perfectly good suggestions that constitute, however, simply good management practice rather than considerations of etiquette.

Perhaps it's unfair to take these business writers to task so harshly. There is some justification in considering some management procedures from the viewpoint of courtesy and general appropriateness.

For our purposes here, coverage in three areas will suffice: dress; introductions; phone usage.

1. Dress.   The key to acceptable appearance largely depends on the "climate" in your company. For example, the informal, even flashy attire that's considered "good form" in an advertising agency, might be inappropriate in a bank.

A change factor entered the picture in the late '60's. The standard white shirt in many instances has been replaced by a whole rainbow range of colors. And in some cases, neckties have vied with the brightest of sunsets. Give some thought to the way you *want* to look. It is possible to be conservative without being "square." It's possible to follow current trends without conforming to the last detail. And "political" consideration enters: it may be advisable for the executive on his way up to be somewhat more conservative than he might like to be, and leave it to better-established executives to be the style innovators and trend setters.

2. Introductions.   Frequently you're called on to introduce people: your secretary to a visitor; a visitor to another executive. Introductions in the business world tend to be informal. But they *should* be audible. In addition to pronouncing names clearly, a title or descriptive phrase is helpful. For example, if you're bringing a customer in to meet one of your company's officers, you might say, as you enter, "Bill, this is Mr. Green, Chief Purchasing Agent of the Acme chain. Bill Smith, our General Manager."

If you are being introduced, any one of a number of traditional phrases uttered in a pleasant tone is acceptable: "Very glad to meet you;" "Yes, I know of your company and think very highly of it," and so on.

Handshaking is almost always in order among men. Women may or may not shake hands, as they prefer.

Finally, if any of the names involved in the introductions are difficult to pronounce, you may want to make it a point of spelling out: "Mr. LeBeau, capital L-e- capital B-e-a-u."

3. Phone usage.   It's in the area of telephone utilization that business practice does tend to vary with practices of the nonbusiness world. Some of the specifics of business phone use involve the executive, some his secretary. In any case, here are some guidelines:

▪ *Prompt response.* People calling you, customers, suppliers, other executives, and so on, get a bad impression when phones ring and go unanswered for any length of time. On the other hand, people appreciate the businesslike and courteous impression made by prompt answering.

▪ *Identification.* The "Hello" response of the everyday world isn't satisfactory on the job. Your secretary will avoid guessing games by answering a ring with: "Production Department, Miss Jones."

▪ *Screening.* Train your secretary *not* to ask, "Who's calling?" It's more acceptable to say, "May I tell Mr. Smith who's calling?" or, "Mr. Smith is attending a meeting. May I have him call you when he's finished?"

▪ *Explain delays.* If you must leave the line, you may want to provide a word of explanation, or at any rate, indicate approximately how long you'll be. Generally, if it's going to require some time to get information, it's wiser to offer to call back.

▪ *Taking messages.* Here's where Girl Fridays may need coaching, particularly if they are beginners in the business world. Train your secretary to spell back names if there is any question and to verify numbers by reading them back to the caller.

As we've said, good manners on the business scene are a simple extension of etiquette in everyday life. And there is no doubt that good manners are an asset to the executive, while lack of courtesy can lose good will, customers, and destroy morale within the executive's own organization.

11. Women in Management

Two developments have changed the all-male ballgame in the executive suite:

- legal pressures, in the form of antidiscrimination legislation.
- increased social consciousness of both men and women caused by the so-called Women's Liberation Movement.

As a result of these and other factors, the upward mobility of women on the work scene has greatly increased—bringing with it disruptions, problems, and a new look in interpersonal relationships. Of course, women have been present on the work scene ever since the Industrial Revolution. But their jobs were generally menial. Following the Civil Rights Act of 1964, barriers against women in the executive echelons gradually weakened. New situations and problems then arose—as you would expect from a change of this magnitude.

It's helpful to both male and female executives to be aware of and be prepared to cope with, the new bisexuality of executive rosters. You'll find the legal aspects of women's new status in business covered in Section 12, *Fair Employment Practices*. The headings below cover some practical problems managers of both sexes face when women make it to the upper echelons.

➜ EQUALITY UNDER THE LAW

The Civil Rights Act of 1964 prohibited job discrimination based on race, color, religion, sex, or national origins. The Equal Pay Act prohibited wage discrimination based on sex. As a result, practices that had previously veiled discrimination—such as the assertion that women "couldn't do" a given job, or that pay differentials were justified because certain elements (often minor) distinguished a male job from a female job—no longer sufficed. Organizations were directed to see to it—by affirmative action—that executive rosters begin to show women holding down higher echelon jobs.

Several key cases pushed by the enforcing agencies levied sizable penalties for noncompliance. Affirmative action programs—that is, plans and projects to recruit, train and promote women into higher echelon jobs—became widely popular on the business scene, particularly in the larger companies.

➲ FOR SOME WOMEN MANAGERS: ROUGH GOING

While antidiscrimination laws are bringing more women into higher echelon jobs, workscene attitudes have not yet adjusted to women's new role. Here is a case history that illustrates one practical aspect of the woman manager's adjustment problem:

Ruth Bertram, well educated, divorced, and in her late 30's, has recently been promoted from assistant to office manager. She is the only female of department-head rank in her organization. She does not have much in common with the other women in the office, who are secretaries and assistants and, for the most part, younger than she. She has, however, developed a friendship with another manager, Tony Frye—a man about her age. They frequently have lunch together and chat in each other's office.

Now there is gossip. A friendship that would be taken for granted between two men is being misinterpreted as an affair. Unfortunately, we have not progressed far from the era when every adult male-female association outside of marriage was presumed to be illicit. Whether it's a holdover from the bad old days, envy, the result of prurient curiosity or boredom on the job, some people still speculate when a male manager and a female manager pair off for lunch.

What can a man and a woman like Ruth Bertram and Tony Frye, who have a nonsexual relationship, do to stop the talk? Some possibilities:

- *Break off their friendship?* But this is the soap opera answer—making a personal sacrifice to prevent scandal. Man and women can be friends without necessarily having affairs.
- *Meet on the sly?* Very bad, because this really would make it look as if they have something to hide. However, it is smart to *avoid* anything that looks more like a date than a business relationship—after-five drinks, for example.
- *Restrict the friendship to business hours?* This way Ruth and Tony give no grounds for surmising about what they may do away from the office. There may still be gossip, but sooner or later the grapevine will switch to hotter topics if they do nothing to feed the remarks.

For the woman, it's a temptation to grasp the first friendly male hand that is extended—and cling to it. But this friend may not be the most helpful in the long run. If other managers then feel shut out, the female manager is even less likely to gain their acceptance.

One realistic remedy: Ruth and Tony should never be exclusive. Inviting other managers to join them regularly gives everyone a chance to see that the relationship is aboveboard. Bringing others into the group has another advantage for the woman manager. In organizations where a woman in management is still a rarity, life can be lonely at the executive level. Adding to her circle of contacts can broaden and enrich her working life.

⮑ HOW THE PAST LINGERS ON

Some women are reluctant to accept promotions. A survey of women in eight large corporations showed that fifty percent of women managers or potential managers have turned down job promotions. A major reason for rejection of the higher job offer: the women believed that the promotions were a "fake," offered to help the organization comply with antidiscrimination pressures, or "were created for women because it looked good," as a kind of tokenism adopted to make the organization seem to be in the forefront of social change.

While this promotion-wariness among women is likely to change, it may persist in individual cases. This attitude is worth remembering if a woman is offered a promotion and refuses it. Of course, men also turn down offers of advancement: because of unwillingness to accept responsibility; not wanting to get too deeply imbedded in the "establishment"; health reasons, and so on. But when a woman turns down an offer of a job of more responsibility, her motivation is likely to be ascribed to the weakness or unpredictability of her sex.

A recommendation to women facing a decision on accepting a promotion: think through the pros and cons on your own. Avoid being persuaded or dissuaded by other people's attitudes or advice that may reflect their own particular biases.

Recommendation to managers who are about to offer a promotion into managerial ranks to a woman: set forth the proposal in the same way you would to a man. However, if the candidate indicates an interest in discussing the special aspects of the new position because she is a woman, level with her and give her full opportunity to clarify her doubts and ask her questions.

⮑ FIVE ASSUMPTIONS TO AVOID IN JUDGING WOMEN JOB CANDIDATES

Antidiscrimination laws aside, people who screen and interview job candidates sometimes proceed on the basis of false assumptions. Here are five that can lead you astray:

1. *Don't* expect to find a woman with qualities just like those possessed by men already holding similar jobs. Almost every job can be done equally well in several ways. A woman can have qualities quite different from male incumbents and still perform satisfactorily. As you would do in any job-filling procedure, list the job demands and gauge the applicant's qualifications as a measure of capability.

2. *Don't* judge the candidate by stereotyped female roles. For example, don't assume that a "masculine"—that is, assertive—type of woman is one you need to be a manager. Or, if you're hiring a person for customer contacts, don't hang your hopes on finding a woman heavily endowed with female charm, as a mainstay of her job tactics.

   In the former case the expectation is that the masculine manner will nullify "female weaknesses." In the second the assumption is that an excess of femininity will help in "manipulating" others. The only cure for this pitfall is to avoid stereotypy—that is, thinking in stereotypes—altogether. Try to see job candidates of either sex as worthy for what they are in themselves. Judge them by what they can do.

3. *Don't* make assumptions about a woman's motivation. For example, it's widely believed that married women coming into the labor force do so for "fur coat money," that is, just to be able to indulge their special acquisitive whims. Another widely-held feeling is that married women with young children inevitably become a high risk in terms of attendance. As long as the woman has made realistic plans for the care of her children while she's working, her attendance will be as good as anyone else's. At one time it was a common assumption that a young woman would stop working when she met and married Mr. Right. Nowadays that's even less likely.

4. *Don't* expect women applicants to be less realistic or hard-nosed about the job you're offering—salary prospects, benefits, and so on—than a male counterpart. Why should they be, now that the law guarantees them equal pay, benefits and so on?

5. *Don't think of women as "little men."* In the dark ages before the Women's Liberation Movement one expert on that intriguing subject known as the "difference between the sexes" maintained that it was really very easy to understand women in terms of what they were and were not capable of:

   "Just think of women as being little men," he maintained. "This explains not only their physical limitations in terms of stamina, weightlifting, and so on, but it also explains their limited ability to plan, make decisions, wield authority, and so on."

The high performance level of today's women managers is the simplest rebuttal to this view.

➜ HOW TO MAKE THE CHANGE

Even at this late date in the history of sex equality, women in upper echelons may represent a break with tradition in individual organizations. Such changes can cause dislocations and upsets of various kinds and degrees. The executives who prepare for the first-time inclusion of women in organizational areas may want to consider two basic methods of making the change:

- *Drastic.*   In some cases the change is best made by quick and decisive action. This can be particularly successful if it coincides with other organizational changes. For example, an organization that is starting a new type of activity, opening up new branches, departments, or other units, can include an appropriate number of qualified women among newcomers being brought in.

  One virtue of fast action is that is prevents the festering and exaggeration that is likely in the time between the word getting around and the actual move. In a waiting period, rumors may start to build up, people opposed have the chance to exacerbate and crystallize their opposition. In some instances, resentment may grow into a power struggle bringing with it all the evils of factionalism.

  A factor in acceptance is the firmness of those in charge. "Yes, Janice Bond is starting Monday as head of Purchasing. I'm sure that with her experience and capabilities, she'll prove to be a worthy successor for Jim Phipps." Such a statement with reinforcement and confidence is owed the newcomers. Any defensiveness or temporizing will weaken their position before they've had the chance to prove themselves.

- *Gradual.*   Where women in management represent an innovation, and no organizational alterations are planned, executive planners may nevertheless prepare moves which will bring women into management positions in a natural way. Clearly, this approach requires time but it does promise the minimum of disruptive problems.

  A gradualistic program would include items like:
  1. The inclusion of qualified women in basic management orientation programs.

2. Special coaching workshops, in which it will be possible to train women in those aspects of management and interpersonal relationships which may represent special obstacles to them.
3. Sponsoring of qualified and interested women employees in management and professional associations.
4. Helping those executives who have the responsibility for maintaining the ranks of executive personnel review evaluation and selection techniques to rid them of sex bias.
5. Inducting one or two women of proven capability, who are almost sure to win acceptance, set patterns and standards of behavior and performance that will smooth the path for others.

Measures like those represent elements of affirmative action, more likely to actually bring women into managerial ranks than passive programs in which firms merely "remove barriers" to equality. Letting "nature take its course" in this situation usually means retaining the status quo.

➲ IF YOU'RE A MALE WORKING FOR A FEMALE BOSS

"Women's liberation has created a new minority, and I'm part of it," asserts a manager. "Who are we? We're males who have female bosses. And like other minorities, we have problems..." Women in management posts may cause the situation alluded to. It may require a psychological adjustment that some male subordinates find difficult.

Of course, the "working-for-a-woman" problem isn't limited to men. In one case a female secretary literally could *not* take dictation from a woman. The few times she was asked to, she became sick to her stomach—clearly a symptom of her psychological trauma.

The overreacting secretary, though a rare case, does suggest the turmoil that may result from what some people see as a reversal of the natural order of things. Actually, there is a range of reactions possible. Some men take the news they will be reporting to a woman by threatening to quit. Others demand a transfer. Sometimes the resentment is more covert.

The fact is that resentment is likely *any* time a new boss takes over. When the person who gets the promotion is a woman, the stereotype of male superiority may increase the sense of being unjustly treated, unappreciated—or, even harder to take—inferior.

Even if a man has no strong negative reaction, he may find that his family and friends do. (In fact, some male subordinates confess that what troubled them most was having to tell their wives they were now reporting to a woman.) Acquaintances declare, "You work for a boss lady? I'd rather starve!" It seems as though the male subordinate lacks machismo if he keeps his cool.

Males, from rank-and-file to executives, who are concerned about their female bosses should consider points like these to ease the pressure:

- *Accept actual feelings.* Unless a man works in an organization where women have traditionally been managers, there's going to be some kind of adverse reaction. And it is far better for a man to be aware of any feelings of hostility than to deny them and have his dealings with the new boss colored by disturbing below-surface emotions.
- *What will it mean in personal terms?* Even if secure enough to feel no threat to his manhood, a man may nonetheless be concerned about his situation. In companies which have promoted a woman because of legal pressure, there can be legitimate concern that top management won't really support her—and that subordinates will suffer along with her as a result of her shaky authority and lack of clout.

In addition, if the only woman a man has known well on a day-to-day basis have been his mother, his wife and his secretary, he may be very uncertain of how to act around a woman superior. But if he is able to face up to his own feelings of discomfort and uncertainty, it will be possible to adjust more easily.

- *See the real problem.* It is a mistake for the male subordinate to see his problem as one of "adjusting to a female boss." The real problem is, "How can I learn to work productively with this particular individual?" It is when the subordinate stops seeing himself as confronting wide-ranging social change, but rather sees the goal as one of developing a practical working relationship that the solution is at hand. Here is one approach to developing a positive relationship. It involves three phases:

    Phase 1: Opening gambits. It is best to let the boss provide the cues as to what she expects and how she will exercise her leadership.

    The subordinate, however, does have some options. He may choose to remain passive and leave it entirely up to his boss to determine the pattern of their relationship. Or he may register a pleasant, accepting attitude. After all, the woman is probably expecting, and dreading, resentment from some of her male subordinates. She'll be looking for cues for her behavior from subordinates, also.

Or, going a step further, a male subordinate can show friendliness. One manager reports he greeted his new boss by saying, "I want to congratulate you on your promotion. I'll give you any help I can..." He wisely did *not* offer to help her learn the ropes but decided to let her ask him, if she chose.

Phase 2: Testing. Will the new boss be formal or informal? Will she run a tight ship? How, and how much, will she delegate? How much initiative does she expect from subordinates? Will she be tough, demanding, or will she prefer a consultative approach?

The answer to these and related questions come through day-by-day contacts. The subordinate usually gets the message automatically. But the more awareness he brings to these contacts, the faster and better he'll understand what's expected.

Phase 3: Optimizing. After some time has passed, the subordinate is in a position to size up the situation between him and his boss by thinking through the answers to specific questions: What are the satisfactory areas of our working together? What areas are unsatisfactory (if any)? Why are they unsatisfactory? What can be done to minimize or eliminate the difficulties? Here the question might be reworded: If my boss were male and I had the same problem, how would I tackle it?

With these rocky spots out of the road, the way is prepared for a good working relationship. The three phases of developing it are, in fact, those a subordinate should expect with any boss. For the secret of adjusting to a woman boss is to regard her, and treat her, as an executive. Whether the approach succeeds depends ultimately on the individuals involved—not on their sexes.

➲ SOME SPECIAL PERFORMANCE OBSTACLES FOR WOMEN

Keep in mind a major fact to avoid misunderstanding, disappointment, or conflict: equality for women and an end of discrimination will *not* transform them into men. They should never be expected to look like the opposite sex, behave like the opposite sex, or necessarily have work styles that are similar.

In specific cases, some standard management situations may represent obstacles to them. For example, in the lower echelons a common problem in sex equality has to do with a woman's ability to lift or carry heavy burdens that may be a part of the job operation. In the upper echelons there are few physical tests that militate against women. But there are some patterns of activity that may represent difficulties, particularly for married women who have responsibility for home and children.

Traveling in the field may mean serious personal disruption for women. Attendance at management or professional seminars or assignments in certain types of company committees may cause family or home problems. Obviously, how much of a problem may be caused by circumstances of this type is an entirely individual matter. But enlightened organizations and executives should take these practical problems into account just as they might give special consideration to male employees in special personal situations.

A possible and touchy complication: hostility by a male manager to a female colleague because she *is* a female. Suspicious and exaggerated reactions may still further complicate the basic situation. For a higher echelon executive, this conflict, usually below surface, represents a problem in forbearance and tact. The best course is to give the woman manager the chance to resolve the problem herself. Supply guidance, if it's asked for. Only as a last resort, and if the hostility of the male manager is clear, should the executive in authority intervene. Perhaps the best approach to the recalcitrant is to remind him that he's terribly behind the times.

◑ THE ROCKY ROAD TO EQUALITY

Women have two obstacles that confront them as they seek true equality in the world of work. One, obviously, is the external blockage, the bias, resentment, and resistance of males who feel threatened by both the thought and the actuality of women in management echelons. Much has been said and written about the *external* obstacles. Less talked about, but more insidious, and for some women an even greater difficulty, is the *internal* or psychological problem.

Women who have reached their maturity in a world which is still sex-differentiated in a thousand different ways will find it difficult to free themselves of these social pressures. For many women the journey from dependency to independency is long, arduous, and beset with basic difficulties. Just consider one major point: Many women have had as their basic role one that is subordinate and dependent on other people—as daughter, wife, mother. In the working world a position most widely held by women is that of secretary—a role which usually makes a woman dependent on a male executive.

From this limiting position, the woman who wants to succeed in management must learn to operate on her own, lead and counsel other people, know and state her own views, and in some cases be assertive enough to persuade others—including her superior—to see things as she sees them. These difficulties, though great, have been successfully surmounted by many women. Individual struggle will become less difficult as many of the old stereotypes weaken and fade away into social history. But for some women, equality will continue to be a two-front battle, external and internal, and this should be kept in mind by both the women themselves and male colleagues.

Men and women should be aware of the possibility of overreaction in attempting to compete in what perhaps is less a male world, but is still bound by some of the old traditions. The ambitious woman may try too hard. Knowing that in some cases she may have to prove herself significantly superior to a man to get equal recognition, she may drive herself into modes of behavior that aggravate her situation. Many businessmen have expressed themselves on the matter of the over-reacting woman manager in words like these: "They are aggressive bitches who can do a good job, but no man would want to marry one."

You can be sure that such views are not objective evaluations but represent male chauvinism at its worst. You'll certainly never hear an aggressive *male* manager described or put down in any such terms. Then why apply it to his female opposite number?

EXPECTATIONS AND JUDGMENT OF PERFORMANCE

"Women will just never perform as ably as men," say some die-hards. "They don't have the mental equipment, the stamina, or the drive."

It's an old bias that may persist even into the distant future. But for the practical executive such rigid views are unacceptable. As would be true of any group being thrust into new situations, obviously there must be a period of adjustment and accommodation. Here are some of the considerations that should be made in instances where women in management represent a recent change:

- *Try to avoid lowering performance standards.* It may seem unfair to expect new women managers to perform at the same level as male old-timers. But it may be wiser to do this than to have it seem that female managers just aren't expected to do as well as their male counterparts. Once this expectation becomes ingrained, it becomes a continuing handicap to the advancement and promotion of other women.
- *Give them time.* There is a distinction to be made between women just starting out in a new responsibility and what's expected of them eventually. It's a recognized technique in sports that

less skilled participants may be given a handicap or assist. This concept should be applied to women only at the start of a training or development period. The ultimate objective should be equality of expectation in terms of performance—objectives accomplished, results achieved, and so on.

- *Avoid a premature overload.* It's an invitation to trouble to give women major responsibilities before they are capable of handling them. The "sink-or-swim" approach to test capability *may* be acceptable under special circumstances such as lack of time or absence of an alternative. Yet, with all the resources used in preparation for management today, there is no reason why women shouldn't be given the benefits of adequate preparation before being placed in demanding jobs.

Finally, it's unwise to keep anyone in a job in which, despite all efforts and help provided, performance expectations aren't being met. The same measurements of adequacy should be applied to women managers as to men. Where failure seems irreversible the policies of transfer or dismissal should be applied the same as they are to unsuccessful male managers.

12. Fair Employment Practices

Starting in the early sixties the Federal Government became directly involved in seeking to insure equality of treatment to all employees in the world of business and organizational life in general. First efforts were directed toward those companies involved in government work. Contractors were required to adopt policies that would guarantee opportunities for members of minority groups.

Since those early beginnings, government control has expanded drastically. It reaches into virtually every phase of company operations. The impact of the 1964 Civil Rights Act has been so broadened by the courts that today the law is used to stamp out job discrimination in all areas: hiring, promotion, training opportunities, and even firing.

Nor is it a simple matter to keep abreast of the law. The prohibitions against discrimination are now embodied in three separate Federal laws and enforcement is divided between the Equal Employment Opportunity Commission (EEOC) and the Wage-Hour Division. What's more, the reach of the law is constantly being broadened by the courts.

Enforcement is growing constantly tougher: the cost of a misstep can be staggering. Penalties of $100,000 and $250,000 in back pay under the Equal Pay Act are not uncommon. Title VII of the Civil Rights Act is being used not only to launch suits, but as a basis for a "fishing expedition" into an employer's personnel records.

With the burgeoning "rights consciousness," not only of minority groups, but employees in general, there will be increasing vulnerability to charges of discrimination in the years ahead. Executives must help rid their firms of outmoded policies, and also eliminate the friction points that may cause a drain on productivity. The laws themselves are summarized on page 224 to provide a broad overview.

➲ TITLE VII OF THE CIVIL RIGHTS ACT OF 1964

Title VII is the broadest of the antidiscrimination laws. It prohibits discrimination with respect to race, color, religion, sex or nationality in the following situations:

- Hiring or firing;
- Setting compensation, terms, conditions or privileges of employment;
- Segregating, classifying or otherwise limiting employees in any way that deprives an individual of employment opportunities or in some other way adversely affects his status as an employee;
- Printing or publishing of advertisements or notices that indicate a preference, limitation, specification or discrimination;
- Apprenticeship or other training or retraining programs.

What is permissible under the law.   Despite the sweeping language of Title VII, there is *nothing* in the act that requires that you hire someone who is *incapable of doing the job*. The Supreme Court has said, "Congress has not commanded that the less qualified be preferred over the better qualified simply because of minority origins." In other words, while race, color, religion, sex or national origin are not acceptable criteria, *ability* is. What's more, an employer may even discriminate on the basis of religion, sex or national origin (but not race or color) if one of these factors is a *"bona fide occupational qualification"* reasonably necessary to the normal operation of his business. The burden of proving the BFOQ exception is on the employer, however.

The courts have clearly stated that if an employer wants to establish that sex is a bona fide occupational qualification for the job, he would have to prove that he had reasonable cause to believe that "all or substantially all women"—or men—would be unable to perform the job safely and efficiently.

SUMMARY OF ANTI-DISCRIMINATION LAWS

Title VII of the Civil Rights Act of 1964

- *Prohibits* job discrimination based on race, color, religion, sex or national origin.
  - *Covers* the following:
  ... Employers engaged in an industry affecting commerce who have at least 25 employees on each working day in 20 or more weeks in the current calendar year (or who met the same test in the preceding year).
  ... Labor organizations that maintain a hiring hall or have 25 members.
  ... Employment agencies.
- *Exempts* specified government agencies, U.S. government-owned corporations, Indian tribes, religious and educational organizations, bona fide private membership clubs (other than labor organizations).
- *Enforced* by the Equal Employment Opportunity Commission (EEOC).

Equal Pay Act

- *Prohibits* wage discrimination based on sex. The prohibition applies to both employers and unions.
- *Covers* all employees subject to the minimum wage provisions of the Wage-Hour Act.
- *Exempts* white-collar executive, administrative, and professional employees and others who are exempt from the minimum wage provisions.
- *Enforced* by the Wage-Hour Division.

Age Discrimination in Employment Act of 1967

- *Prohibits* job discrimination based on age, but protection is limited to those who are at least 40 years old but under 65.
  - *Covers* the following:
  ... Employers in an industry affecting commerce who have at least 25 employees (including officers) in 20 or more weeks in the current calendar year (or who met that test in the preceding year).
  ... Labor organizations that maintain a hiring hall or have at least 25 members.
  ... Employment agencies.
- *Exempts* the U.S. government, U.S. government-owned corporations and state and local governments (but it does cover the U.S. Employment Service and state and local employment services receiving federal assistance).
- *Enforced* by the Wage-Hour Division.

Reprinted with permission of the Research Institute of America

Obviously, you are on safer ground if you analyze the job itself to find out just what skills are needed rather than to make a general assumption about the capacities (or incapacities) of a job applicant. The Washington State Board Against Discrimination gives the following example of the identification of specific skills: An airline that operates between Japan and the United States must have Japanese-speaking stewardesses. What's required in this case, however, is competency in speaking Japanese, not Japanese national origin—unless the airline can show that only someone of Japanese ancestry can properly serve the airline's Japanese clientele.

RACIAL DISCRIMINATION

Title VII clearly bans overt job discrimination based on race—for example, paying minorities less for the same work, denying them advancement by locking them into low-paying, menial jobs, and the like. But many companies have encountered trouble in the courts with more subtle forms of discrimination, and in these cases it was frequently unintentional.

Moreover, many traditional business practices have been called into question—such as requiring new employees to have a high school diploma and to pass standard aptitude tests. If such requirements act to weed out minority members, they will be regarded as discriminatory unless the employer can clearly demonstrate that they are essential to performance on the job. Where past practices have led to a pattern of "de facto" discrimination, the employer would have difficulty defending himself against charges brought by a rejected candidate.

Recruitment. Any recruitment methods that tend to screen out minority applicants may be questioned. Be wary, for example, of relying exclusively on word-of-mouth recruiting—the fairly common practice of telling employees about job openings and having them notify their friends. If all or most of the employees are white, this might be considered evidence of discrimination. The EEOC has consistently taken the position that if an employer with an all-white workforce relies solely on word-of-mouth recruiting, he is being discriminatory even in the absence of any other evidence.

Screening. Standard procedures that may have been acceptable in the past can cause trouble under today's laws. The Supreme Court has said that an employer violates Title VII if he uses broad-gauge employment qualification standards that have the effect of discriminating against minority groups—such as requiring a high school diploma or a specific score on a general aptitude test.

This doesn't mean that tests can't be used, but they must be related to the requirements of the job. "What Congress has forbidden," the Court said, "is giving testing or measuring procedures controlling force unless they are demonstrably a reasonable measure of job performance."

Needless to say, requirements for a college degree should also be reexamined in the light of the Court's ruling to see whether jobs really require a college background. EEOC had earlier ruled that such a requirement for a sales representative was discriminatory because relatively few minority applicants could meet that standard. The commission also noted that the requirement had been instituted only a few years earlier and that it could hardly be justified on the grounds of business necessity since the sales supervisor had no degree.

Experience requirements may also be questioned if they aren't reasonably necessary for the job. For example, the EEOC has ruled that a company discriminated by rejecting a minority applicant who lacked the four years' experience that had been set as one of the job requirements. The evidence showed that a few years earlier the company had waived this requirement in favor of a 90-day trial period in order to get needed workers.

Turning down an applicant on the basis of an arrest record can also be unlawful, according to a federal district court. A black applicant had a record of prior arrests, none of which had resulted in conviction, but the company's policy was to refuse to hire anyone who had been arrested "on a number of occasions." The court rules that even requesting this type of information in job interviews or on application forms is unlawful. Regardless of how fairly such a policy is applied, it tends to discriminate against minorities which may have a rate of arrests substantially higher than that of whites. The decision did state that a company can inquire about any criminal convictions of an applicant or employee and that requests for information about prior arrests are permissible in situations that involve national security clearance regulations.

Job classifications and seniority. Any employment practices that "limit, segregate, or classify" employees on the basis of race in any way that might tend to deprive them of employment opportunity or in any other way affect their status as employees are specifically prohibited by Title VII.

Title VII *does* permit differences in pay—or terms, conditions or privileges of employment—that are based on a *bona fide seniority system.* However, as one court pointed out, a seniority system can't be considered bona fide if it has discriminatory effect.

One of the most significant implications of the above decisions is that the courts have provided justification for the EEOC to look back at a company's *past* policies—*before Title VII went into effect*—in order to evaluate its present practices.

Training programs. The carry-over effect of past discriminatory practices can also cause violations by restricting training opportunities. In one company, for example, most of the apprenticeship programs were conducted in departments that were predominantly white (because of past restrictions on transfer privileges for minorities.) The program was held unlawful because it gave preferential treatment to white applicants. This means that segregation by race in collective bargaining units, seniority lines or lines of progression is clearly unlawful.

Working conditions. Any physical segregation of employees by race with respect to restroom and locker facilities, restaurants, recreational activities and the like are in clear violation of Title VII.

The following forms of segregation are also considered discriminatory:

- Segregated Christmas parties.
- Segregated houses and churches in a company-owned community (these are considered "privileges of employment").
- Segregated payroll lines and employee identification systems.

An employer is expected to take *positive steps* to prevent the pattern of segregation from perpetuating itself. For example, even where the employer has removed racial designations from toilet and locker room facilities, discrimination will be presumed to exist if employees continue to use the facilities on the same segregated basis as before. The employer is also responsible for any harassment of minorities for using formerly white washrooms. Even subtler forms of behavior by white employees can be attributed to the employer—for example where minority members didn't use snack-bar facilities because white employees gave them the impression that they weren't wanted. An employer is responsible if his employees use racial insults or in any other way harass other employees because of their race. In short, he is expected to "maintain a work environment free of racial intimidation."

Mere announcement of a nondiscriminatory policy isn't enough. According to the EEOC, the employer must take steps to insure that the policy is observed at all levels. A company that failed to support a black supervisor who was subjected to harassment by white employees was held to violate Title VII.

➲ NATIONAL ORIGIN DISCRIMINATION

The EEOC has issued "Guidelines on Discrimination Because of National Origin," which say that the commission will "apply the full force of the law" to eliminate such discrimination.

The guidelines say that one indication of possible discrimination in this area is the use of tests in the English language when (1) English is not the individual's first language or mother tongue, and (2) skill in English isn't necessary for the job. The use of tests that aren't job-related has in any case been outlawed by the Supreme Court.

The commission will also examine "with particular concern" cases in which equal employment opportunity is denied because the employee or job applicant:

- is married to a person of a specific national origin or is otherwise associated with members of such a group;
- is a member of a lawful organization identified with or seeking to promote the interests of national groups;
- has attended schools or churches commonly utilized by persons of a given national origin;
- belongs to a class that tends to fall outside national norms for height and weight, where such height and weight specifications are not necessary for the performance of the work involved.

Discrimination on the basis of citizenship, the guidelines continue, has the effect of discriminating on the basis of national origin. Therefore, a lawfully immigrated alien, domiciled or residing in the United States, may not be discriminated against on the basis of his citizenship.

In a separate ruling, the EEOC has said that an agreement to hire a U.S. citizen or resident for each nonresident hired doesn't violate Title VII. Such discrimination against nonresidents as a class isn't directed at the citizens of a particular country or even at aliens in general.

Also, employers in situations affecting national security can refuse to hire someone who doesn't get security clearance. For example, an employer who had contracts with the Atomic Energy Commission did not violate Title VII when he refused to hire a person who couldn't get CIA clearance because he had relatives behind the Iron Curtain.

Many of the rulings issued by the EEOC on individual instances of national origin discrimination have been concerned with discrimination against Spanish-Americans. The following practices were ruled discriminatory:

- *Discharge of Spanish-American employees for violations of company rule:*   Non-Spanish employees who violated the same rule were retained.
- *Harassment:*   Other employees corroborated a Spanish-American employee's charge that two supervisors had made derogatory remarks about Spanish-Americans.
- *Refusal to hire because of appearance and manner:*   An appli-

cant for a job as manager spoke with a noticeable Spanish accent, but was as well qualified in terms of education and experience as some of the company's managers and assistant managers. The company hired some Spanish-Americans who had no noticeable accent. The EEOC ruled that this one was apparently turned down because of his appearance and manner of speaking.

- *Ban on speaking Spanish on premises:*   Spanish was banned both at work stations and during lunch and other breaks. The employer said that the rule was imposed because the supervisors didn't understand Spanish, but he supplied no evidence of business necessity for the rule, especially as it applied to nonworking hours. The EEOC did state, however, that there may be occasions when business necessity will permit an employer to forbid employees from speaking a language unfamiliar to their supervisors, but such a rule must be applied only during working hours.

- *Denial of pretest training:*   A Spanish-American employee was denied promotion because he refused to take a truck-driving test without some preliminary training. Although the company claimed that it had no formal training program, some drivers had given informal driving lessons to non-Spanish applicants for these jobs.

SEX DISCRIMINATION

Stereotypes of women and traditional concepts of job roles may be the biggest obstacles to compliance with Title VII's ban on sex bias on jobs. Traditional ideas about "male jobs" and "female jobs" are being challenged on all sides. In short, you must treat women on the same basis as men in hiring and on the job itself, unless you can prove that sex is a bona fide occupational qualification for the job.

To reinforce these points, the EEOC has issued Sex Discrimination Guidelines (which must be accorded "considerable weight.") The guidelines warn that the following attitudes or practices may be illegal acts:

- *Assumptions about the comparative employment characteristics of women in general*—for example, refusing to hire a woman on the grounds that the female turnover rate is higher than the male.

- *Stereotyped characterizations of the sexes*—such as the belief that men are less capable than women of assembling intricate equipment or that women are less capable of aggressive salesmanship. Individuals must "be considered on the basis of individual capacities and not on the basis of any characteristics generally attributed to the group."

The last point is especially significant because generalizations about women as a group don't stand up in court. For example, one court countered an employer's claim that a job was "too strenuous for women" with questions like, "What do you mean by 'strenuous'?" "How do you know that *all* women can't perform the job?" The court admonished the employer for relying on stereotypes in assuming no woman can safely lift 30 pounds but all men can.

■ *Basing hiring decisions on the preferences of customers, clients, coworkers, or the employer himself.* Exceptions are permitted only where sex is a bona fide occupational qualification. Here's one case where it wasn't:

A woman had been refused a job as "courier guard"—that is, a driver of a security truck used to transport valuable commercial papers between banks. The employer acknowledged that sex was the reason for turning her down but contended that the trucking service would lose customers, who would feel that the woman wouldn't be able to provide the degree of security needed. Moreover, the employer argued, the work would expose women to too many risks. The EEOC ruled that these arguments had failed to prove the employer's case because he hadn't come up with factual evidence showing that all or nearly all women wouldn't be able to perform the job safely and efficiently.

Another EEOC ruling shows how traditional ideas can cause job erosions and result in a charge of discrimination: A woman had been promoted to the job of editor-writer, with the understanding that she would perform a substantial amount of writing. She had been asked, however, to perform some clerical functions as the need arose. These requests gradually increased until, finally, clerical work took up most of her time. When she complained, her supervisor responded "That sort of work is woman's work. You wouldn't expect one of the men to be willing to do it." The EEOC stated that such treatment is in direct conflict with the requirements of the Civil Rights Act.

Job Classifications. The Sex Discrimination Guidelines prohibit employers from classifying jobs as "male" or "female" and from maintaining separate lines of progression or separate seniority lists that are based on sex if this practice would adversely affect any employee. Exceptions are allowed only where sex is a bona fide occupational qualification for the job. Therefore, *these practices are unlawful:*

- Barring a woman from applying for a job labeled "male" or in a "male" line of progression (and vice versa).
- Barring a man scheduled for layoff from displacing a woman with less seniority on a "female" seniority list (and vice versa).

The guidelines also prohibit any *seniority system* or line of progression that distinguishes between "light" and "heavy" jobs if it (1) operates as a disguised form of classification by sex, or (2) creates unreasonable obstacles to the advancement of members of either sex into jobs they could reasonably be expected to perform.

The EEOC position on segregated seniority lists has received court backing. An employer was guilty of discrimination when his separate seniority lists resulted in the layoff of women who had greater seniority than some of the men who were retained.

A seniority system that perpetrates past discrimination against women is unlawful. In this case, promotions, transfers and layoffs were all based on departmental seniority, which continued the effects of the original classification system in which women had been placed in segregated classifications and departments. As a result, women with greater plant-wide seniority could not replace men in other departments.

A similar pattern appeared in another case. The women in this case had formerly been confined to segregated departments or denied transfer privileges to some all-male departments. To comply with the act, the company attempted to desegregate the departments by opening up transfer privileges to the women. However, seniority continued on a departmental basis, so that a woman who transferred would lose seniority and pay privileges. The court ordered the company to permit the women who had been hired before the change-over to transfer on the basis of their plant-wide seniority and retain this accumulated seniority in the new department.

Advancement opportunities. The EEOC has issued the following rulings on advancement opportunities:

- There can be no discrimination in terms of advancement opportunities. If supervisory training is available to members of one sex, it must be made available to members of the other.
- Permitting women to advance to a higher job classification only on a temporary basis—and at their old rate of pay—may violate the act. An employer was found to be in violation when some of his temporary assignments of women employees lasted more than a year.
- Differences in the rates of promotion of men and women can indicate discrimination unless the difference is based on ability or

some factor other than sex. For example, one employer was found to be in violation when he promoted male employees from four months to one year earlier than female employees who had comparable qualifications and equivalent performance ratings.

■ An employer had merged previously segregated job classifications. However, two intermediate levels of jobs in the line of progression required the lifting of heavy weights, which the woman could not or would not do. The EEOC ruled that the employer was discriminatory because these jobs barred the women from access to the top-level jobs, which they were able to perform.

Discrimination resulting from marriage. Any company rule that forbids or restricts the employment of married women but not married men is unlawful. But the EEOC says that there may be some circumstances in which such a rule could be a bona fide occupational qualification—if it's justified in terms of the job itself rather than some general principle such as the desirability of spreading work.

The EEOC has ruled that the following policies violate the act:

■ Requiring married women to be discharged one year after marriage if the husband is physically able to work. (The policy was not applied to married men.)

■ Policy providing for the employment of a married woman only if a single person is not available. This is a violation unless the same rule is applied to men.

■ Rule banning the employment of male employees' wives and requiring that female employees resign when they marry male employees. But this policy on marriage between employees would be lawful if the company left it up to the couple to decide which spouse should resign. If they couldn't agree, it would be permissible for the company to require that the junior of the two employees resign.

■ A number of airlines require stewardesses to quit when they marry. The EEOC has consistently ruled that this policy is discriminatory if the same rule isn't applied to male flight attendants—even if the stewardess had signed a pre-employment agreement saying that she would resign if she married.

Pregnancy and maternity leave. The EEOC has stated that "as a general rule," an employer may not fire a female employee compelled to stop work because of pregnancy, unless it offers her a leave of absence and reinstatement without loss of seniority or other benefits.

But this is not a hard and fast obligation. The commission points out that it aims to be fair to both employer and employee. Thus, it recognizes that women who are pregnant when hired may merit less protection than those who become pregnant after they are hired, and that employees with longer service may warrant more favorable treatment than newer workers. It has expressly stated, for example, that a company which grants no leaves before 12 months of service may apply the same rule to maternity leaves.

EEOC views pregnancy as a temporary disability rather than "sickness." Thus an employer may grant maternity leaves without pay, even though he provides pay to employees on sick leave. Furthermore, an employer may have a medical and hospital insurance plan which covers the expenses of delivery, but excludes disabilities related to pregnancy, childbirth, miscarriage and abortion.

The EEOC formerly held that a five- or six-month leave starting 90 days before delivery would be permissible, but a federal district court has said that any mandatory policy requiring women to quit a certain number of months before delivery is illegal unless the employer can prove that the employee's efficiency is impaired because of her condition. The employee in this case, who was required to start her maternity leave two months before delivery, was awarded back pay and accumulated sick and vacation leave.

(Also, see *Women in Management* starting on page 212).

⊃ EQUAL PAY ACT

Many employees are protected under both the Equal Pay Act and Title VII of the Civil Rights Act. Specifically, the Equal Pay Act covers all employees who are subject to the minimum wage requirements of the Wage-Hour Law. It does not cover such exempt salaried workers as executive, administrative and professional employees. Nor does it cover outside salesmen or others who are exempt from the minimum wage.

Title VII, on the other hand, applies to *all employees* of employers with at least 25 employees—including those who are exempt from the Equal Pay Act. Therefore, any employee who is subject to the minimum wage requirements *and* works for an employer with at least 25 employees is covered under both laws.

The Equal Pay Act, of course, is concerned with *sex discrimination in wages*. The jurisdiction of Title VII, on the other hand, extends beyond wage payments to discrimination in hiring, firing, promotions and anything affecting the "terms, conditions, or privileges of employment."

To avoid conflicting interpretations where employees are covered under both laws, the EEOC has announced that it will adopt the interpretations made under the Equal Pay Act—but only where the juris-dictions actually overlap. (The Equal Pay Act is enforced by the Wage-Hour Division which has more clout than the EEOC.)

What the Equal Pay Act prohibits. The act prohibits an employer from paying wages to employees of one sex at a rate less than he pays to employees of the opposite sex if they are working on jobs that re-quire *equal skill, effort and responsibility* in performance and if those jobs are performed under *similar working conditions.*

The only exceptions allowed are payments made pursuant to (1) a seniority system, (2) a merit system, (3) a system that measures earnings by quantity or quality of production, or (4) a differential based on "any other factor other than sex." *An employer cannot reduce the wages of any employee in order to comply with the act's requirements.*

The act bans discrimination "within any establishment." According to the Wage-Hour Division, an "establishment" is any "distinct physi-cal place of business" rather than an entire business. For example, if you have three plants (or stores, offices, warehouses, etc.) at separate locations, each of them is considered a separate establishment, and it isn't necessary to make comparisons between wage payment in one plant and another.

⊃ HOW JOBS ARE COMPARED

To be equal, jobs need not be identical, but only "substantially equal." As one court puts it, "insubstantial differences in the skill, effort and responsibility requirements of particular jobs should be ignored." In comparing jobs, the key questions that should be asked are these:

- *Do the jobs require equal skill, effort and responsibility?*
- *Are they performed under similar working conditions?*

The equal pay rules won't apply unless the jobs match on *both* of these tests. For example, two jobs may be performed under similar working conditions and require equal effort and responsibility, but if they demand different skills—or a different degree of skill—they won't be subject to the equal pay rules.

In determining whether jobs require equal skill, effort and responsi-bility, it's important to *look at the jobs as a whole and examine their characteristics over a full work cycle.* For example, in a situation where men and women operate the same type of machines for three weeks, but in the fourth week the women ship parts and the men set up the machines, the jobs would have to be compared over a period of at least four weeks.

Job content is the controlling factor in determining whether two jobs require equal skill, effort and responsibility. It's risky to rely on such criteria as job classifications, point values assigned under an evaluation system, and job titles, all of which may be misleading.

➲ AGE DISCRIMINATION IN EMPLOYMENT ACT

The Age Discrimination in Employment Act protects persons who are at least 40 years old but less than 65 against discrimination based on age in the following situations:

- Hiring or firing;
- Setting compensation, terms, conditions or privileges of employment;
- Segregating, classifying or otherwise limiting employees in any way that deprives an individual of employment opportunities or in some way adversely affects his status as an employee;
- Printing or publishing of advertisements or notices that indicate a preference, limitation, specification, or discrimination.

Compensation includes all types and methods of remuneration for employment. An employer *cannot reduce the wages* of any employee in order to comply with the act's requirements. For example, if a 62-year-old worker is being paid 50 cents an hour less than a 30-year-old who is doing the same work, the older worker's pay must be raised. Any attempt to avoid compliance by transferring one of the employees to other work would appear discriminatory.

How the ban on age discrimination works. No employer may discriminate against anyone in the protected 40-to-65 age group by giving preferential treatment because of age to someone younger or older. Nor can you discriminate on the basis of age between one person and another within the 40-to-65 protected group. For example, if you have two job applicants, one 42 and the other 52, you can't turn down either one on the basis of age. The hiring decision must be based on other factors, such as capability and experience.

It is possible, however, to indicate a hiring preference for persons 40 to 65 years of age, so long as there is no discrimination within that age group. Indicating a preference for persons receiving social security old-age benefits is considered discriminatory. On the other hand, the Age Discrimination Employment Act doesn't prohibit a refusal to hire someone under 65 who is getting social security benefits and is restricted in the amount of wages he can earn without losing benefits.

The act provides no protection to those outside the 40-to-65 age group. For example, age discrimination between a 25-year-old and a 35-year-old is not barred. The Wage-Hour Division has ruled that the following practices would be considered *discriminatory:*

- A union contract clause setting a 1-to-5 ratio of employment for men of 55 or over to younger men—even though its purpose may be to guarantee some work to those 55 and over.
- A union contract assigning a particular type of job to workers 50 and over.
- A union contract clause setting up an upper age limit of 35 for entrance into maintenance crew positions—unless one of the exceptions discussed below is applicable.

However, there is nothing in the Age Discrimination Act that prohibits the following practices:

- Discrimination on the basis of age where *age is a bona fide occupational qualification reasonably necessary to the normal operation of the particular business;*
- Any differentiation that's based on *reasonable factors other than age;*
- Observing the terms of *a bona fide seniority system* or any bona fide employee benefit plan, such as a retirement, pension or insurance plan, which is not a subterfuge to evade the purposes of the act. However, *no employee benefit plan can be an excuse for failing to hire anyone in the 40-to-65 age bracket.*

Age as a bona fide occupational qualification. As under Title VII, the bona fide occupational qualification (BFOQ) exception is construed narrowly, and the burden is on the employer to prove that the exception applies. In the following examples, age is an acceptable "BFOQ:"

- Complying with federal laws or regulations that set compulsory age limitations for hiring or that set compulsory retirement ages, without referece to the individual's actual physical condition at retirement age, when such conditions are clearly imposed for the safety and convenience of the public. For example, airline pilots who are within the jurisdiction of the Federal Aviation Agency can't engage in carrier operations as pilots after they reach 40.
- Hiring actors required for youthful or elderly characterizations and persons used to advertise or promote the sale of products appealing exclusively to either youthful or elderly consumers.

➲ HELP-WANTED ADVERTISING

The antidiscrimination laws place tight restrictions on help-wanted advertising. The EEOC has ruled that the following types of ads violate Title VII:

- *An ad specifying race or placed in racially separated lists.*
- *An ad indicating a preference for religion, sex or national origin* unless one of these factors is a bona fide occupational qualification. For example, an ad for employees trained in a particular foreign country is discriminatory unless the preference is based on the particular nature and quality of the foreign training.
- *Ads placed in classified columns headed "Male" or "Female,"* unless sex is a bona fide occupational qualification for the job.

The Age Discrimination Act bans such age specifications in help-wanted ads as "age 25 to 35," "girl," "boy," "ambitious young man," "junior executive," "age over 65"—in short, any indication of age preference that would discriminate against the 40-to-65 age group that the act is intended to protect. Also suspect are "retired person" and "supplement your pension." The only clear age preference you can mention is for the entire protected group—"age 40 to 65"—but you can't discriminate within the group by specifying, for example, "age 50" or "age 40 to 50." You can also specify a minimum age if it's less than 40—such as "not under 18" or "not under 21." In addition, you can indicate "college graduate," but not "recent college graduate." Asking the applicant to "state age" isn't actually a violation, but the Wage-Hour Division has said that such ads will be "closely scrutinized."

Use of the term "Girl Friday" isn't considered unlawful under the Age Discrimination Act. But it probably would be a violation of the sex discrimination provisions of Title VII. Many companies resolve the problem by advertising for "Gal/Guy Friday."

➲ BOOBY TRAPS IN APPLICATION BLANKS AND INTERVIEWS

Pre-employment inquiring regarding an appliants' race, color, religion or national origin can cause trouble. Such inquiries will weigh against the company—unless made in conformance with requirements of a local, state or federal government agency—particularly when found in combination with other evidence of discrimination. Special care should also be taken so that those who interview job applicants don't inadvertently stray into areas of inquiry which are touchy.

While the EEOC has not spelled out the do's and dont's in this sensitive area, you can get a fairly good indication of what the trouble spots are from the following summary of questions which the New York Commission Against Discrimination has held to be unlawful:

- Original name of an applicant whose name has been changed by court order or otherwise.
- Birthplace of applicant, applicant's parents, spouse or other relatives.
- Requirement that applicant submit birth certificate, naturalization or baptismal record.
- Inquiry into an applicant's religious denomination, religious affiliations, church, parish, pastor, or religious holidays observed.
- An applicant may not be told "This is a Catholic, Protestant or Jewish organization."
- Inquiries regarding complexion or color of skin.
- Requirement that an applicant affix a photograph to his employment form after interview but before hiring, or at his option.
- Inquiry into whether an applicant's parents or spouse are naturalized or native-born citizens; the date when any of the above acquired citizenship.
- Requirement that applicant produce his naturalization papers or first papers.
- Inquiry into applicant's lineage, ancestry, national origin, descent, parentage or nationality, or the nationality of applicant's parents or spouse.
- Inquiry into language commonly used by applicant.
- Inquiry into how applicant acquired ability to read, write or speak a foreign language.
- Name of any relative of applicant, other than applicant's father and mother, husband or wife, and minor dependent children. (This ruling prohibits such inquiries as "maiden name of applicant's wife," "maiden name of applicant's mother," "name of applicant's relatives," and "names of applicant's close relatives.")
- Address of any relative of applicant, other than address (within the United States) of applicant's father and mother, husband or wife and minor children.
- Requirement that applicant list all clubs, societies and lodges to which he belongs.
- Inquiry into an applicant's general military experience.

However, the EEOC has said that an employer may inquire about an applicant's military service. It has also stated that a woman may be asked her maiden name, provided the information isn't used to discriminate.

2

REVIEWS
AND
APPRAISALS

"How am I doing?"

The serious-minded professional executive can't help but ask this question. It's the key to his progress and achievement.

Section II of *The Executive Deskbook,* makes it possible for you to fill out answers to your personal capability in specific and significant areas of your executive job.

The reviews and appraisals that you find in this section give you a chance to assess your capability in key professional areas. In some cases, the self-ratings give you numerical evaluations. These need not be taken too seriously. But as an approximation of how well you are doing, your scores can be extremely helpful in rule-of-thumb assessments. Further, in pinpointing weak and strong areas, you can derive the benefits of remedial moves that can further strengthen your professional capabilities.

*   *   *   *   *

➜ SPOTTING COMMUNICATIONS WEAKSPOTS

A key function of every executive is to receive and give information. How well are you doing? The questions below can turn up some useful answers:

1. In communications with your subordinates, do you often get:
   a. inaccurate information?
   b. more than you need?
   c. less?
2. Are you receiving only *routine* material, suggesting a hardening of communications arteries?
3. Do your subordinates complain that they get information late?
4. Do your people often have to check for:
   a. additional information (for example, to supplement a report)?
   b. clarification of a communication you've sent them?
5. From your superior do you usually get:
   a. all the information you need?
   b. information as soon as you need it?
   c. more information than you actually use?
   d. ambiguous, garbled, or unclear information?
6. In communications to your superior:
   a. do your replies to his reports or memos tend to be late?
   b. do phone calls to him take up more time than warranted?
   c. are you making the best use of written reports, phone calls, and face-to-face discussion?
7. In your communications with fellow executives:
   a. are you handicapped by any persistent gaps in information?
   b. are you sending any reports that no longer fill a purpose?
   c. are you receiving any reports that need revision?
   d. do you know of any change in method of communications that would improve results (e.g., switching from memos to conferences)?
8. Are your outside contacts (with customers, suppliers, and so on):
   a. snowing you under?
   b. frequent enough to provide satisfactory results?
   c. close enough to permit personal relationships?

➜ YOUR DECISION-MAKING PRACTICES

Your decision-making success depends on how well you can evaluate or compare alternative solutions to your problems, despite time pressure and insufficient data.

1. Do you avoid leaving yourself left high and dry, because of failure to decide on a course of action *in time?*
2. Similarly, do you avoid making decisions *before* you have to, and later receive information that would have changed your actions?
3. In developing alternative courses of action to given problems, do you make use of the experience and knowledge of—
   a. your superior?
   b. colleagues?
   c. professional sources of know-how?
   d. your subordinates?
4. In evaluating the advantages and disadvantages of alternatives do you—
   a. list the pros and cons of each possibility in writing (at least for critical decisions)?
   b. check the opinions of experts or people with relevant experience?
   c. try to quantify as many factors as possible, to make comparisons easier and more meaningful?
5. In your final selection of a course of action, do you consider the possibility of combining the favorable aspects of two or more alternatives?
6. In analyzing decisions that misfired, was the reason:
   a. misunderstanding the objectives you were trying to achieve?
   b. miscalculating the difficulties of the situation?
   c. overestimating the abilities of your subordinates?
   d. underestimating their abilities?
   e. failing to keep up with new developments affecting your decision?

➲ PLANNING

The ability to study cause and effect, to see short-range difficulties in the light of long-range goals, is a key to overall executive accomplishment.

1. Do you review objectives periodically, so that your planning can be updated?
2. Do you take advantage of group brainpower by permitting subordinates to participate in planning procedures?
3. Would you benefit by formalizing your planning procedures, that is, allocating specific time periods to planning activities?
4. Do you use the basic "tools" of planning—calendar, pencil,

paper, charts, graphs, pertinent records of past performance, and so on?

5. Is your planning flexible enough to meet changing conditions—higher standards, shorter deadlines, and so on?

6. Are your planning methods organized well enough for you to be able to explain them to someone else?

7. Do you try to develop the skills of your subordinates as an aid to achieving your most ambitious plans?

8. Do you devote "training time" to helping your subordinates plan their activities?

9. Are you planning the activity of any subordinate who should be on his own?

10. Are any of your subordinates performing planning functions that you should be doing?

11. Do you ask your superior for enough information to make your planning sufficiently long-range?

12. Do you consult your superior to get his suggestions on your planning activities—covering everything from objectives to resources to methods and evaluation of results?

➲ ORDER-GIVING REVIEW

How good is your command of the order-giving process? Check—

1. Before giving orders, do you—
   a. clarify the end results you're after?
   b. pre-think the moves required to meet objectives?
   c. decide on the right people to do the job?
   d. help make needed resources available to them?

2. In giving orders or instructions, do you—
   a. suit the type of order to the individual: a direct order for the beginner, "result-wanted" order for the veteran, etc.?
   b. indicate, wherever necessary, the additional information (data, reference material) they'll need to finish the job?
   c. try to put into your instructions the challenge that will create the strongest motivation for the individual?
   d. provide written instructions, and other "support" material, as needed?

3. In setting goals for subordinates' activities, do you—
   a. let them join in a discussion of the relevance and importance of goals?
   b. permit those with initiative enough leeway to exercise it?
   c. give those who lack self-confidence the opportunity to check back with you as often as will be helpful?

4. To aim at better teamwork, do you—
   a. give your group the opportunity, where possible, to share in planning operations?
   b. keep group goals clearly in view at all times?

➲ PROBLEM-SOLVING

Unsolved problems are stones in the road of progress. The executive administrator is confronted by an unending parade of problems day in, day out. Are you able to keep the stones out of the road? As an indication:

1. Do you go looking for problems in order to account for:
   a. plans that haven't jelled?
   b. unanticipated developments?
   c. unexpected behavior on the part of your people?
2. Do you agree that a problem generally holds the clue to its solution?
3. When you're faced by a problem, do you automatically:
   a. start digging out the relevant facts?
   b. mentally line up the people who can help solve the problem?
   c. try to approach the situation on a logical, systematic basis?
4. Do you motivate the problem-solving activities of your subordinates by communicating to them the excitement and challenge of facing up to a tough problem?
5. Do you give your unconscious a chance to work on your problems by generating mental input—focusing on the circumstances and facts of the difficulty, thinking about the problem, and not trying to think through to a solution, leaving that to your unconscious mind?
6. As a starter for creative problem-solving, do you examine and challenge the assumptions you may have about both the circumstances of the problem, as well as the possible solution?

➲ ARE YOU GETTING RESULTS FROM YOUR LEADERSHIP

Of all management skills, leadership is most highly valued—and most difficult to define. Of course, a good leader may be easy enough to identify:

> "His people will do anything he asks of them."
> "He knows how to make his group pull together."

But even when we watch good leaders in action, we find it difficult to pinpoint exactly *what* they do and *how* they do it. Nevertheless, while there's a lot about leadership we don't know, some insightful checkpoints can provide a rough rule of thumb measure of this crucial skill. Try the quiz that follows, sticking reasonably close to your own experience.

	True	False
1. I do a good job of getting my people to cooperate in achieving goals	——	——
2. My people don't hesitate to bring their really tough work problems to me	——	——
3. When the heat's on, I can get my people to go full steam without any gripes from them	——	——
4. When I'm not around to supervise personally, my subordinates go on working pretty much as usual ..	——	——
5. I have a good record of helping individuals improve their job performance	——	——
6. I have never had a justified complaint about showing favoritism	——	——
7. I can usually get people to accept changes, even if they have to make a big adjustment	——	——
8. In case of an argument or controversy involving other departments, I back up my people when I know they are right	——	——
9. I have relatively little trouble in getting my people to level with me	——	——
10. I use encouragement often	——	——
11. My subordinates seem to take criticism from me and respond constructively	——	——
12. I find it easy to get volunteers	——	——
13. I make a special effort to be fair in assigning tasks, equitably	——	——
14. My people feel I'm readily available for assistance, as they need it	——	——
15. I am proud of my staff and don't hesitate to show it	——	——

Scoring: Give yourself 10 points for each item marked true, then rate yourself on the scale below.

130 to 150—You're an outstanding leader, a combination of Solomon and Caesar.

100 to 120—You're good, with only a slight case of Achilles' heel.

Under 100—You're not sure of your leadership ability, and this results in job headaches.

If you're dissatisfied with your score, go back over all the questions. Each one highlights a major opportunity for leadership performance. Questions you answered incorrectly are prime areas for improvement.

➡ A PERFORMANCE REVIEW CHECKLIST FOR YOUR SUBORDINATES

Executives with department heads, supervisors, foremen, and other lower-echelon managers reporting to them, may want a performance checklist that these subordinates can use to show how they're doing in a given time period—quarterly, semiannually, and so on. Here are the kinds of items that form the basis of such a performance review, and the ratings that can pinpoint areas requiring consultation with you.

	Excellent	Satisfactory	Requires Att'n	Top Priority
1. Holding cost line	☐	☐	☐	☐
2. Cooperation from work group	☐	☐	☐	☐
3. Suggestions and ideas from work group	☐	☐	☐	☐
4. Ability to handle rush or emergency orders	☐	☐	☐	☐
5. Keeping up with work	☐	☐	☐	☐
6. Flexibility of work group	☐	☐	☐	☐
7. Improving employee skills (Training, job rotation, etc.)	☐	☐	☐	☐
8. Relations with line departments	☐	☐	☐	☐
9. Relations with staff and service departments	☐	☐	☐	☐
10. Staying on top of personal workload	☐	☐	☐	☐
11. Equipment maintenance and performance	☐	☐	☐	☐
12. Self-improvement, updating of management skills	☐	☐	☐	☐
13. Other (add your own)	☐	☐	☐	☐
14. Other	☐	☐	☐	☐
15. Other	☐	☐	☐	☐

➡ BROADENING YOUR HORIZONS

Keeping up with—or keeping one jump ahead of—developments in your business and profession, is an important element in every executive's personal anti-obsolescence program. The questions below point up some of the key areas for updating:

	Yes	No

1. In your industry, have you increased your contacts by:
   a. reading the trade journals in your field? ☐ ☐
   b. increasing your participation in a professional group or association of men who do similar work? ☐ ☐
   c. attending conferences and lectures, or interviewing experts, to keep up with changes in your industry? ☐ ☐
2. Inside your own company, have you taken advantage of progress-boosters, like these:
   a. talking shop regularly with your colleagues? ☐ ☐
   b. making changes in your way of handling assignments? ☐ ☐
   c. taking on new assignments?
3. In your quest for job knowledge, have you:
   a. visited other companies that are now working on problems you may soon be encountering? ☐ ☐
   b. kept up with the stream of ideas available in current management literature—for example, *Harvard Business Review, Fortune, Business Week* and *Nation's Business?* ☐ ☐
   c. investigated what's available at local schools?
   d. made suggestions, either to a top company executive or to schools, for studies of interest to you? ☐ ☐
4. In pursuit of your professional interests, have you:
   a. experimented in the application of new methods to executive problems? ☐ ☐
   b. experimented in the development of new methods to complete your daily tasks? ☐ ☐
   c. tried as much as possible to substitute method and system for casualness and the impromptu solution? ☐ ☐
   d. kept in touch with the kind of thinking going on at Arden House, Harvard Business School, the University of Chicago's Management Development Program, and so on? ☐ ☐

In trying to solve the problem of tomorrow, you will have to look two ways at once. Keep one eye on the growing professionalization of executive activity and standards; keep the other eye on home base.

➲ HOW FLEXIBLE ARE YOU?

Answer the questions below as accurately as possible. Even if you're able to spot the "right answers," try to indicate what you would actually do in the situation described. You'll find scoring directions at the end of the quiz.

1. You're in a room with three or four other executives. They're all wearing gray flannel suits; yours is brown tweed. Your reaction, if you noticed their garb at all, would be:
   a. To smile to yourself at their conformity.
   b. To suggest jokingly that at your next meeting they appear "out of uniform."
   c. To feel uncomfortable at being incorrectly dressed.
   d. To make a mental note to wear your gray flannel next time you are going to be in similar company.
2. Your office is to be moved to a different floor because of some structural changes being made in the building. Your feeling is likely to be:
   a. Regret that you'll be leaving a place to which you've become accustomed.
   b. "Fine! New surroundings will be a welcome change."
   c. Interest in seeing that the new setup will be as good as the old.
3. You're in a conference called to decide whether or not the company should expand into a new field. Your probable course, all other things being equal, would be:
   a. To argue for the move.
   b. To argue against the move.
   c. To argue for the move, on condition that a careful study indicates good chances for success.
4. Your boss calls you into his office. "Jack," he says, "I've been wanting to talk to you about your job, but I don't know just how or where to begin. Now I want you to ask me for a raise. I think that will trigger the things I have to say." Your move is to say:
   a. "Boss, I'd like to have a boost of five thousand dollars a year, retroactive to the first of the year."
   b. "I couldn't, Boss. Let's wait until you can get going under your own steam."
   c. "Boss, our relationship must be getting awfully weak if you can't come right out and tell me what you want to say."

5. Your boss calls you into his office. "Henry," he says, "let's go through our usual routine of discussing last week's problems. I'm not sure we're getting much benefit from this procedure, but I feel it's better than not doing anything at all." Your reply is:

   a. "Sure, just as you wish . . .," and then you launch into the kind of monologue that has featured the sessions.

   b. "Since we're not getting satisfactory results, why not change our approach? How about . . . ," and you suggest a couple of alternative methods that you think might yield more information.

   c. "If you feel it's a waste of time, why do it at all?"

6. A customer is on the phone, telling you he must have delivery on an order by the end of the week. You tell him you can't make the stuff up to the standard of quality he wants and still ship within the time limit he has set. He insists; you insist. Finally:

   a. You tell him, "I'm sorry, Mr. White, but you're being unreasonable. No matter how much we'd like to, we just can't satisfy your request." And that's your final word.

   b. You ask him whether he could use material of the lower quality that would result from a speeded-up process.

   c. You say, "There is a possibility that we could get the work out on time, but it would mean running on a three-shift basis, and we're only set up for two. Would you be willing to pay the extra cost involved in our arranging a three-shift schedule?"

7. You've just got a new secretary. She's a good, capable girl who insists on dusting your desk every morning. The trouble is, she has her own ideas of how your desk equipment should be arranged: she puts your in-out box at the right instead of the left, puts your phone at the back of the desk, although you generally keep it toward the front, and so on. Would you:

   a. Let her have her way.

   b. Make it very clear that you have your personal preferences in the matter of desktop arrangement, and order her to place the items the way you've always kept them.

   c. Ask her why she feels her arrangement is better than the one you've been using.

8. You've made it a practice to have lunch with one of your colleagues every Tuesday. He calls you in the morning to say he can't make it. Which would be your likeliest move:

   a. Phone another friend or acquaintance and try to set up another lunch date.
   b. Feel quite disconcerted, go to lunch alone, and find yourself at loose ends for the entire hour.
   c. Go to lunch alone and enjoy the unaccustomed pleasure of an hour's solitude.
9. You get out of bed one morning and see it's a little late; you shave, gulp breakfast, and dash off to the station. To your surprise you notice the platform is practically empty; then you realize it's Sunday morning. Would you:
   a. Try to sneak back into bed without waking your wife, so that could keep the incident a dark secret.
   b. Feel the incident proves you're too deep in a rut, and cast about for some way of easing up.
   c. Decide to go into town anyway, to clean up a couple of overdue matters at the office.

Scoring: First, realize that any one question by itself isn't too significant. Many of us can be flexible in some areas—matters of dress, personal working habits, for example, and inflexible in others—time schedules, and off-the-cuff reactions to abrupt changes.

However, a very high score in the quiz is probably a favorable indication of your flexibility in general; a very low one is apt to be unfavorable. Rate yourself as follows:

Start by giving yourself a perfect score, 90 points. Then, *subtract 10 points* for these "wrong answers": 1c or d; 2a; 3b; 4b; 5a; 6a; 7b; 8b; 9a.

Here's the rating scale:

70 to 90: You're as adaptable as a good boxer.

40 to 60: You tend to freeze a bit at the edges; ease up.

Below 40: A bit of rut-busting might do you a world of good.

➲ PRE-INTERVIEW CHECK LIST

Before you begin an interview, check these points:
   1. Do you know as much about the interviewee as is necessary in the context of the interview? For some situations, these points are helpful:

name and title
nature of his responsibility or function
name of his company and what it does

his superior
his business or work experience
his special interests
his accomplishments
2. Will the place selected be suitable?
3. Are there others who should be informed of the interview?
4. Are there others who should be present during the talk?
5. Is the information or data you may want to use at hand?
6. Have you taken steps to minimize interruptions?
7. Do you have a list—mental or written—of the points you want to cover?
8. Do you know the objective you're after?
9. Do you know the objective of your interviewee? What does he want to gain from the meeting?
10. Should you decide in advance to what extent you want to help satisfy his objectives?
11. Are there others who should be informed of the outcome of the interview?
12. Any follow-up steps to be taken—memos sent off, ideas to be followed, etc.?
13. Should a record of the interview be made?
14. If the interview is one of a series, should you note the ideas you've gained that should be reflected in subsequent talks?

➔ **HOW EFFECTIVE IS YOUR INTERVIEW TECHNIQUE?**

	Yes	No
1. Do your interviews generally run about as long as you feel they should?	☐	☐
2. Do you concentrate on helping the interviewee relax?	☐	☐
3. Do you check your notes during the meeting to make sure you cover the points and subpoints of your objective?	☐	☐
4. If unavoidable interruptions occur, do you try to minimize the annoyance for the interviewee—give him a book or magazine to glance at or, still better, material pertinent to your meeting?	☐	☐
5. Do you consider the advisability of terminating an interview short of its goal, if an unanticipated problem arises—unusual nervousness, or emotional upset of the other person, for example?	☐	☐

6. Do you strive for a positive and usually a satisfying

ending to your interview—a pleasant word of thanks, or assurance of an action desired by the interviewee, if that's in the cards? □ □

7. For repetitive interview, would a checklist of points to cover be helpful? □ □

8. Are you aware of "stress interview" techniques— that is, pressuring the interviewee—so as to *avoid* them, as being unfair and unproductive? □ □

  Yes is the preferred answer, except for 7, where either answer is O.K. *No* answers suggest points requiring remedy.

➲ FOLLOW-UP

How do you think you rate in your knowledge of follow-up procedures? Here's a chance to rate yourself.

Everybody's always telling everybody else to follow up. But what nobody tells anybody is exactly *how* you do it. The questions below can help you check yourself on some of the ABC's of the process.

                 Yes No

1. You give two subordinates assignments. One man is an old-timer, the other has been on the job only six months. Would you, in all cases, check back on the new man rather than on the old-timer? □ □

2. Do money considerations play a part in follow-up practices? □ □

3. Does the fact that a particular job has been done again and again make follow-up unnecessary? □ □

4. Is resentment at having you "breathing down their necks" a necessary consequence of follow-up? □ □

5. Is it possible to toss the "follow-up ball" to the subordinate doing the assignment? □ □

6. Can you delegate the follow-up responsibility? □ □

7. Let's look up the ladder for a moment. Is there anything you can do to ease the follow-up burden of your superior? □ □

Answers:

1. *No.* For example, if the old-timer was on a job with which he was unfamiliar, and the new employee was on his regular assignment, chances are it would be wiser to check the old employee.

2. *Yes.* Where sizable sums figure in the outcome of work being done, it's mandatory for you to keep a closer check.

3. *No.* In addition to the possible dollar penalties of something going

wrong, any critical operation—one involving risk to the employee, for example—demands your continued attention.

4. *No.* The manner you use in your follow-up can go a long way toward offsetting employee sensitivity.

5. *Yes.* Executives frequently use the device of having subordinates check back with them to report on developments or results.

6. *Yes.* In many routine jobs it's definitely in the cards for you to have an assistant or an experienced employee do the checking for you.

7. *Yes.* Give him the information he needs—in the form of a progress report, for example—as soon as it's available.

Scoring: Give yourself 10 points for each correct answer.

70: You're perfect.

40 to 60: You're good.

0 to 30: Rereading the questions and answers can improve both your score and grasp of the follow-up process.

➲ HOW TO BENEFIT FROM FAILURE

The worst has happened. You've fallen on your face and you have that "bottom-has-dropped-out-of-everything" feeling. You can't look your colleagues in the eye.

But before laying out the price of a one-way ticket to Shangri-la, see if supplying the answers to some simple questions doesn't help, and without giving up the comforts of home:

1. Just what has been lost as a result of your failure? Write out this answer. Be specific. Mention amounts, time losses, delays in schedule, and so on.

2. Did you include "self-confidence" in your list above? If not, it's probably a serious omission. Add it.

3. Do you agree that as a result of your failure, you're wiser than you were before?

4. Write out what you've gained, point by point, from your failure?

5. If you find that you can't list anything in No. 4, just consider the items submitted by an executive who had failed in his all-out attempt to sell his boss on a program designed to expand the facilities in his department:

   a. learned a lot about the dollar worth of present physical equipment

   b. learned what was available in the market today

   c. from boss's objection, got a better understanding of top management's views on cash investment

   d. improved my ability to present a project in written form

e. realized for the first time that my boss has absolutely no imagination

f. from boss's questions, realized the need to supply and dramatize facts to support my contentions

g. put myself on record as being interested in building the area of my responsibility

6. Compare your answers to No. 1 and No. 4. Doesn't No. 4 constitute a more important factor in your future moves than No. 1?

7. Can you minimize or eliminate the items of loss you've noted in answering No. 1?

8. Can you apply the items, noted in your answer to No. 4, in any future activity?

9. Don't you agree that the extent to which failure persists as an influence on your behavior is largely within your control?

If you can answer yes to No. 9, your Failsmanship is already of a high order.

⮕ HOW WELL DO YOU RELATE TO YOUR SUBORDINATES?

Here's a chance to get some insight on how good you are at working with your people. The questions are simple, but practical:

	Yes	No
1. Is everyone on your staff aware of your genuine interest in him as an individual?	( )	( )
2. Do you know both first and last names of all those in your group?	( )	( )
3. Have you shown sufficient interest in them (without being nosy) so that you know—		
a. names and ages of their children	( )	( )
b. where their children go to school or work	( )	( )
c. something about their home life and :problems	( )	( )
d. their outside activities, talents, and hobbies	( )	( )
e. their health	( )	( )
f. their personal aspirations	( )	( )
4. Have you developed the right amount of friendliness without overfamiliarity?	( )	( )
5. Do you go out of your way to be personally helpful on things that don't relate to the job?	( )	( )
6. Are you willing to go all out for your people if the facts warrant it, even though it means some inconvenience for you?	( )	( )

7. Do you go out of your way to establish mutual interests with each subordinate—
   a. stressing a sincere interest in his career objectives   ( )   ( )
   b. showing an unaffected interest in his personal interests, hopes, and so on   ( )   ( )
8. Do you try to keep the communication lines sufficiently open and used, so that the times you seek out contacts with subordinates are not something special and ominous?   ( )   ( )
9. In the interviews that you have with subordinates, do you try to create a relaxed, unhurried air that helps each man feel at ease and emphasizes your receptivity?   ( )   ( )

Scoring: Give yourself 10 points for each question answered yes. Then rate yourself on the following scale:

90–100   You're good with your people, and they can be a fountainhead of strength and support to you.
70–80   You're pretty good. Try just a bit harder.
Below 70   You're not deriving all the benefits you can from your people. Reread the quiz questions which you didn't answer yes. Each one suggests an area in which you have an opportunity to strengthen your rapport with people.

➲ YOU'RE A GOOD CONFERENCE LEADER: TRUE OR FALSE?

The dozen items below can test your conference leadership knowledge and skill. Indicate whether you believe each statement to be true or false. Then check your score according to the directions that follow.

	True	False
1. You may do nothing between your introduction and summary except ask questions, and still do a good job of leading a conference.	T	F
2. Differences of opinion generally hamstring a conference.	T	F
3. When you "know the answer," you should save time by telling the conferees, rather, than use the slower method of leading them to think their way to the answer.	T	F
4. The leader should state his view to encourage the conferees to state theirs.	T	F
5. When a conferee is "wrong" or advances an unpopular opinion and is attacked by the group, you have a responsibility to defend him.	T	F

6. A side discussion can be stopped without chastising the participants.	T	F
7. Vote taking is the only approved device for settling disagreements.	T	F
8. Even the long-winded conferee should be given full opportunity to say his piece.	T	F
9. "Atmosphere" changes in a conference can be detected before they erupt.	T	F
10. The best number of conferees is twenty-five.	T	F
11. An articulate expert is a constant help to a conference leader.	T	F
12. The leader is a dead duck if the conference gets out of control.	T	F

Scoring: To see how good you are as a conference leader, score your answers as follows. Give yourself 10 points for each questions correctly answered. It may be that you may disagree with some of the "right" answers given below. If you disagree violently, stick by your own answers and give yourself full credit. But generally, we believe you will find the answers as given to be acceptable:

1. True. Socrates did it all the time, and look what a reputation for wisdom he gained! And the modern leader finds it an effective method.
2. False. They're an important asset. If everyone agrees, no one will go out smarter than when he came in.
3. False. The answer they think out acquires real meaning and acceptability.
4. False. There will always be a number of insecure individuals who will refrain from ever doing anything that even remotely smacks of bucking the boss or leader.
5. True. Actually he's doing the group a favor—making them think.
6. True. For example, if you can assume they're talking about the conference subject, state that everyone would like to hear the idea they're discussing.
7. False. If there's that much lack of agreement, more discussion is needed.
8. False. The uncontrolled rambler is a prime conference killer. You must help him get his point briefly.
9. True. Learning to recognize "feeling words," negative interactions, and subsurface meanings equips you to predict and counteract them.
10. False. Experience recommends six to twelve as optimum in most cases.
11. False. The expert is best rendered inarticulate, so others can think and contribute.
12. False. The fact that a conference occasionally does wrench loose from its mooring is proof of its spontaneity. And it's seldom a problem to restore peace and direction.

Rate yourself on the following scale:

100 to 120 . . . . outstanding
 70 to 90 . . . . good
 40 to 60 . . . . poor
Below 40 . . . . suggest you reread questions answered incorrectly
                   as a start in strengthening weak points.

➜ YOU'RE A GOOD CONFEREE: TRUE OR FALSE?

	True	False
1. The conferee who does not have the problem being discussed can be a valuable contributor.	T	F
2. People sitting next to you influence you more than do those across the table.	T	F
3. A conferee who hears all that's said knows what is happening in a discussion group.	T	F
4. Conferences can be a promotion-gaining vehicle for a conferee.	T	F
5. Skilled conference leaders make good conferees.	T	F
6. The fellow conferee who disagrees with your view is more help than one who agrees.	T	F
7. It is all right to tell a joke during a conference.	T	F
8. It's a good idea to "study up" on a subject before a discussion.	T	F
9. If you see that everyone in the group but you is heading in a direction you believe is wrong, you should keep quiet for the sake of peace and unanimity.	T	F
10. Any single conferee can make or break a conference by being either aggressively negative or aggressively positive.	T	F

Scoring: To see how good you are as a conferee, give yourself 10 points for each question correctly answered. You may disagree with some of the "right" answers given below. If you disagree violently, stick by your own answer and give yourself full credit. But generally, we believe you'll find the answers given to be acceptable.

1. True. He has the great advantage of objectivity, can see the problem without emotional obstructions.
2. False. Tests show that the greatest interaction is between conferees sitting directly opposite one another.
3. False. Often, occurrences beneath the surface affect a conference more than visible factors do.
4. True. Many firms use conferences as a means of detecting superior and promotable people.
5. False. While their knowledge of problem handling, etc., equips them

to help the leader eliminate disruptions, they sometimes cannot overcome the impulse to step in and start leading the discussion.
6. True. He obliges you to think harder and deeper in order to support
your position.
7. True. A funny story is a big help, if it's relevant, illustrative, or seems
to ease tension.
8. True. You're better equipped to participate.
9. False. If you believe your contrary view is valid, you do a disservice if
you don't speak up, even though it may mean that, in a way, you pit
yourself against the group.
10. True. One person can liven it up if it's dull, sour the whole group,
raise spirits if defeatism is setting in, etc.
Rate yourself on the following scale:
   80 to 100 . . . . outstanding
   50 to 70 . . . . just about O.K.
   Below 50 . . . . poor; suggest you reread questions answered incor-
                          rectly as a start in strengthening weakpoints.

⊃ CHECK YOUR DICTATION PRACTICES

A review of your dictating procedure may help you spot habits or
practices that, in the interest of efficiency, should be changed. The
list below touches some of the high spots:

1. Are your dictation periods timed so that they fall in the best possible spot in your daily routine? (For example, does your timing allow ample leeway for transcription before the last mail?)	yes	no
2. Do you make every effort to prevent unnecessary interruptions while you're dictating?	yes	no
3. Do you have at your fingertips all the information you require for the dictation you plan to give?	yes	no
4. Do you clearly state your instructions for each piece of dictated material—whether it's a memo, a letter, a report, or other type of communication?	yes	no
5. Do you clearly state your priorities—which items are to be rushed, which can be left for last?	yes	no
6. Do you ask for a rough draft when you anticipate changes in your copy?	yes	no
7. Do you spell out unusually difficult words, proper names, and technical phrases, and enunciate clearly all critical figures?	yes	no
8. If you use a stenographer, do you regulate your dictation speed to her shorthand rate?	yes	no

9. When appropriate, do you give your stenographer an opportunity to ask questions on points that may not be clear?   yes   no
10. Do you indicate minor corrections in such a way that letters and reports need not be retyped?   yes   no

Although you may have answered all the questions, keep in mind the possibility that some of your replies should be considered subject to review by your stenographer or transcriber. *Yes* is clearly desirable in each case.

➔ TENSION QUIZ

Here's an amazing fact: many executives, including those laboring under greatest tension, don't know they're tensed up. You may have to check to see how badly tension gets you down. The questions and multiple-choice answers below can help you find out the truth about yourself.

1. Your superior has asked you to see him. As you sit outside his office, what would be in your mind?
   a. "I wonder what's wrong."
   b. "I hope the boss has good news for me."
   c. Your mind turns to other matters completely unrelated to the coming sessions.
2. An employee asks for permission to see your superior, because he wants to complain about your handling of a situation. You're sure in your own mind that you are beyond blame. Which move would you be most likely to make?
   a. Tell the employee flatly that he is not to go to the boss.
   b. Try to persuade him that it would be better if you and he settle the question between yourselves.
   c. Say, "I always want you to feel free to see the boss at any time. Go right ahead."
3. You've suggested a new service policy to your boss. He likes the idea and suggests that you explain it to the board of directors. You're now sitting in a conference room with a dozen big shots. You feel:
   a. As though you'd like to sink into the floor.
   b. Completely calm.
   c. Somewhat jittery, but exhilarated at the challenge you're facing.
4. You're sitting home reading. It's eleven P.M. Unexpectedly, the phone rings. Which reaction would be most likely for you?
   a. "I wonder who's calling at this hour?"

b. "Oh, oh. Here comes trouble!"

c. "Probably a wrong number."

5. In the course of discussing a problem, you suggest a solution. A fellow executive takes violent exception to the idea, attacks it as "stupid." Your reaction:

a. You drop your wraps and come out fighting for your idea.

b. You're so upset that it takes a few seconds for you to recover.

c. You laugh and say: "Now that you've told us what's wrong with the idea, Bill, let's see if we can't incorporate the good points into our solution."

6. You've recently chosen a new assistant. He turns in an outstanding performance. Your reaction:

a. You're very pleased.

b. You go out of your way to tell your boss about your assistant's accomplishments.

c. You think maybe he's been more successful than you really want him to be. Now the man is beginning to show you up in your own executive performance.

7. You and two other executives are being considered for promotion. The phone rings and it's the call that's to give you the decision. As you answer:

a. You feel pretty good because you're reasonably sure you got the nod.

b. Your hand is shaking and you almost drop the receiver.

c. You're reasonably calm, because you know even if you missed out this time, eventually you'll make the grade.

8. You have to make a key decision that will affect the operation of your department for the entire year. Now, as in other decision-making situations, you are:

a. Nervous and worried.

b. So intent on digging into the facts and figures that you're not particularly aware you're doing anything special.

c. In a Napoleonic mood, in which you feel yourself to be master of the situation.

Scoring: Unlike most other self-tests, a "normal" score in this test is not one where all your answers indicate an absence of anxiety or tension. You'll find this fact reflected in the scoring directions below.

Answers that indicate you are predisposed toward tension: 1a, 2a, 3a, 4b, 5b, 6c, 7b, 8a.

For each question answered as above, deduct 10 points from a total of 80. Then rate yourself.

40 or less: You're too anxious.

50 to 70: You're anxious, but about average.

80: You're *too* perfect. Chances are you didn't answer the questions frankly, or you approach crises with an unnatural calm.

⮕ THE SKILLS RATING CHART

There are many different sets of categories management experts have developed that represent executive skills. The one used below represents twenty-one job-oriented areas of executive activity. Taken together in this quick quiz form, they give you a chance to rate your executive performance. You'll find an interpretation of your score following the items. To answer, ask yourself, "How do I rate my past performance in the given area?"

Skills Rating Chart

	Low	Medium	High
1. *Using the expert*—getting information, opinions, ideas from well-informed people inside or outside your company.	□	□	□
2. *Building reputation*—making yourself known; developing a favorable name for yourself in the company.	□	□	□
3. *Activating*—getting your people to understand and follow your instructions.	□	□	□
4. *Imparting information*—making yourself understood by subordinates or superiors.	□	□	□
5. *Judging people*—gauging individuals so as to be able to establish good relations and increase job satisfaction.	□	□	□
6. *Working with subordinates*—establishing cordial and effective relationships with those who work for you.	□	□	□
7. *Interviewing*—talking with people face-to-face.	□	□	□
8. *Listening*—learning from the words of others how they think and feel.	□	□	□
9. *Getting cooperation*—motivating people to join you in accomplishing departmental goals.	□	□	□
10. *Maintaining good relations with your superior*—being both friendly and businesslike in your dealings up the line.	□	□	□
11. *Using working time effectively*—being able to get 60 minutes of work out of every hour.	□	□	□
12. *Decision-making*—arriving at a logical conclusion and sticking to it.	□	□	□

13. *Planning*—developing a course of action to accomplish a definite objective. ☐ ☐ ☐

14. *Controlling paper work*—maintaining the flow of interoffice communications, reports, and the like, to and from your desk. ☐ ☐ ☐

15. *Getting information*—uncovering the facts you need to advance your work. ☐ ☐ ☐

16. *Delegation*—making subordinates responsible for some of your activities, while retaining control. ☐ ☐ ☐

17. *Problem-solving*—licking the tough situations that interfere with efficiency. ☐ ☐ ☐

18. *Pacing your energy expenditures*—conserving yourself so as to be able to complete the day without undue fatigue. ☐ ☐ ☐

19. *Concentration*—being able to stick with a given task. ☐ ☐ ☐

20. *Memory*—remembering events, incidents, ideas, plans, or promises. ☐ ☐ ☐

21. *Self-scheduling*—accomplishing the objectives of your job by efficient allotment of your time. ☐ ☐ ☐

Selecting skills to improve. Some executives feel that after making an overall assessment of their abilities, the next step is to concentrate on the weak spots.

This may be best. But note suggestions concerning your ratings in each of the three columns:

■ *Skills rated "high.*" The items marked "high" are the ones in which you have the strongest natural proficiency. There's a tendency to pass over these. "Why bother doing anything about them?" the reasoning goes. There are some good reasons:

1. *Locating fertile ground.* Since these "highs" are likely to represent natural strong points, you may find that with only slight effort they can be made outstanding.

2. *Magnifying your strong points.* The parts of your job in which you've already been doing well may prove to be the best areas to work in. You're likely to be at an advantage, and you put yourself in a position to extend past successes.

Say you have a knack for "getting information" (#15 on the list). By concentrating on this item, you may win special assignments from your superior, involving trouble shooting or analytical inquiries, for example.

■ *Skills rated "medium.*" These may be your real danger areas.

In some cases the tip-off to trouble lies in the thought, "Let well enough alone."

Look over each item you've rated in the "medium" column. Supply actual working situations involving these skills. For example, if you've rated "imparting information" (#4 on the list) in this column, visualize the handicaps you've run into as a result. Ask yourself this question:

Do your instructions fail to get across, causing an assistant to fail to correctly carry out an assignment? An affirmative reply can set you on the road to new insight and remedy.

▪ *Skills rated "low."* These may be the toughest items to work on. Chances are that they are the areas in which you have least natural proficiency or experience.

Face that fact frankly. That means improvement in these areas may require an uphill battle. You may have to go all out for a comparatively moderate gain. Yet, if the skill involved is a key to the objective you've set for yourself, it may be well worth the effort involved.

In general, selecting the skills to improve should be guided by these additional considerations:

Which do you *use* most?

Which play the most important role in the operation of your department?

And finally, this key question that takes your personal objectives into account:

Which are the most important in helping you advance toward your specific goal?

➲ ARE YOU LISTENING?

From interviewing to handling complaints, success in many executive activities depends on *how well you listen.* The other fellow's opinions, information, suggestions, can pay off in a big way if you're "receiving" properly. But these same ideas don't have a chance if they fall on deaf ears. Here's a quick quiz that shows where you stand on this important skill.

1. Do you choke off an employee's conversation
   to—
   . . . ask questions?   ☐ Yes   ☐ No
   . . . correct what he says?   ☐ Yes   ☐ No
   . . . tell him *your* views?   ☐ Yes   ☐ No
2. Do you brush aside a subordinate's arguments
   because you're right?   ☐ Yes   ☐ No

3. Do you frequently have to backtrack because you misunderstood the information or instructions you received?　　☐ Yes　　☐ No

4. Are you quick to label a conversation or a speaker dull or boring?　　☐ Yes　　☐ No

5. Do you tend to squirm or fidget while others are speaking?　　☐ Yes　　☐ No

6. Do you "always know what they're going to say before they say it?"　　☐ Yes　　☐ No

7. Do you fail to listen for "feelings" or emotional content, as well as for sense?　　☐ Yes　　☐ No

8. Do you neglect to ask for a repeat or a restatement, when you haven't heard, or are not clear on meaning?　　☐ Yes　　☐ No

9. Do you think it's all right to only half listen to a conversation because you're already forming your answer to what's being said?　　☐ Yes　　☐ No

10. Do you prefer talking to listening?　　☐ Yes　　☐ No

Scoring: Give yourself to 10 for each question answered No. 100-80 is good; 70-50 is poor. Anyone with a score below 50 is generally out of touch with people.

3

KEY
MANAGEMENT
CONCEPTS

With the work of Frederick Winslow Taylor, the management of the business corporation developed a scientific orientation. Taylor's approach, called "Scientific Management," brought the idea of system and method to the working world.

Since Taylor's day, the science of management has moved ahead on the basis of concepts and innovative thinking contributed by industrial psychologists, management experts, and others dedicated to the world of the corporation.

In this section, you will find the major foundation stones of contemporary management wisdom. Taken together, they form the theoretical background on which progressive management practice is based today.

* * * * *

● MANAGEMENT BY OBJECTIVES

Basically, *Management by Objectives* is a simple concept: it is job performance and achievement guided by results desired. There are two types of application.

Unit performance. The method may be used to set guides and evaluate results for departments, divisions, or whole companies.

Individual performance. The Management by Objectives idea may be applied to the work of individual executives, managers, and employees. It is in this latter application, as a tool for motivating and measuring individual performance, that Management by Objectives can help the executive develop and evaluate subordinates.

An early innovator in the field, General Mills of Minneapolis, started to apply the Management by Objectives concept in 1957:

People from front line management echelons upward set job objectives for themselves after their immediate superiors presented them with statements of their accountability. An "accountability" is a result that the company expects for the satisfactory performance of the job. Each job at General Mills has from three to ten accountabilities. Accordingly, each manager of the company is annually presented with a list of three to ten results that he must accomplish—whatever the means he chooses to accomplish them.

A company spokesman gives an example: "I'm responsible for insuring that our salary structure compares favorably with our competitors'. A front-line manager might be held accountable for maintaining an effective work force."

After the front-line manager has drawn up his statement of accountabilities, he writes out certain specific objectives; for example, "To improve the performance of employee John Doe by January 1." The manager creates as many of these specific goals as he thinks necessary to satisfy every accountability the company has placed upon him.

When he finishes, he meets with his superior to discuss whether the accomplishment of these objectives will satisfy the accountabilities. If need be, he modifies his objectives: adds more or changes some.

The method can be summed up in three steps:

Superior and subordinate work out realistic performance objectives. They agree on the means for achieving specified results.

At the end of the agreed-on period, actual results are compared to expected results.

The manager commits himself to specific, measurable action with specific time limits. In so doing, he obviously takes the risk that he may fail and *that his superiors will know he has failed.*

Observers of the management scene has noted these problems in connection with Management by Objective:

Heel-dragging participation. In one company that tried to pursue an MBO program, resistance showed up during the orientation workshops. Some recalcitrants were insecure managers, afraid to give up the comfortable old ways. Others were afraid to be under the spotlight of having to tell their superiors what results they would achieve. And there were others who had been on plateaus. They weren't happy about having to stretch themselves—which MBO forces on a manager.

The participation of some managers was only half-hearted. As one executive observed: "They would get a business call and have to leave. Or they would prolong the conversation about the need for objectives so as not to have to write any. We encounted many delaying tactics."

The setting of low standards. In discussions with his boss, the subordinate sometimes committed himself to objectives that involved no challenge, hoping thereby to overachieve.

One executive reports on these situations: "Men would become embarrassed, found difficulty talking about their conceptions—or misconceptions—of the job. Or a superior and a subordinate would both get embarrassed because both had misunderstood the subordinate's job. Sometimes the subordinate and his boss would realize, simultaneously, that the boss had failed as a manager— because he had not communicated what was expected of the subordinate."

The problem of quantification. The difficulty in quantifying objectives can be a big stumbling block. For example, an executive of the Internal Revenue Service New York office, commented: "We tried to implement MBO for our group supervisors. But we found it difficult to set an objective for morale and attitude, which are the two most important contributions of our people." There are other jobs for which morale, willingness, call it what you will, is important. This can be a soft spot in Management by Objectives.

Clearly, the value of MBO is largely comparative. But it is still superior to past methods for goal-setting and performance measure. Until a better tool comes along, it is likely that applications of MBO will proliferate.

SENSITIVITY TRAINING

Sensitivity training developed in the management field out of a felt need. A growing segment of management came to believe that an executive's effectiveness depends largely on his interpersonal relationships. The problem of effective leadership then becomes one of the executive relating more effectively to his subordinates, colleagues, and so on. It is to this problem that sensitivity training addresses itself.

Sensitivity training got its start about 1946, as a result of work done by psychologist Kurt Lewin of M.I.T. In that year, Lewin and others conducted a workshop at the State Teachers' College in New Britain, Connecticut.

The workshop was divided into several groups, each with its own research observer. In the course of the workshop, Lewin became aware of two things. People who had been part of the same group experience had differing perceptions of what actually had occurred. And discussion of "my perception of reality" produced some startling interactions. One example, as recorded by the research observer:

> At 10:00 a.m. Mr. X attacked the group leader and then X and Mr. Y got involved in a heated exchange. Some other members were drawn into taking sides. Other members seemed frightened and tried to make peace. But they were ignored by the combatants. At 10:10 a.m., the leader came in to redirecet attention back to the problem, which had been forgotten in the exchange. Mr. X and Mr. Y continued to contradict each other in the discussion that followed.

> Immediately Mr. X denied and Mr. Y defended the correctness of their views. Other members reinforced or qualified the data furnished by the observers. In brief, participants began to join observers and training leaders in trying to analyze and interpret behavioral events . . . participants reported they were deriving important understandings of their own behavior and the behavior of the group.

Lewin and his training staff felt a powerful process of reeducation had been hit upon. Group members, if confronted with their own behavior and its effects, might achieve highly meaningful learning about themselves, about the responses of others to them, and about group behavior and group development in general.

What had been created in 1946 is known today, variously as laboratory training, sensitivity training, and the T-group (training group); and it promises methods of altering the behavior of groups and individuals, and increasing their operating effectiveness.

"Sensitivity training," says Chris Argyris of Yale, one of its proponents, "is one of the most effective tools we have for developing human relations skills."

These are some of the benefits claimed:

▪ It improves an executive's control over personal frictions among subordinates.

▪ It gives him the ability to work more understandingly—and constructively—with his superior and colleagues.

■ It enables him to get subordinates and colleagues to "level" with him, be more open in day-to-day dealings.

The T-Group Experience   About 60 percent of the total time of a typical sensitivity training course is spent in T-group meetings. In each group there is a staff member, usually an industrial psychologist, who guides the group to some extent. It would be a mistake to call him a leader, because he does little or no leading. At the first session, the staff man usually explains that the group will study behavior, that there is no agenda, and that any learning that occurs will depend upon the group itself. With that, he stops talking.

Since each unit is composed of different individuals, no group will operate in exactly the same way. Often a period of silence occurs— embarrassed, even awkward. Eventually, someone may suggest a topic to discuss, or the members will introduce themselves, or a participant will take it upon himself to try to lead the group. Whatever happens, the actions and statements of individual members are fair game for exploration.

It usually isn't long before the talk is free-wheeling. One contributing factor is, of course, the desire of the participants to gain as much as possible from the training. Another is the relative anonymity of the setting—executives from many companies who've just met and who'll be together for only a brief period. As a result the comments become open and personal.

Individuals who have participated in sensitivity training dwell at length on the vividness and depth of the experience. As a matter of fact, a more or less constant refrain from T-group participants is, "It's impossible to describe. You have to experience it to really understand what it's like."

To some extent, this is true. The T-group, with its ten or twenty participants and a psychologist-leader or trainer, is a microcosm, a small world with rules different from those "outside." As indicated, the usual amenities like politeness and small talk are absent.

In place of ordinary social conversation and small talk, participants begin reacting to one another in deep and significant ways. Complete openness, for example, is aimed for. And after a preliminary period of caution, participants feel free to level with one another, *really* voice their true opinions. This freedom to express what one really thinks and feels is based on trust in the group. T-groupers know they will not be penalized for honesty. It's at this point the life of the T-Group can be highly personal, revealing, and instructive.

As one participant expressed it: "The few days I spent in a T-group gave me more information about my co-members than I had learned about people I had worked with for ten years." Because such close knowledge is gained, faults and virtues, strengths and weaknesses become apparant. An individual sometimes gets a more accurate, even disturbing, picture of himself than he's ever had before.

During the final week, the T-group members try to relate what they've learned about themselves, about each other, and about group dynamics to their jobs back home. For many managers, the result is personal growth and improved on-the-job relationships.

To understand why the compressed experience of a sensitivity session may be more helpful than uninterrupted immersion in real life—to understand, in short, why *this* particular compressed experience is a better teacher than "real" experience—it is necessary to understand, first, how the simulation works.

Participants in a typical group at a recent session at Bethel, Maine, headquarters of the National Training Laboratory seminars, included a minister, personnel director, a research scientist, two managers, and a trainer of hospital nurses.

Here's one participant's description of his experience, his increased self-awareness:

"At first, I was my usual self: hostile, aggressive, angry. In the past I'd always said 'I don't care what so-and-so thinks, I'll be myself.' You can say this. But you can't say, 'I don't care what *people* think.' You do care when everybody starts telling you the same thing.

"That's what happened. Ten people told me they disliked me—they'd disliked me from the beginning. When several people tell you something like that you have to say to yourself, 'Maybe they're right.' It's *not* one man's opinion. You begin examining yourself. I did, and I decided that my hostile manner was a thing I wanted to change about myself."

Instant feedback is what this man got from the group—something he had never gotten before. In the "real" world people are seldom told about their less desirable traits. Even when they are, there's a tendency to reject the statement as that of an "enemy." But the T-group is seen as helpful. The simulation of the T-group encourage candor, and the revelations and insights that emerge produce a desire to change.

A T-group is also referred to as a *behavioral laboratory*. And what participants soon come to realize is that this phrase is *literally* accurate. They can experiment with behavior. They can say what they really think, unlike the rule in the "outside" world. For example:

Participant A (to B):   There's something about you I don't like.

Participant B: Well, what is it?

Participant A: I'm not sure . . . something about your size . . . yes, that's it . . . You seem so big, powerful . . . I'm afraid we might get into a fight. . . .

With the skillful help of the leader, Participant A, for the first time, becomes aware that he reacts negatively to men, who, because of their size, burliness, or other physical aspect, suggest aggressiveness. With this insight, he is able to comprehend for the first time why he avoids (or works poorly with) men who seem to be threateningly aggressive.

Similarly, Participant B develops new insights. He learns how his appearance and behavior might affect other people, and realizes why some individuals seem to become defensive in dealing with him. He can't change his appearance, but his new awareness helps him tone down his approach to people.

Note the benefits that emerge from this brief T-group interplay:

Participant A becomes aware of an *attitude* of *his* that affects his relationship with other people.

Participant B becomes aware of how some people *react* to *him* because of his physical appearance.

These two results taken together constitutes the "sensitivity," the increased awareness of interpersonal relationships by the T-group members.

In the T-group world, an individual may have *several* personal revelations in a few hours. Accordingly, the compression of experience is substantial. Most of us may go through *years* of real-life experience without a single such revelation.

Two Key Facts.   Although this controversial training method has been winning wider acceptance, problems continue to hinder progress. Two hard facts emerge:

Sensitivity training works.   A recent two-week program of sensitivity training at Bethel, Maine, sponsored by the National Training Laboratory, boasted a completely filled out roster of 120 participants. At the end of the two weeks, a sampling of opinion among the participants drew reactions that ranged from extreme enthusiasm to opinions such as, "Quite interesting;" and "Fairly helpful." The point is, these latter views were the *most negative* expressed.

None of the participants felt the experience was a waste of time or harmful in any way. The large majority dwelt on the success of the program in increasing the individual's self-awareness, and sharpened perceptiveness to the feelings and attitudes of others. And these people did not talk in generalities. They pinpointed specific benefits they had gained that increased their abilities in dealing with people.

Applications are a problem.   Not only the participants, but the professionals who conduct T-group sessions stress the obstacles to applying the benefits on the job.

The lore of the building trades provides a simple parallel: "You can't add new to old," says the plumber, the carpenter, and the stone mason. Anyone who has made a plumbing installation knows the problems of adding new fittings, pipe joints and so on, to old lines— which may have different diameter pipes, different threading, and so on.

Similarly, it's difficult to have managers, back from T-group training, apply immediately what's been learned. Old habits, traditions, values, and points of view cannot be readily meshed with new ways of relating and working with one another. When "they're all out of step but Jim," no matter how keen a cadence Jim is treading, Jim can't really hope to have people change to conform to his style. However, if these obstacles can be minimized, it seems likely that the T-group experience may become an accepted, even essential preparation for the business world.

➲ THE MANAGERIAL GRID

Dr. Robert R. Blake and Dr. Jane S. Mouton, professors at the University of Texas and associates in the management consulting firm of Scientific Methods, Inc., Austin, Texas, have developed an approach based on a so-called "organic theory of change." They reject a static, mechanic view of the organization, seeing it, rather, as a developing set of interdependent net works of people. Their main emphasis, therefore, is on improving work relationships.

Dr. Blake and his associates feel that the most effective type of management is that of an integrated team operation, both from the standpoint of production and of an organization's ability to adapt swiftly and appropriately to rapidly changing conditions.

The "managerial grid" approach (see illustration p. 217) has two basic premises: (a) a manager or management can be measured according to two variables—a concern for people and a concern for production; (b) the best management is team management. If one accepts these premises, then the grid can be a useful tool in analyzing the manager's efforts as well as those of his subordinates.

On the grid, "concern for people" is measured vertically on a line divided into nine sections: "concern for production" is measured

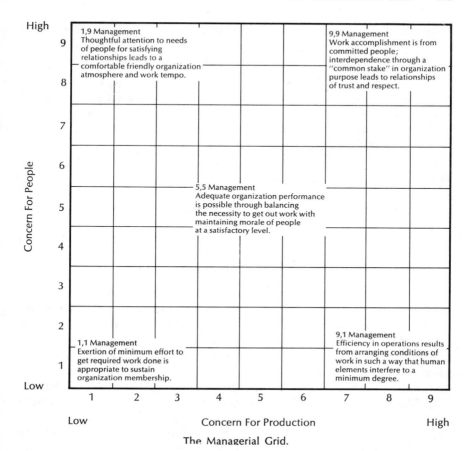

The Managerial Grid.

horizontally on a line similarly divided. The resulting grid has 81 "positions" which can be used to delineate various styles of leadership. Here are major styles discussed by the authors:

Task management. Down in the lower right-hand corner of the grid one finds 9,1 management. It is characterized by strong emphasis on the task to be performed. People in themselves are of little consequence, except to the extent that they impede or further production. They are there to be used, somewhat like machines, and they should be replaced if they don't function effectively.

This type of leadership is strictly authoritarian. Subordinates are expected to carry out their orders unquestioningly and all conflict is suppressed. As a result, subordinates tend to lose initiative, their creative, approach to problems; and any increased skill and knowledge they develop is likely to remain untapped. One consequence of this type of leadership is the "gradual shift of many working and managerial persons in the direction of a 1,1 accommodation."

Country-club management. Contry-club management, located at 1,9 in the upper left-hand corner of the grid, is the very opposite of task management. Here the emphasis is all on people, the theory being that if they are kept contented and happy, high production will automatically follow. But whether production follows or not, the attitudes and feelings of people, "are valuable in their own right. They come first."

One possible consequence of this style of leadership is that production will suffer at the expense of harmonious human relations. But even here, conflicts are likely to be smoothed over and buried rather than resolved. And when this type of organization is called upon to increase efficiency, it is frequently unable to respond. As a result, it tends to succomb to competitive pressures.

Impoverished management. Impoverished management, located in the lower-left-hand corner of the grid, couples low concern for production with low concern for people. This type of manager does just enough to get by. To all intents and purposes, he is "out of it." He avoids involvement and concern because this, "can only lead to deeper frustration and discouragement."

An organization is seldom managed this way because, as Mouton and Blake point out, "a business operated under 1,1 concepts would be unable to survive very long." But an individual can sometimes persist for quite a long time as a 1,1 manager in a bureaucratic or country-club atmosphere. However, it's a situation of failure, not only for the individual, but for the company, since it involves the loss of a "potential productive contribution."

Dampened pendulum management. In the middle of the grid at 5,5 is located the middle of the road, or dampened pendulum type of management. It avoids swinging to the extremes of 9,1 or 1,9. The 5,5 manager is aware of a conflict between people and production and tries to effect a happy compromise, to play it safe by not overemphasizing one or the other. Real problems are apt to be muted, and the climate is frequently paternalistic.

While 5,5 management is likely to be superior to any of the extremes mentioned so far, it too, has its limitations. According to the authors, "5,5 provides a poor basis for promoting innovation, creativity, discovery, and novelty. All of these are likely to be sacrificed by the adherence to tradition and 'majority' standards of conduct. Long term, then, the 5,5 or status quo, results in a gradual slipping behind as more flexible, progressive organizations take advantage of new opportunities or better management practices."

Team management.   The obvious goal of good management lies in the upper right-hand corner of the grid at 9,9. Here there is a high concern for both people and production. The result is a team approach to management where the "needs of people to think, to apply mental effort in productive work and to establish sound and mature relationships . . . with one another are utilized to accomplish organizational requirements."

Some of the gains attributed by the authors to a change toward 9,9 management are: (a) increased profitability; (b) improvement of intergroup relations; (c) more effective use of team action; (d) reduced frictions and increased understanding among individuals; and (e) increased individual effort and creativity and personal commitment to work.

In short, under team management, "the needs of individuals to be engaged in meaningful interdependent effort mesh with the organization requirements for excellent performance."

The managerial grid is a tool to help analyze one's managerial style, the styles of other managers, or the total management of a company. It's a way of structuring one's thinking about styles of management, and as such, both an analytical and constructive tool.

➲ SELECTIVE LEADERSHIP

The executive seeking practical guidance in leadership finds slim pickings in management literature. He'll have no trouble in gathering numerous *general* statements: "A leader must be enthusiastic;" "A leader must know how to motivate his people;" "A leader must be able to empathize." and, as has been indicated in previous pages, the list of traits of the leader, or the situational factors that the leader must master to be effective, are readily come by. But theoretically sound and practically effective approaches are notable by their absence. Into this vacuum, Auren Uris, in the early 1950's, described in *How to Be a Successful Leader* (paperback edition titled *Techniques of Leadership*) a systematic approach for leadership on the work scene. The concept, called "Selective Leadership," offers the executive an approach that has been used successfully in fields as varied as child rearing and the supervision of scientists working in a business setting.

Selective Leadership is a method that stems from experiments by psychologist Kurt Lewin at the University of Iowa. To explore the nature of leadership, Lewin set up two experimental groups:

1. One group was dominated by an "autocratic" leader, who determined policy; decided what was to be done and how it was to be done; assigned tasks and chose the work companions for each member; and was highly personal in his praise, criticism and general comments.

2. The second group was led by a "democratic" leader, who brought up matters of policy for group discussion; encouraged group members to participate in decisions; permitted individuals to choose their own work companions; and was highly "objective" in his comments.

Then came an unplanned and unexpected development: one of the individuals playing the role of "democratic" leader was found to be creating an atmosphere different from that of the other "democratic" leaders. He exercised virtually no control over the group. He permitted group members to shift for themselves to a large extent; and he had them tackle the problems that arose as best they could. The group's response to this technique differed from the reactions of other democratic groups. Lewin accordingly set up a third kind of group under this type of leadership, termed "laissez-faire."

Observers noted certain significant differences in atmosphere, behavior, feelings, and accomplishments among the three groups:

Autocratic. Group members were quarrelsome and aggressive. Some individuals became completely dependent upon the leader. When the leader was absent, activity tended to stop altogether. Work progressed at only a fair rate.

Democratic. The individuals got along with one another on a friendly basis. Relations with the leader were freer, more spontaneous. The work progressed smoothly and continued even when the leader was absent.

Laissez-faire. Work progressed haphazardly and at a slow rate. Although there was considerable activity, much of it was unproductive. Considerable time was lost in arguments and discussions between group members on a purely personal basis.

Although each method seems to have built-in strengths and weaknesses, as you will soon see, each method has its value.

Actually, the three methods developed in the University of Iowa investigations provide the framework of the Selective Leadership approach. Selective Leadership welds the three Lewin concepts into a unified and systematic method that has scored outstanding success in the management field.

Using the Selective Leadership approach, the manager *selects* which-ever one of the three tools is most appropriate. For the sake of clarity, let's define the three tools as follows:

1. Autocratic leadership.   The leader mainly seeks obedience from his group. He determines policy and considers decision-making a one-man operation—he, of course, being the one man.

2. Democratic leadership.   The leader draws ideas and suggestions from the group by discussion and consultation. Group members are encouraged to take part in the setting of policy. The leader's job is largely that of moderator.

3. Free-rein leadership (Lewin's "laissez-faire" method).   The leader functions more or less as an information booth. He plays down his role in the group's activity. He exercises a minimum of control.

These definitions provide the basis for a systematic approach to leading people. Autocratic, democratic, or free-rein methods may be considered as *three tools* of the management leader.

Contrary to common belief, the three approaches are *not* mutually exclusive. No one has to choose either the autocratic, democratic, or free-rein method. That would be like telling a golf player he must choose between using a driver or only a putter; in the course of a game he will use both.

Note Manager X in action:

- He *directs* (autocratic method) his secretary to make a report.
- He *consults* (democratic method) with his employees on the best way to push a special order through the shop.
- He *suggests* (free-rein method) to his assistant that it would be a good idea to figure out ways in which special orders may be handled more smoothly in the future.

This type of leadership suggests that mastery lies in knowing *when* to use *which* method. In short, Selective Leadership is a logical adap-tation of autocratic, democratic, and free-rein techniques to appro-priate situations, seeking to put leadership on a rational basis.

(A description of Selective Leadership as a working procedure is included in Section I, Part 7.)

➲ MANAGEMENT BY EXCEPTION

Lester R. Bittel, author of *Management by Exception*, published by McGraw-Hill in 1964, describes the concept in these terms: manage-ment in its simplest form is a symptom of identification and commu-nication. It tells the executive when his attention is needed in a particular activity or aspect of an activity, and conversely to remain silent when his attention is not required. The primary purpose is to simplify the management process; to permit the manager to find the problem that needs his attention, and avoid those which are routinely handled by his subordinates.

Bittel views *Management by Exception* as having six key elements:

1. Measurement. Assign value—often numerical—to past and present performances. Without measurement of some sort, it would be impossible to identify an exception.

2. Projection. Analyze those measurements that are meaningful to business objectives and extend them into future expectations.

3. Selection. Pinpoint the criteria management will use to follow progress toward its objectives.

4. Observation. That phase of measurement that informs management of the current state of performance.

5. Comparison. Actual performance compared with expected performance identifies the exceptions that require attention and reports variances that exist.

6. Decision-making. What action must be taken to
 ▪ bring the performance back into control, or
 ▪ adjust expectations to reflect changing conditions, or
 ▪ exploit opportunity.

⤵ MASLOW'S HIERARCHY OF NEEDS

Industrial psychologist, A. H. Maslow, has made a major contribution to motivational theory on the work scene.

Maslow developed the "basic needs" concept that helped executives understand some puzzling factors about employee motivation. For example: money was supposed to be the great incentive. Yet, strangely, when people were asked what was most important to them in their jobs, money often took third or fourth place. Factors like "challenging work," "chance for advancement," and even, in some cases, "a good boss," ranked higher.

Dr. Maslow sugested a theory that explains the seeming contradiction. He suggested that there is a hierarchy of needs that exists for the human being. We give precedence to the first of these needs until it is satisfied. When the first need is satisfied, the second becomes dominant, and so on through the sequence. Here's Maslow's list:

Physiological needs—hunger, shelter, sexual gratification.

Safety needs—these represent our needs for protection against danger and threat, either from the environment or from people.

Social needs—after the physiological and safety needs are fairly well-satisfied, the needs for love, affection, and "belongingness" tend to emerge.

Esteem needs—these have to do with the wish that most of us have for self-respect and the good opinion of others.

Self-fulfillment—last on the list, but perhaps of most significance for future managers is the need for "self-actualization." This concerns the individual's feeling about the value and satisfaction of his work.

Failure to understand this need often lies behind the manager's complaint: "We've given our people everything: good pay, pleasant working conditions, all the physical comforts possible on the job— and yet they're dissatisfied." Dr. Maslow's concept explains the reason. It's precisely because employees have had the four basic needs sufficiently satisfied that the fifth—the need for self-fulfillment—emerges. It will cause discontent unless and until the manager finds ways of satisfying it.

➲ HERZBERG'S MOTIVATOR/HYGIENE FACTOR CONCEPT

Dr. Frederick Herzberg, chairman of the Psychology Department at Western Reserve University, developed the concept that many management experts feel clarifies what makes an employee satisfied or dissatisfied in his job.

Herzberg developed the idea that two sets of conditions affect a man at work. He calls one set *motivators,* the other, *hygiene factors.* The first group is positive, with the power to satisfy an employee. The second group, hygiene factors, is negative, can dissatisfy or demotivate. Of the former, the five most important, according to Herzberg, are achievement, recognition, the work itself, responsibility, and advancement. Of the latter, the five most important are company policy and administration, supervision, salary, interpersonal relations, and working conditions.

The distinction between them says Herzberg, is that the first set of factors (the motivators) "describe man's relationship to what he does; his job content, achievement on a task, recognition for task achievement, the nature of the task, responsibility for a task, and professional advancement or growth in task capability."

The dissatisfiers (or hygiene factors) describe an employee's "relationship to the context or environment in which he does his job."

They "serve primarily to prevent job dissatisfaction while having little effect on positive job attitudes."

This is a most important distinction. Dr. Herzberg's study shows that "the factors involved in producing job satisfaction are separate and distinct from the factors that lead to job dissatisfaction." The lack of satisfiers does not lead to dissatisfaction; the presence of hygiene factors does not lead to satisfaction, but to no dissatisfaction.

In other words, the presence of good company policies and administration, good supervision, good salaries, good interpersonal relations, and good working conditions will not motivate people over the long haul. What does motivate people is the challenge and pleasure they get out of the work itself, the sense of achievement they get from doing the work, recognition for a job well done, a feeling of responsibility, and the desire for advancement.

➲ THEORY X, THEORY Y

Toward the end of the '50s, management experts here began to focus on the climate of work as a motivational factor. Behind this interest was an awareness that neither cash, nor stock incentive, nor punishment are effective as motivators in the long run. Professor Douglas McGregor of the Massachussetts Institute of Technology superceded these "pushing" types of motivators by the concept of a climate of concern that helps the individual develop his own internal reasons for wanting to excel.

Professor McGregor first explained his Theory X and Theory Y concepts at talks at MIT, and then expanded his ideas in a book, *The Human Side of Enterprise.*

McGregor's now-classic work suggests that two different approaches, or philosophies of management, are possible in business. Each is based on a set of assumptions about people. One can see the differences in approach—and at the same time test one's own assumptions about people—by looking at McGregors's descriptions:

Theory X Assumptions about People	*Theory Y Assumptions about People*
1. Human beings are inherently lazy and will shun work if they can.	1. For most people, the expenditure of physical and mental effort in work is as natural as for play or rest.
2. People must be directed, controlled, and motivated by fear of punishment or deprivation to impel them to work as the company requires.	2. Man will exercise self-control in the services of objectives which he accepts.

3. The average human being prefers to be directed, wishes to avoid responsibility, has relatively little ambition, and wants security above all.

3. Under proper conditions, the average human being learns not only to accept responsibility, but also to seek it.
4. The capacity for exercising imagination, ingenuity, and creativity exists generally among people.

Which set of assumptions is true? Neither one, in a clear-cut objective way. But in general, managers tend to evaluate people either by the Theory X or Theory Y assumptions. And whichever position a manager takes, there are direct consequences in the way he handles his people. For example, consider the implications of McGregor's first assumption:

"Tom Smith is inherently lazy and will shun work if he can," (Theory X). If Tom Smith's boss believes he has an allergy to work, Tom Smith will be managed by a considerable amount of direct and close supervision. Rigid work schedules must be set for him. His progress and level of performance must be checked continually. These methods belong to the Theory X arsenal of management techniques.

Compare this with the second assumption:

"Tom Smith is energetic, enjoys his work, and prides himself in doing it well," (Theory Y). If Tom Smith's boss sees Tom as this type of person, he will spend considerably less time on direct supervision. Tom will be given objectives of assignments, and left to work out the ways of achieving them. He will also be trusted to turn out a satisfactory amount and quality of work, without overly frequent checking. These methods represent the Theory Y approach.

McGregor's ideas caused a furor in management circles. Many people, including management practitioners and consultants, contest McGregor's view that Theory Y is best for managing people.

One of the more articulate opponents of Theory Y is the well-known management consultant, Dr. Robert N. McMurry. In a recent issue of *Business Management,* Dr. McMurry points out a psychological basis for the superiority of Theory X:

"There appears to be little awareness that . . . the so-called victims (employees managed by Theory X) might relish their bondage. Why? For the simple reason that the rigid structure in which they find themselves is not fettering, but reassuring. It is even conceivable that rank and file employees deliberately seek regimented jobs because these positions are more comfortable and less demanding than jobs requiring initiative, creativity, and decision-making."

In general, critics of Theory Y describe it as being impractical, unrealistic, out of place in today's world of business. Moreover, the anti-McGregors argue, Theory X, whatever its shortcomings, works. Actually, objective observers now believe that these opposed views are more the result of misunderstanding and failure to agree on basic terms than of the irreconcilability of the two approaches.

Psychologists and management experts are still discussing the pros and cons of McGregor's Theory X-Theory Y concepts. Yet Theory Y has not achieved the impact expected by some. True, many managers now give a responsible employee considerable latitude in his work, but more often than not, they've never heard of McGregor. What has failed to develop is any degree of broad and general application of Theory Y that might lend eventual support to either side of the argument.

In other words, practicality and personal preference rather than theory—either X or Y—rules. Managers and executives develop their personal leadership styles that often are a mixture of both X and Y assumptions about people. We have not yet developed a concept of climate building that is sufficiently surefire as to result in general acceptance and use.

➲ PARTICIPATION

Psychologists working in the field of group dynamics have long been aware that people behave differently in groups than they do as individuals. For example, studies conducted during World War II showed that housewives who participated in group discussions on the dietary value of citrus fruits tended to use citrus fruits to a greater degree than matched groups that were simply lectured at, on the same subject, by dieticians.

The implication for management was clear: if employees were given the chance to participate in decision-making, they would accept the fiscal decision and be more wholehearted in working towards its implementation. Change, a continuing preoccupation of business, might then become more acceptable at the lower echelons.

Yet here again the easy answer does not always apply. For example: Professor Arnold S. Tannenbaum of the University of Michigan describes an experiment in which a company divided its clerical staff into two groups, one to be managed participatively, the other in the usual way, with management making all decisions. In the participative group, the clerks discussed and decided things like rules for office conduct, size of work groups, length of coffee breaks, and so on. The other group was not allowed to participate in decisions.

The results? Although productivity in each group went up and the clerks in the participative group enjoyed their work more, productivity in the nonparticipative group rose most.

Professor Tannenbaum accounted for the results by suggesting that productivity went up in the participative group because of increased job satisfaction and in the other group because of the manager's increased control. Tannenbaum further suggested that output might have gone up more in the participative group, if the supervisor had realized that the purpose of participation was not to make personnel happy, but to improve their functioning inside the organizational context.

Academic findings and discussions aside, the practicing executive knows from experience that participation can help achieve a number of extremely desirable objectives:

- *Communication.* By letting employees in on the "ground floor" of a problem or development, they're getting direct and early information, as compared to the garbling and confusion that may result from attempts at communication after the fact.

- *Feedback.* The executive who gives his subordinates the opportunity to participate in discussions of problems, plan developments, and so on gains the benefits of the ideas and suggestions of his people, as well as the modifications or extensions of his own ideas.

- *Training self-respect and dignity.* Subordinates who have a chance to join you in discussions become exposed to your values, attitudes, and experiences in a most constructive situation. In addition, their response to being treated as "equal," as "being important enough to become important factors" in planning and other important activities will clearly have a desirable influence.

- *Motivation.* Perhaps the greatest benefit of the opportunity for participation by your people is the great sense of responsibility and willingness with which they undertake tasks that grow out of their participation.

⮑ THE PARETO PRINCIPLE

Vilfredo Pareto, a nineteenth century economist, analyzed the distribution of welfare in his time and discovered that most of it was in the hands of a few people (the vital few), while the vast majority (the trivial many) existed in poverty.

In his book "Managing for Results," Peter Drucker suggests that many management problems lend themselves to this approach. Drucker points out, "In the marketplace, a handful of products in the line produce the bulk of sales volume; a few salesmen out of the total roster produce ⅔'s of all new business."

The Pareto principle can be applied to any management problem that can be quantified or broken down into units of relative importance. For example, a company asked its key officers to list the obstacles to increased profitability. When the lists were tabulated, they showed a total of 37 problems—too many to handle at once. The list was sent back to the company officials with the request that they rate the problems in order of importance. The second set of lists showed that five of the problems fell into the category of the *vital few*. The rest fell into the category of the *trivial many*. The above example demonstrates the four basic steps involved in applying the Pareto principle:

First, make a written list of the factors, units, or components involved in the problem.

Second, arrange these items in order of importance relative to the problem.

Third, identify the vital few.

Fourth, identify the trivial many.

Another illustration of the application of how the four steps above apply: the president of a clock-making company eliminated one-third of the regular models when he found they added up to only 4 percent of the company's volume. Within six months, the company was doing a larger, more profitable volume.

In another case, the company alayzed 2,753 orders. The top 13 percent accounted for 66 percent of the sales volume in dollars, while the bottom 69 percent of the orders brought in only 7.1 percent of sales . In this case, the vital few, while accounting for 66 percent of the results, involved only 13 percent of the sales costs. The trivial many, bringing in only 7.1 percent of the sales were responsible for 68 percent of the costs. As Drucker puts it, "Results in costs stand in various realtionship to each other." In this case it is clear, cutting of sales costs, to be most effective, must come from the trivial many.

➜ THE "HALO EFFECT"

When one trait of a person or aspect of a situation influences your judgment of another trait or another aspect, you have the "halo effect" in action. It's a management problem in cases like these:

▪ *Interviewing prospective employees.* An executive permits the pleasant appearance and oral skills of an applicant to blind him to the fact that the man has a murky work history.

And, of course, the "halo effect" can work in the opposite way: an unattractive appearance or manner may blind one to an applicant's assets.

■ *Making assignments.* A subordinate does an excellent job of investigating and reporting a space situation in his company. His boss promptly gives him another task: analyzing poor reactions to requests for suggestions from the staff. The subordinate gets nowhere. Eventually his boss realizes that he's fine when dealing with tangibles: space, inventory, and so on. He's a babe in the woods in human relations situations.

■ *Judging job performance.* "Barry's turning in a terrific job," a sales manager tells the V.P. in charge of sales. "This is the third week he's among the top 3 producers."

"You're overlooking something," observes the V.P. "His cancellation rate from customers is tops also."

It's important for the executive not only to understand how the "halo effect" works but also to be aware of preventive measures:

1. Keep the "halo effect" in mind when rating people. Remind yourself from time to time that a man who's industrious is not necessarily cooperative; that a man whose job knowledge is excellent doesn't necessarily apply himself. And, remember that the man who is eager to please is not necessarily the best one for a demanding assignment.

2. Judge employees on one trait at a time. This is an added safeguard. Let's say you're rating the group's cooperation and initiative. By rating everyone on *cooperation* first, you get around the danger of letting Smith's cooperation rating influence his mark for initiative. By the time you get back to Smith to rate his initiative, you've broken through the "blinding" of the "halo effect."

3. Avoid putting similar traits close together if you make up your own rating form. For example, it's a good idea to follow a work performance trait like *job skill* with a personality trait like *initiative*.

The "halo-effect" concept is a good reminder that our judgments are susceptible to illogical pressures. Awareness of the "halo effect" phenomenon can be a major protection against unbalanced judgment.

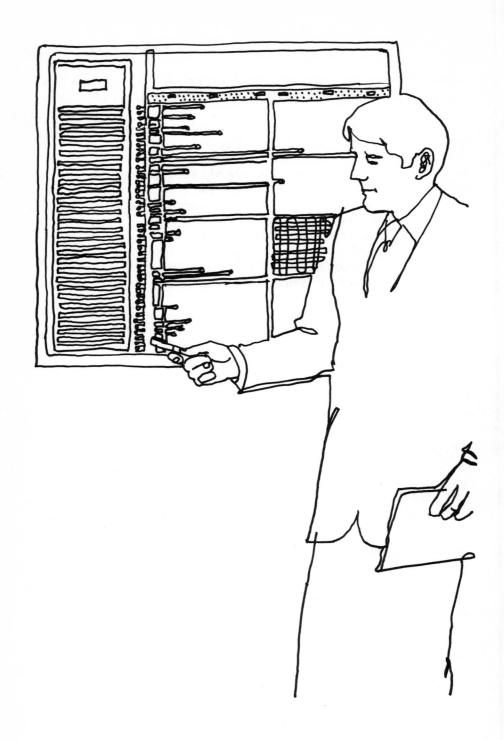

4

MANAGEMENT
TOOL
KIT

"Man is a tool-using animal . . . without tools he is nothing, with tools he is all," said Thomas Carlyle.

Increasingly, the executive is getting to be a tool-using professional. As a mater of fact, the proliferation of tools available to the executive today reinforces the professionalism of his calling.

In the pages that follow, you will find a sample group of practical tools executives use to improve communications, expedite planning, help develop training needs, and so on Each one of these tools individually can help you cope with specific management problems. Taken together, they represent an executive tool kit that can help sharpen your tool awareness and serve as a guide for the development of your self-developed tools.

* * * * *

➲ COMMUNICATIONS CHANNEL CHOOSER

Method	Advantages	Disadvantages
Phone	Speed. Permits give and take of questions. Doesn't call you away form your desk.	Words and figures might be misunderstood or garbled. Usually no record of conversation.
In Person	Visual. You can "show" and "explain." In many cases permits better meeting of the minds, closer rapport.	You may have to leave your office, lose time. The time may be inconvenient to either of you. Requires spontaneous thinking.
Informal Note or Memo	Brief. It can be "for the record"—in his files and a copy in your own.	You don't get an immediate reply. Your memo is at the mercy of a routine delivery and the bulk of his mail.
Formal Report	Complete. Permits time for organization of material. Can be reported to others.	Sometimes requires considerable time. May make for slow writing at one end, slow reading at the other.

➔ **COMMUNICATIONS ANALYZER**

Chart I—Sending

Name of Communi- cation	To Whom Sent?	About What?	Method (Phone, written, face to face)?	Frequency (How often sent)?	Apply all questions to each item in the first column.
					Yes No
					1. Is the communi- cation really needed (that is, used) by the person receiving it? ☐ ☐
					2. If it is a request for information, are you sending it to the best source? ☐ ☐
					3. Does the com- munication ask for information already on hand in another form? (For example, payroll records may serve as an attendance record.) ☐ ☐
					4. Are you commu- nicating too frequently about the same things? (A monthly report substituted for a weekly one may cut the job by 75 percent.) ☐ ☐
					5. Are your com- munications frequent enough? ☐ ☐
					6. Are you using the best method of communicating for this material? (See the Channel Chooser Chart.) ☐ ☐

➲ **COMMUNICATIONS ANALYZER**

Chart II—Receiving

Name of Communi-cation	From Whom?	About What?	Method (Phone, written, face to face)?	Frequency (How often received)?	Apply all questions to each item in the first column.
					Yes No
					1. Do you really need this communication (That is, do you use the information it contains)? ☐ ☐
					2. Does it get to you on time (when it's scheduled to). ☐ ☐
					3. In time? (Geting to you "on time" may still not be in time to do any good.) ☐ ☐
					4. Does it contain all the information you need? ☐ ☐
					5. Do you need all the information it contains? (If not, you can take a load off the other fellow.) ☐ ☐
					6. Does everyone who needs some or all of the information receive it? ☐ ☐
					7. Should you be passing along some of the information it contains? ☐ ☐
					8. Are you getting this communication in the best possible form for your needs? (For instance, you can't file a phone call for record-keeping.) ☐ ☐

⮕ PERT

The U.S. Navy calls this management tool "PERT," which stands for Program Evaluation and Review Technique. The Navy used the approach to expedite its gigantic Polaris missile program. It can also be used to overhaul an office or plan a factory project.

PERT works like the housewife's approach to preparing a multi-course meal. She uses several burners and the oven simultaneously, starts the things that take longer first, and ends up at dinner time ready to serve.

Here's how to apply PERT to a task:

1. List everything that has to be done. To take a simple example: Let's say you plan to transfer cartons of stored material from one room to another. These are the things you would have to do—

get a hand truck;

get two employees to do the moving;

make sure new area can take the load;

move cartons to the new locations;

sort and label the cartons;

check amount of material to be moved;

get okay by supervisor;

stack cartons, using the new system.

2. Put the jobs in sequence. Go over your list of job steps and put them in the sequence in which they must be done.

In the list above, for example, the first step would be to make sure that the material you want to store will fit into the new area.

3. Estimate time for each step. Express the time in minutes, hours, days, or as you will, and indicate time alongside each step on the sequence of operations you've listed. Now your list looks like this:

A. Check amount of material (.8 hours)

B. Check capacity of new areas (.4 hours)

C. Get truck (.2 hours)

D. Get employees (.1 hours)

E. Move material (5 hours)

F. Sort and label (2 hours)

G. Okay by supervisor (.5 hours)

H. Stack (3 hours)

4. Make an arrow diagram. The PERT chart or "network" is a key step, shows how the various parts of the job interrelate. To draw the chart:

Use an arrow to indicate each step in the operation. The lengths of the arrows don't matter. But the *direction* of the arrow shows you how the step relates to the rest of the job.

Construct the diagram by asking three questions of each element in the sequence:

   . . . *What immediately precedes this element?*

   . . . *What immediately follows it?*

   . . . *What other elements can be done at the same time?*

Here's how a PERT chart for the carton-moving operation might look:

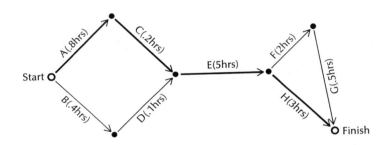

Note some of the things the chart tells you at a glance. First, Step E, the actual moving, can't take place until after Steps A-D are completed.

Second, it shows the general scope of the operation. Third, it helps you determine *the critical path.*

The critical path is the total of the longest consecutive jobs. In our chart, the critical path is shown by the heavy line. Knowing the critical path, you're now in a position to do several things:

   . . . Estimate the total time for the job. In our example, it would be nine hours.

   . . . Spot bottlenecks. Every operation on the critical path is, theoretically, a bottleneck. Operations *not* on the critical path (these are called *slack paths*) may generally be done at the same time as those on the critical path.

Since they take less time, it is the critical path that limits your schedule.

   . . . Expedite the schedule. You have two alternatives, if you want to shorten your completion time: (a) have steps on the slack paths performed as much as possible at the same time as those on the critical path; (b) shorten critical path operations by making them crash activities, i.e., putting more men or equipment on the job, devising a more efficient method, and so on.

Used wisely, PERT can also help you keep costs down. You could, for example, devise two alternative charts, representing two different ways of getting a job done. Comparing man-hours, possible overtime, and other cost elements, and stacking completion time of one method against the other, you can come up with figures that tell you whether a "normal" production or a souped-up schedule is more desirable from a dollar and delivery standpoint.

➲ EMPLOYEE SKILLS AND ASSIGNMENT CHART

When you're under time pressure, it can be difficult to make work assignments efficiently. You may forget that Tom, who is temporarily out of your sight, might be best man for a given assignment, and you may put Harry on it instead. Results may be unsatisfactory.

A simple chart can take some of the hit-or-miss quality out of job assignments. Here's a sample:

Names of Employees	Operation 1	Operation 2	Operation 3	Operation 4
Brown, C.	A	B	B	A
Coughlin, L.	C	A	A	—
Green, P.	B	A	B	B
Kinkead, R.	A	—	—	C

Legend: A—Fully competent
B—O.K. with slight assistance
C—Can do the job only with close supervision

You make the chart work by these steps:

■ **Step 1.** List each employee on your staff down the left-hand column.

■ **Step 2.** List each task or operation in your area, one task to a column, as in the chart.

■ **Step 3.**   Using the symbols "A," "B," or "C," give each employee a rating for each departmental task, if that employee is *at all* able to do the task. Meaning of the symbols:

A: Fully compentent.

B: Knows the operation but needs a few pointers.

C: Can do the job, but only with supervision or with the assistance of a co-worker.

The rating symbol should be entered in the space *opposite* the employee's name and *below* each job. If he can't handle the job at all, leave the space blank.

When the chart is fully filled out, you may want to decide that you'll use "C" people only in pinches—when the work just has to be done and there's no one else to do it. You may also want to establish restrictions on the use of "B" people. Generally, assign "A" people, unless there's a reason for not so doing—lack of availability or higher-priority assignments.

The chart can have a secondary use: pinpointing training needs. If you don't have enough "A" people for a given task, it might be a good idea to undertake to upgrade the skills of "C" and "B" individuals.

➲ PLANNING GUIDE

This form is illustrative only. In the average case, a plan for a project of any size would require many pages.

1. Project Name:

. . . .

2. Purpose:

. . . .

3. Personnel:

. . . .

. . . .

4. Facilities:

. . . .

. . . .

5. Methods:

. . . .

. . . .

. . . .

6. Estimated Costs:

. . . .

. . . .

7. Schedule—Preparation:

. . . .

. . . .

Assignments:

. . . .

. . . .

8. Controls:

. . . .

. . . .

9. Evaluation of Results:

. . . .

. . . .

➲ SIX CHECKPOINTS FOR YOUR PLANNING

Here's a brief checklist to use before, during, and after planning. It can pinpoint a weakness, eliminate a kink that might wreck an effective program.

1. Should you subdivide? You may benefit by dividing a large-scale program. Each subplan is parcelled out to a competent subordinate. The advantages: (a) no one man is snowed under by a load of details; (b) you benefit from the ingenuity of others and your people will cooperate more fully because they've had a voice in planning.

2. Do you need an alternative plan? There are cases in which you must not fail. It's certainly a good idea to backstop yourself: locate a source for additional equipment; or, train extra people who can lend a hand, just in case.

3. How far can you pretest? Engineers have shown the way: . . . *Rough planning.* Before you get lost in details, block out the program in its basic form. Suppose you are trying to edvelop a better method of indoctrinating new employees. It may be enough to simply work out four or five basic areas to be covered such as: (a) introductions to other employees; (b) helping the newcomer to get acquainted with physical layout, wash rooms, etc; (c) reviewing department functions; (d) reviewing company history; (e) explaining his function in the scheme of things.

... *Dry run.*   Where feasible, a run-through of your plan helps you check methods, procedures, reactions.

... *Models.*   Want to see your troubles before they get to you? No matter how well you can visualize, it pays to use—

a. *Scale models.* Let's say you're planning a new floor layout. You can spot flaws by laying out the room dimensions and using cardboard cutouts to represent equipment, workstations, and employees. Insufficient space in the aisles, awkward relationship of equipment, etc., will be revealed.

b. *Working models.* By having a carpenter make up one version of a projected auxiliary warehouse, an executive could check for feasibility.

... *Component tests.*   When your car is serviced, it's under the microscope piecemeal: motor, tires, control mechanisms. Similarly, if your plan were to involve a series of report forms, you could scrutinize each one to see how well it furthers your overall objectives.

4. Should you bring in your assistant?   The quickest way for a subordinate to develop a broader view of departmental problems is for you to delegate part of the planning to him. Do you have anyone you want to develop in this fashion?

5. Should you "step-plan"?   The situation may not allow you to lay out a complete course of action. Your efforts may involve two or more phases. You may have to stop after each part has been completed to appraise results before you can map the next step. Know the reassessment points in advance.

6. Does your plan need booster-shots?   Programs once started tend to run out of gas. If your plan covers an extended period of time, keep in mind the possible need to remotivate your people.

EMPLOYEE SKILLS DEVELOPER

List the names of staff members whose skills you would like to improve. Under the section titled "Present Skills," list the various skills used in your departmental operations. Under the next section, titled "Extra Skills To Develop," list the skills you anticipate will be needed in the near future. Then, fill out the chart, using the following suggested code—

EMPLOYEE'S NAME	Present Skills						
	GRINDING	DRILLING	LATHE #1				
Jim Jones	P	✓					
Jack Lee	T,	✓					
Fred Smith	✓	✓	✓				

✓ = employee has this skill

P = employee has the potential to develop this skill

T = employee is being trained by you (or your assistant) to learn this skill.

To indicate the state of the employee's training, you may want to use a simple rating from 1 to 5, with 1 equalling the beginning of training, 5 equalling the final stage. Thus you might put a T_3 next to an employee who is midway in training.

EMPLOYEE'S NAME	Present Skills			Extra Skills To Develop				Remarks		

Plans for Training.   Many executives consider training to be a continuing process. Even so, changes in overall company plans or changes in departmental operations may dictate "emergency" training programs. In either case, the questions below can suggest worthwhile points for action.

1. Are the right people doing the training in your department?

Notes: . . . .

. . . .

2. Are you making use of the help available in your company: your boss? your colleages? your highly skilled subordinates? Personnel?

Notes: ....

....

3. Are you giving encouragement to those of your staff who feel their jobs are dead-end—showing them how they can train to get to the next step?

Notes: ....

....

4. Are you emphasizing refresher training?

Notes: ....

....

5. Are you using assignment rotation as a means of expanding employee skills?

Notes: ....

....

6. Do you have anyone working at a job requiring fewer skills than he has? If so, can he be transferred to more demanding work?

Notes: ....

....

➲ THE FLOOR-PLAN CHART

When filled in, this chart will show in visual form the layout of all or part of your office or department, and will help you consider possible changes. It will also picture where the work originates and the steps followed to completion, and it will spotlight sources of trouble— badly located aisles, storage areas, and so on.

Wherever you have a problem that's rooted in poor layout, such as improper placement of equipment, a floor-plan chart can help. Here's how to proceed.

1. The Floor Plan. Draw a floor plan for your department. It doesn't matter how rough the drawing, but keep it in proportion, if possible. Use a ruler to draw the straight lines—walls, and so on. If

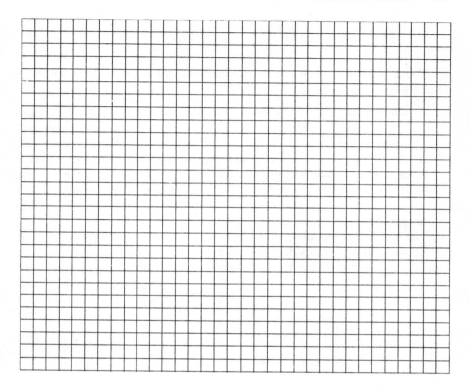

you know the dimensions in feet, draw the area to scale. Once the general dimensions are worked out, draw in all the major equipment—desks, files, and so on.

2. Sequence of Operations. On another sheet, list the steps the work goes through.

Here's a list drawn up by the head of a production department producing spiral tubing:

 a. Receive factory order.
 b. Order material from stockroom.
 c. Store material on shelf until needed.
 d. Move material to spiral machine.
 e. Fabricate tubing on spiral machine.
 f. Store tube lengths.
 g. Move tube lengths to slitting machine.
 h. Slit tubes to size.
 i. Spotcheck tubes for length and O.D.
 j. Move tubes to assembly table.

k. Assemble cap on one end of tube.
l. Final-inspect tubes.
m. Pack and send to Shipping.

When you've written out the steps, show the flow of the work, as in the drawing below.

3. Making an Improvement. The Floor-Plan Flow Chart can pay off substantially. In the situation illustrated (see Figure 1), the production head saw that the work was moving too long a distance, so he redid his drawing, and the actual arrangement, to look like Figure 2.

Note the improvement: by changing the location of the storage shelves, the distance between operations was cut considerably.

Of course, it's unwise to carry out such changes without consulting your subordinates, who may resent being left in the dark. To overcome any kickback later, give them the chance to work with you on improving the weak spots revealed by the chart. It's particularly advisable because the changes you're liable to make are the kind that affect

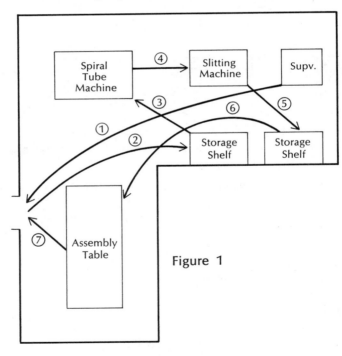

Figure 1

Original Floor-Plan
Flow Chart—Spiral
Tube Department.

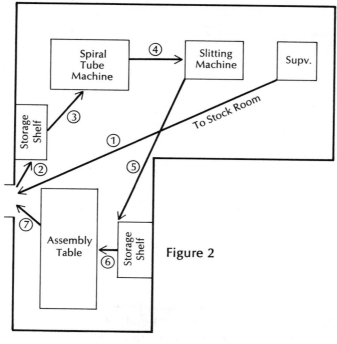

Figure 2

Improved Floor-Plan
Flow Chart—Spiral
Tube Department.

them personally. Logical or not, the attachments people develop for
"their" work sites are pretty strong. A one-sided decision to move a
chair, a table, a machine, may cause more upset than the improvement is worth. Explanation and discussion can avoid this trouble.

➲ ATTENDANCE ANALYZER

Insert the appropriate information. An explanation for calculating an
absentee rate (note the formula along the bottom of the chart) will be
found in detail after the form. You may want to duplicate this form and
use one copy at the end of each month.

Directions for calculating absentee rate:

If absence is a serious problem for you, we recommend that you
duplicate the form above and keep accurate records, month to month.
Executives find that record-keeping is often, of itself, a helpful remedy
for diminishing absenteeism.

Name of Subordinate	Days Absent for Month of_____	Excused? Reason	Unexcused	Result of Discussion / Action to be Taken		Follow-Up, Remarks

$$\text{ABSENTEE RATE} = \frac{\text{Man-Days Lost: _____}}{\text{Man-Days Scheduled: _____}} \times 100 = \quad \%$$

The chart provided is self-explanatory, though a note should be added about the column marked "Result of Discussion." It is based on the notion that it is a good practice to have a returning employee see his superior before starting back to work. This interview will not only tell you the reason for the absence, but impress the employee with your concern.

The Absentee Rate is found by 1) taking the man-days lost in your department, 2) dividing them by the man-days scheduled, and 3) multiplying that figure by 100.

Here is how one manager performed this calculation, a man with twenty employees in the department, each scheduled to work eight hours a day, twenty-four days a month. At the end of one month, recently, he found that seven of his employees hadn't been absent at all, but that five had been out one day each; four two days each; three three days each; and one man, twenty days. So he roughed out the following chart:

No. of Employees	Days Absent	Man-days lost
7	0	0
5	1	5
4	2	8
3	3	9
1	20	20
	Total	42

Next, he figured out the number of man-days that were scheduled for this month: he multiplied the number of people in his department (20) by the number of work days in the month (24), to get 480. Filling in the formula, this manager's final calculation was:

$$\frac{42}{480} \times 100 = 8.75\%$$

An 8.75% absentee rate is very high (the national average is 4%). If your rate rises above 4% for any month, consider this recommendation: Concentrate on the men with the highest number of absences, whether excused or unexcused. Studies show that these same men will be repeaters unless checked.

➲ IDEA STIMULATOR: GETTING IDEAS FROM YOUR SUBORDINATES

Here is a form executives have used to facilitate the flow of ideas from their subordinates. The example below shows how the form looks when filled out:

Subject: Plan to change locker room location.

Problem: Present location is inconvenient.
Time lost by workers between work area and lockers totals about 12 minutes per day per worker. (Include additional points as required.)

Proposal: Move lockers to B storage room; using present locker room for storage.

Advantages: Lockers would be next door to work area. (Include additional points as required.)

Disadvantages: Change would occupy two men for three days. (Include additional points as required.)

Recommendation: Locker location should be changed because it will save time and wil! be a morale builder worth the expense involved.

Ed Loman,
Supervisor

➲ EXECUTIVE TOOL RACK

Executives who have been able to figure out new applications for old standbys, such as charts and graphs, have successfully de-kinked knotty tasks that previously slowed them down.

The executive who looks for help in the form of tools tends to develop a concept of efficiency, of "the better way" that is reflected in his overall performance.

Tool Catalogue.   Below you'll find a list of devices that are to be found in executive offices everywhere. There isn't an executive alive who uses all or even most of them. But your use of a single one may prove to be the answer to an unsolved problem of efficiency that may have been bothering you for a long time. As you go down the list, keep in mind your own operations and the possible assistance you may gain by an application or adaptation of each item.

Charts and graphs.   All types and sizes of these are for organization control, production control, quality control, keeping track of orders received, processed, and shipped; overtime, and stock needed.

Phone adaptations.   You can have conference phones that sit on the desk and require no handling; double phones for three-way talks; phone side-switches to tell the switchboard whether the executive is in, away or available by auto-call; timers to limit long-distance calls.

Blackboards and easel charts.   You can use these behind the desks, as well as in conference rooms, for problem-solving, illustration, etc.

Slides rules, adding, or calculating machines.   These make for easy computation in planning. "I run up a column of figures a dozen times a day," is a fairly typical statement from a top-level executive to explain the presence of equipment you wouldn't expect him to have.

Work tables.   You can get them man-sized, medium, or small to use as a second desk, a clear work area, for quick huddles, blueprint examination, and so on.

Cameras.   Movie, candid, and still types can be used for getting visual evidence of a damaged shipment, supplies received in poor condition, safety malpractices, and many other occasions.

Clocks.   Include an alarm clock, to remind you when it's time to set out for an important meeting or date, Wrist models are becoming popular.

Projectors.   Slide or movie projectors are becoming more common in executive offices. As an adjunct to conferences, or as a briefing or training device, their rich possibilities are largely unexplored.

Dictating machines or recorders.   The use of a dictating machine for letters, and so on, is standard. But executives have found that putting a conference "on tape," for example, provides a verbatim record that at times is highly desirable.

The possibilities for each tool itemized above are by no means exhaustive. Your ingenuity in seeking out new uses may make a measurable improvement in your personal effectiveness, or that of your subordinates.

➲ WEEKLY SCHEDULING FORM

Many executives view their day as being divided into four parts, as indicated in the form below. In scheduling your week, you may use color coding to denote: important meetings or appointments, occasions for which some preparation is necessary, regular meetings such as conferences, or periodic discussions with staff or other executives. (This form may be photocopied.)

	Monday	Tuesday	Wednesday	Thursday	Friday
Morning					
Pre-Lunch					
Post-Lunch					
Late afternoon					

➲ PERSONAL AND WORK RECORD OF YOUR STAFF

It's helpful to have at hand information about your subordinates, from the day they came with the company to auxiliary skills. The Roster Record is a convenient form for keeping such data. One caution: if you enter confidential notations, such as salary, or your evaluation of capabilities, the Record should be secured in a locked drawer or file. This form may be reproduced or photocopied.

ROSTER RECORD

Name, etc.	Date Data	Education and Previous Experience	Work Record (Attendance, health, promotions, raises)
☐ Mr. ───────	Came with company ───		
☐ Miss ───────	Joined your staff ───		
☐ Mrs. ───────	Transferred ───────		
Home address: ───	Separated ───────		
───────	Birthday ───────		
───────			
Telephone: ───			
───────			

ROSTER RECORD

Name, etc.	Date Data	Education and Previous Experience	Work Record (Attendance, health, promotions, raises)
☐ Mr. ☐ Miss ☐ Mrs. —————— Home address: —————— —————— —————— —————— Telephone: ——————	Came with company —————— Joined your staff —————— Transferred —————— Separated —————— Birthday ——————		

ROSTER RECORD

Name, etc.	Date Data	Education and Previous Experience	Work Record (Attendance, health, promotions, raises)
☐ Mr.	Came with company ————		
☐ Miss	Joined your staff ————		
☐ Mrs. ————————	Transferred ————		
	Separated ————		
Home address: ————	Birthday ————		
————————			
Telephone: ————			

ROSTER RECORD

Name, etc.	Date Data	Education and Previous Experience	Work Record (Attendance, health, promotions, raises)
☐ Mr.	Came with company ——		
☐ Miss	Joined your staff ——		
☐ Mrs. ——	Transferred ——		
	Separated ——		
Home address: ——	Birthday ——		
——			
——			
Telephone: ——			
——			

ROSTER RECORD

Name, etc.	Date Data	Education and Previous Experience	Work Record (Attendance, health, promotions, raises)
☐ Mr. ☐ Miss ☐ Mrs. _____ Home address: _____ _____ _____ Telephone: _____	Came with company _____ Joined your staff _____ Transferred _____ Separated _____ Birthday _____		

ROSTER RECORD

Name, etc.	Date Data	Education and Previous Experience	Work Record (Attendance, health, promotions, raises)
☐ Mr. ☐ Miss ☐ Mrs. _____ Home address: _____ _____ _____ Telephone: _____	Came with company _____ Joined your staff _____ Transferred _____ Separated _____ Birthday _____		

➲ SELECTIVE DIRECTORY

Use the form below for recording addresses and so on of customers, colleagues, key employees, special contacts—a streamlined directory you'd like to keep at your fingertips.

Name	Address	Telephone Number	Remarks, Reminders

Name	Address	Telephone Number	Remarks, Reminders

INDEX

317

NOTES

NOTES

NOTES

NOTES